THE MARK OF THE SACRED

Cultural Memory
in
the
Present

Hent de Vries and Mieke Bal, Editors

THE MARK OF THE SACRED

Jean-Pierre Dupuy

Translated by M. B. DeBevoise

STANFORD UNIVERSITY PRESS

STANFORD, CALIFORNIA

Stanford University Press
Stanford, California

The Mark of the Sacred was originally published in French under the title La marque du sacré © 2008 Carnets Nord.

Support for this translation was provided by Imitatio, a project of the Thiel Foundation.

Printed in the United States of America on acid-free, archival-quality paper

Library of Congress Cataloging-in-Publication Data

Dupuy, Jean Pierre, 1941– author.
   [Marque du sacré. English]
   The mark of the sacred / Jean-Pierre Dupuy ; translated by M.B. DeBevoise.
      pages cm. — (Cultural memory in the present)
   "Originally published in French under the title La marque du sacré."
   Includes bibliographical references.
   ISBN 978-0-8047-7689-9 (cloth : alk. paper)
   ISBN 978-0-8047-7690-5 (pbk. : alk. paper)
   1. Religion and sociology. 2. Catastrophical, The. 3. Faith and reason.
4. Holy, The. I. DeBevoise, M. B., translator. II. Title. III. Series: Cultural memory in the present.
BL60.D8613 2013
201'.7—dc23

                                                                    2013007537

ISBN 978-0-8047-8845-8 (electronic)

Contents

Note on the Translation   ix

Foreword to the American Edition   xi

Prologue: The Form of the Sacred   I
From Archimedes to Münchausen 2—*Anatomy of a Global
Panic* 6—*When Satan Casts Out Satan* 13

1. Imagining the End: A Personal Journey   21
    Staring at Catastrophe 21—*Apocalypse Now* 31—
    Illich and Girard 34—*The Education of a Prophet
    of Doom* 43

2. Science: A Theology in Spite of Itself   54
    The Purported Neutrality of Science 54—*The Theological-
    Scientific Problem* 57—*Why We Need the Future* 60—
    When Technologies Converge 63—*Beyond the Obsession
    with Risk* 66—*The Matrix of the Transhumanists* 79—
    The Responsibility of Science 85

3. Religion: Natural Versus Supernatural   90
    Looking in the Wrong Place 91—*Religion as Collective
    Effervescence* 95—*Sacrifice and Murder* 100—*Sacrificial
    Thought and the Confusion of Categories* 105—*Religion
    and Morality* 109—*Scapegoats and Sacrificial Victims* 116—
    The False Promise of Salvation by Morality 119

4. Rationality and Ritual: The Babylon Lottery   125
   Chance as a Solution to the Theological-Political Problem 125—
   Reason and the Rite of Election 130—*The Lottery
   in America* 138—*What Political Philosophy Can Learn
   from Anthropology* 146

5. Justice and Resentment: Corruption of the Best   151
   Justice Is Not Reducible to Logic 153—*Social Inequality
   and Humiliation* 157—*What Economics Can Learn
   from Anthropology and Political Philosophy* 165

6. The Nuclear Menace: A New Sacrament for Humanity   175
   From bin Laden to Hiroshima 175—*Theoretician
   of the Atomic Age* 178—*The Impotence of Deterrence* 185—
   The End of Hatred and Resentment 193

   Epilogue: Variations on *Vertigo*   195
   Self-References 195—*On Madeleine's Mode of Existence* 198—
   Catastrophe and Time 201—*The Object of Desire* 205—
   The Sense of the Past 209—*Alcmena's Paradox* 212

Note on the Translation

This translation of *La marque du sacré* constitutes a revised edition of the work first published in Paris in 2009. The French text has been altered in several places by the author himself, and other small, but significant changes have been made for the sake of clarity, with his approval. I am grateful to Jean-Pierre Dupuy for his extensive comments on an annotated draft manuscript.

Most of the estimates of the rate of climate change in the French edition have been removed. The temptation to replace them with current estimates has been resisted, since these too will soon be superseded by new research and readers can in any case consult updated reports through a variety of published sources. The present position of the minute hand on the Doomsday Clock has nevertheless been noted to reflect the most recent appraisal of the scale of the dangers facing the world, and web-page addresses given in the notes have been amended as necessary. Minor errors of fact in the original edition have been silently corrected.

Bibliographic information has been considerably expanded as a courtesy to both scholars and general readers, and standard English translations of works in French and German cited wherever possible. With regard to quotations from the Old and New Testaments, I have relied on the Revised Standard Version of 1952 in preference to the New King James Bible and other still newer editions.

Foreword to the American Edition

    This book treats a series of questions that concern all of mankind. To what do we owe our faculty of reason—that power of thought in which we take so much pride, and which philosophers since Aristotle have considered to be uniquely human? Is rationality equally distributed among all peoples? Was it inborn in us from the beginnings of our existence on earth, or did it first blossom only with the invention of two things for which the Western world is pleased to take credit: democracy and philosophy? Did it, in either case, subsequently achieve its fullest flowering as a consequence of modern advances in science and technology? If it did, must we say that instrumental rationality—the ability to relate ends to means that is peculiar to *Homo œconomicus*—represents the unsurpassable culmination of human reason? Or is it merely a degraded and inadequate facsimile?

    Whether reason is innate or acquired, we know that it can be lost, individually and collectively. But what does this tell us about the nature of reason? Not only the murderous rages, the genocides and the holocausts, but also the folly that leads humanity to destroy the conditions necessary to its survival—what do these things teach us about the absence of reason? In 1797, Francisco Goya made an etching to which he gave the title *El sueño de la razón produce monstruos*. It shows a man fallen asleep in his chair, his head resting heavily on a table, surrounded by terrifying creatures of the night, owls and bats. A large cat looks on. With this arresting image an artist who had upheld the ideals of the French Revolution in opposition to many of his countrymen expressed his horror at the awful massacres of the Terror. The title is generally translated as "The Sleep of Reason Produces Monsters." But the Spanish word *sueño*, as it happens, may mean either sleep or dream. In this second sense Goya's title acquires a much more disturbing meaning. It is not the eclipse of reason that produces monsters;

on the contrary, it is the power of reason to dream, to fantasize, to have nightmares—to unleash the demons of the imagination.

To all these questions there is a simple reply, or at least a reply that is simply stated: reason, like all human institutions, has its source in religion. It is the same answer one finds in the French tradition of social science inaugurated by Émile Durkheim and Marcel Mauss. Durkheim, in his great work *The Elementary Forms of Religious Life,* congratulated himself on having established that "the fundamental categories of thought, and therefore of science, have religious origins." As a result, he concluded, "it can be said that nearly all great social institutions are derived from religion."[1] If Durkheim was right, as I believe he was, the adventures and misadventures of human reason will make no sense to us unless we examine them in the light of his discovery.

Even though the topics I discuss in this book are of universal importance, the conclusions I draw cannot help but arouse sharply differing reactions among my readers, depending in large part on the place of religion in public life that they are accustomed to regard as proper. In the Western world, probably no two countries are separated by a greater distance with regard to the place reserved for religion than the United States and France, as Alexis de Tocqueville was perhaps the first to point out when he traveled through America in the 1830s. The gap between them is hardly smaller today than it was in Tocqueville's time. It may be well, then, to say a few words at the outset in the hope of preventing at least the grossest misunderstandings.

France is proud to describe itself as a secular country. It is telling that the meaning of the phrase *pays laïc* cannot easily be conveyed in English. Secularism in the French sense does not signify the neutrality of the state, as it does in America. The doctrine of the neutrality of the state, due to classical liberalism, assumes that the state is incompetent to decide what constitutes the good life, and therefore cannot take sides between competing conceptions. In France, by contrast, secularism is understood to be a fundamentally anti-liberal and "perfectionist" concept. On this view, the state has both the authority to say in what the

---

1. Émile Durkheim, *Les formes élémentaires de la vie religieuse,* 6th ed. (Paris: Presses universitaires de France, 1979), 598.

good life consists and the right to command obedience to its will in the public sphere. It is here that the problem of religion makes itself felt most acutely. The republican tradition in France makes conformity to reason the sole qualification for taking part in public life. Condorcet expressed the idea beautifully: "Generous friends of equality, of liberty, unite to demand from your governors an education that will make reason the property of the people."[2] Thus the ideal of the French Revolution—rationality as the highest public virtue.

Now, to the French secular mind, religious faith of every kind seems profoundly irrational. Religion and its visible signs therefore have no legitimate place in the public sphere in France, where education is obligatory and free of charge for all. The thought of a president of the republic taking the oath of office on a Bible is unimaginable. Were the president to conclude his inaugural address with the words "God save France," there would be rioting in the streets. When the nation's currency was the French franc, the idea that banknotes might bear the legend "In God We Trust" would have been simply inconceivable. These commonplaces of American political culture are deeply shocking to my fellow *citoyens,* no less shocking than the recent French law prohibiting the display of emblems of religious affiliation in schools, whether the Islamic veil, the Jewish skullcap, or Christian crucifixes greater than a certain size, seems to many of my American friends. For someone like myself, who loves both countries, this mutual incomprehension is disheartening.

Tocqueville was forcibly struck above all by the religious faith of the American people. Having come to America to study democracy, he came afterward to think that the former was the necessary condition of the latter. As he so memorably put it, "I doubt whether any man can endure, at one and the same time, complete religious independence and complete political freedom; and I am led to believe that, if a man is without faith, he must serve another, and, if he is free, he must believe."[3] Some of the most eminent political philosophers in France today have strongly

2. Marie Jean Antoine Nicolas de Caritat, marquis de Condorcet, *Cinq mémoires sur l'instruction publique* (1791), ed. Charles Coutel and Catherine Kintzler (Paris: Garnier-Flammarion, 1994), 104.

3. Alexis de Tocqueville, *De la démocratie en Amérique,* vol. 2 (1840), 1.5 (Paris: Garnier-Flammarion, 1981), 31.

criticized Tocqueville on this point.[4] The true spirit of democracy, they say, was there to be found in his own country, post-revolutionary France. A democratic society is not one that is in harmony with its basic principles, as American theorists such as John Rawls have maintained. Just the opposite is true: it is one in which these principles are perpetually called into question, a social and political regime marked by conflict and division over the very values on which it is founded; indeed, it is of the essence of democracy that such questioning should be constant and open-ended. In Tocqueville's time, France was torn between those who favored democracy and those who opposed it. This very tension, it is said, worked to strengthen democracy. French political thought today, or at least its most secular element, therefore concludes it is futile to suppose, as Tocqueville did, that religion can erect a durable barrier against the subversive influences that erode the foundations it has given itself. God and religion will inevitably perish as a result of the growth of democracy.

In America, the growth of religious fundamentalism in recent decades, and the excesses to which it has given rise, have produced by way of reaction an assault against religion in which God has become, or become once more, the perfect scapegoat—and all the more perfect as he is believed not to exist. The titles of bestsellers that line the shelves of American bookstores—*The God Delusion, God Is Not Great, The End of Faith, Breaking the Spell*—do not deal in nuance. Together, they amount to a declaration of war against the religious foundations of American democracy.

It is tempting to imagine that the secular crusade of the French Left and the anti-religious crusade of the American Left are somehow similar. And yet they have nothing in common. Few books by religion-bashers in England and America are translated into French. The ones that are sell poorly, and their ideas have no resonance whatever in the quarrels over secularism that regularly enliven French political debate. There are two reasons for this. The first is that scholars and intellectuals in France have a hard time taking seriously what they consider to be the work of mere pamphleteers, whose outstanding characteristics are, on the one hand, a lack of culture, and, on the other, a weakness for arguments that rely on

---

4. See, e.g., Marcel Gauchet's essay on Tocqueville in Mark Lilla, ed., *New French Thought: Political Philosophy* (Princeton, N.J.: Princeton University Press, 1994), 91–111.

biological theories of evolution and research in the cognitive sciences. But this is nothing new. Attempts to reduce social phenomena and the symbolic dimension of human existence to purely natural causes have never gotten a warm welcome in France.

The second reason has to do with the history and sociology of religion, which, it must be admitted, is not the strong point of the new atheists in England and America. One often has the impression that they take particular delight in making Christianity out to be no less irrational than any other religion, and therefore one more reason for dismissing religion in all its forms. French thinkers from Durkheim onward, by contrast, deepening an insight famously associated with Max Weber, have argued that secularization—what Weber called the disenchantment of the world—was a paradoxical consequence of the spread of Christian faith that, in its turn, prepared the way for the flourishing of economic rationality. Indeed, it is not uncommon today to hear Christianity described as "the religion of the end of religion." The blindness of the new atheists to the fundamentally distinctive nature of Christianity is taken in France to disqualify them from taking part in the debate about the nature of religion and its future.

I mention all these things here in order to remind my American readers that one can hardly write a book on the religious origins of human reason without taking into account the settled prejudices of one's audience. Nevertheless, in the pages that follow, I touch only in passing on questions that are primarily of interest to historians and sociologists of religion. I concentrate on a different set of questions, philosophical questions, which are logically prior to the ones that concern historians and sociologists. I begin by considering a notion that lay at the heart of religious anthropology when it was still recognized as a discipline in its own right, namely, the sacred. I do not dispute the vagueness of this concept, nor do I try to give an exhaustive account of what it involves. Instead I characterize its formal properties, and go on to show that human reason preserves the mark of its origins in the sacred, however much it may regret this fact. I then take up in turn several related kinds of rationality in which the mark of the sacred may yet be plainly seen, in science, politics, economics, and strategic thought.

Along the way I develop three lines of argument: first, that the Judeo-Christian tradition cannot be identified with the sacred, since it is responsible for the ongoing desacralization (or disenchantment) of the world that epitomizes modernity; second, that desacralization threatens to leave us defenseless against our own violence by unchaining technology, so that unlimitedness begins little by little to replace limitedness; third, the greatest paradox of all, that in order to preserve the power of self-limitation, without which no human society can sustain itself and survive, we are obliged to rely on our own freedom. It will be clear, I think, from what I have already said about the differences between France and America, that in making these claims I come directly into conflict with both French secularists and American religion-bashers, since they all consider religion to be the height of irrationality, whereas they themselves adamantly believe in Reason, pure and immaculate; with religion-bashers, in particular, since they fail to see what even secularists accept, namely, that Christianity has been the driving force in bringing about the secularization of society; with secularists, in particular, since they fail to see that reason in its various forms continues still today to display the mark of the sacred; and, of course, with religious fundamentalists of all faiths, since they resemble their rationalist adversaries in regarding reason and the sacred as strangers to each other, locked together in a merciless struggle to the death. That's a lot of people to take on at once.

One last thing. The task of bringing over not only my words, but the intricate structure of my arguments and their subtlest shades of meaning, from the language and culture of France to the language and culture of America has required a translator of exceptional talent. Once again I am pleased to be able to give my warmest thanks to Malcolm DeBevoise.

Paris, December 2012

THE MARK OF THE SACRED

Prologue

> Man believes either in a God or in an idol.
> —Max Scheler, *On the Eternal in Man*

One truth stands out before all others when one considers human history in its full sweep: our societies are machines for manufacturing gods.

Why should this be so? How exactly are gods made? These questions ought to be at the heart of the humanities and the social sciences, and yet they are not. It is as though the fierce determination of secular positivism to free itself from every last relic of religious thought shapes the choice of subjects that these disciplines judge worthy of study. On the positivist view of the world, the religious outlook is outmoded, an aberration. From this it concludes that nothing of value can be expected from a scientific approach to the study of religion. But what if, quite to the contrary, the science of religion and the sciences of humanity are one and the same? What if, in order to understand human beings, it turns out to be absolutely necessary to understand why they invent gods?

In this book I am not concerned with the relationship between reason and faith, an ancient quarrel that is still far from being exhausted. I am interested in a prior (or, as lawyers would say, pre-judicial) question having to do with the nature of reason. I shall argue that what we call reason preserves indelible traces of its origin in religious experience. Following Durkheim, I regard religion as being defined less by beliefs than by actions, less by faith than by ritual. It will become plain that when reason treats religion as something foreign, whether in order to reject it or, on the contrary, to imagine some form of peaceful coexistence with it, reason shows itself to be a kind of faith—*bad* faith.

From Archimedes to Münchausen

Human societies have always found ways to act upon themselves through some external agency, long identified with divinity. What we call modern society, or simply modernity, abandoned this conception in favor of a secular perspective in which human beings take the place of gods. In saying that they are able to produce their own exteriority, I mean that human beings can project themselves, go beyond themselves, as it were, in order to exert a power over themselves. In this sense their abilities have much less in common with the physics of Archimedes than with the imaginary exploits of Baron Münchausen.

Archimedes thought that he could move the world through his own strength alone, provided that he had a lever and an *external* fulcrum. Baron Münchausen, for his part, claimed to have *pulled himself out* of a swamp by his own hair (or, according to another version, by his bootstraps).[1] One is given to imagine that he had somehow managed to split himself in two, so that the hand that grabbed hold of a part of his body belonged to an alter ego. A miraculous and impossible feat, of course—and yet all human societies have been able to accomplish the like of it. Indeed, this may well have been the condition of their becoming societies in the first place.

The figure I introduce here, in a preliminary sort of way, is not one of my own invention. It has long been known to philosophy. Hegel called it "self-exteriorization" *(Entäusserung)*, Marx "alienation" *(Entfremdung)*, Hayek "self-transcendence." But it was the French sociologist and anthropologist Louis Dumont

---

1. Rudolf Erich Raspe published *The Surprising Adventures of Baron Münchausen* in London in 1785. The tales were translated back into German, and added to in a definitive edition that appeared in Göttingen the following year. Since then, owing to some perplexing detours through quantum mechanics and the emigration of German scientists to the United States before World War II, the related notion of "bootstrapping" has become a familiar part of the English language. Thus, for example, to use a common expression borrowed from computer science, one "boots up" a computer by starting its operating system: a simple program activates another, more complex program.

who came closest to apprehending it in its pure form. He called it "hierarchy," while noting that this term was meant in its etymological sense of a sacred order (from the Greek word formed by combining *hierós*, sacred, and *árchein*, to rule).[2]

Dumont considered himself a holist, which is to say that he asserted the logical and ontological priority of the whole of society to its individual elements. Yet, unlike Durkheim, he did not interpret the transcendence of society in relation to its elements as a simple function of exteriority. He assigned it a form—a hierarchical form. But what is hierarchy? Far from being a succession of levels in which a higher level includes or dominates a lower level, hierarchy, in Dumont's phrase, is an *encompassing of the contrary*. A linguist, for example, if he were speaking strictly, would say that the French language does not contain a masculine gender and a feminine gender, but rather an "unmarked" and a "marked" gender. The unmarked gender encompasses the totality of subjects, regardless of their sex. The marked gender, on the other hand, applies only to the female sex. It follows from this that the masculine, which is the form of the unmarked gender, represents at one level the totality, and by virtue of this encompasses the feminine; whereas at another level, that of the proper subset (a mathematician regards the set of odd integers, for example, as a proper subset of the set of integers) and its complementary subset (the set of even integers), it is opposed to the feminine. The coincidence of the whole and one of its proper subsets (which, for a mathematician, implies the idea of infinity) is what permits the whole to stand in opposition to the complementary subset. The whole, in other words, encompasses its contrary—the part that does not coincide with the whole.

Hierarchy in this sense, Dumont holds, is inverted within itself. The reversal of sign is associated with a change in level: what is superior at the encompassing level becomes inferior at the encompassed level, and vice versa. Dumont elaborated the logic of this way of looking at the world in connection first with the relationship between religious and political authority in India, and then with the doctrine of Pope Gelasius, enunciated five hundred years after Jesus Christ: "In matters of religion, and

---

2. See Louis Dumont, *Homo Hierarchicus: The Caste System and Its Implications*, rev. ed., trans. Mark Sainsbury et al. (Chicago: University of Chicago Press, 1980), 65–66.

hence absolutely, the priest is superior to the king or emperor to whom public order is entrusted. But *ipso facto* the priest will obey the king in matters of public order, that is, in subordinate matters."[3] This hierarchical form—which, following the example of certain logicians, might better perhaps be called "tangled hierarchy"[4]—is summarized by an elegant formula: "Priests are superior, for they are inferior only on an inferior level."[5]

Dumont reasons here as an anthropologist of traditional societies, in which a religious principle promotes social cohesiveness. But it is when he ventures onto the terrain of philosophy that a still more arresting image occurs to him, one that perfectly captures what he means by hierarchy. Discussing the metaphysical system of Leibniz, in which he sees a modern version of a premodern conception of the world, he takes up the question of theodicy, or divine justice, and the vexed problem of reconciling the presumptive benevolence and omnipotence of the Creator with the inescapable fact of the existence of evil on earth. Leibniz's solution is well known for having been ridiculed by Voltaire: the world in which we live is the best of all possible worlds. What appears to us as evil seems to be so because we have only a finite, individual view of the world. But if we could have a view of the totality—if we could look at the world from the divine point of view—we would see that what appears to us as evil is a necessary sacrifice for the greater good of the totality. Had evil not been permitted to intervene, our world would not have been the best of all possible worlds. Dumont is therefore led to characterize the essence of theodicy by this memorable phrase: "[G]ood must *contain* evil while still being its contrary."[6] Here the verb "contain" has the sense of encompassing, and the relation it describes is hierarchy, which is to say the encompassing of the contrary.

It has always seemed surprising to me that Dumont and his school of anthropology should have seen hierarchy as nothing more than the sign of a stable order, guaranteed by religion. One has only to recognize that the verb "contain" has another meaning—of blocking, inhibiting,

3. Louis Dumont, *Essays on Individualism: Modern Ideology in Anthropological Perspective* (Chicago: University of Chicago Press, 1986), 252–53.

4. See, e.g., Douglas Hofstadter, *Gödel, Escher, Bach: An Eternal Golden Braid* (New York: Basic Books, 1979).

5. Dumont, *Essays on Individualism*, 46.

6. Ibid., 251. The emphasis is mine.

repressing—in order to construe hierarchy, understood as the encompassing of the contrary, in an entirely different and much more disturbing sense, namely, as a system that is constantly in danger of being overturned. Just so, the most stable social order is the one that *contains* the threat of its own collapse, in the two senses of the verb "to contain."

If one considers hierarchy only in its relation to order, as Dumont does, it is one of the most familiar ideas in the philosophy of history and society. It has been developed in different ways and under various names—ruse of reason, ruse of history, dialectical materialism, the "invisible hand" of the economists. In each case one finds the same idea, which is the foundation of modern rationalism: evil is, at bottom, only a lesser evil, a necessary evil, for it is placed in the service of the good; evil is only apparent, for it is an integral part of the good. But once a hierarchical order enters into crisis and, under the pressure of the ensuing panic, totters on the edge of collapse, a quite different picture emerges. Its levels, distinct and well ordered until now, come to be confused with one another in a way that reveals their kinship. Whereas before good was thought to govern evil, its contrary, now evil seems to have governed itself—by distancing itself from itself, by putting itself outside of itself—with the result that the higher level, having been self-externalized, so to speak, takes on the aspect of the good.

This idea can be stated less abstractly if we consider the singular relationship, which I will later have occasion to treat in greater detail, that unites murder and sacrifice in a society where sacrifice constitutes the founding ritual. In that case sacrifice *contains* the outbreak and spread of murder; though it is in one sense just another murder, it promises to put an end to violence. Capital punishment performs the same function in certain criminal justice systems. But when the religious order ("hierarchy") is overthrown by disorder and violence, when the administration of justice loses its transcendent authority, ritual killing can no longer be distinguished from murder. *Before* the onset of crisis, however, sacrifice was both murder and something other than murder.

The crisis that accompanies the collapse of a hierarchical order bears a name that has come down to us from Greek mythology: panic. The myth itself contemplates only exteriority, for it places the blame for the violent breakdown of hierarchy on an eponymous divinity, Pan—god of shepherds, half-man, half-goat, a gifted musician, a democrat, a famous lover of nymphs—whose sudden appearance behind a grove was said instantly to inspire terror. As an empirical matter we know that panic is internally generated, in the sense that its destructive force is unleashed only to the extent that it was previously *contained* by the order that it brings crashing down. Spectators at a sporting event, for example, who are known to resist panic even in the event of an earthquake, are liable to throw themselves headlong into a murderous stampede if the competitive tensions of the event itself exceed a certain threshold. For those who remain blind to the logic of self-exteriorization that underlies human violence, Pan is a perfect scapegoat—the evil genie who has escaped from his bottle.[7]

Yet like Pan himself, who is at once civilized and a source of terror, panic is not only a force of destruction. The etymology of the word itself suggests a phenomenon whose effects are all-encompassing and serve to bring forth a new order, a new totality, a new direction or orientation, even if it is only flight from danger. Here the relation between a disordered set of individual behaviors and an emergent pattern of order is one of self-transcendence; its form is hierarchical, in the sense I have just described, namely, that the emergent order appears to govern individual behaviors from the outside, even though it is itself a consequence of the synergistic coordination of these same individual behaviors. Since these behaviors represent disorder, the emergent order *contains* them, in the two meanings of the word. In this case order does not, as Dumont supposed, contain disorder while at the same time being its contrary. Instead disorder steps outside of itself, as it were, so that it stands in a relation of exteriority to itself, and in this way creates an ordered, self-regulating system.

Anatomy of a Global Panic

I write these lines in the autumn of 2008, in the midst of a panic that threatens to bring about the collapse of the world economy. The commentaries that the crisis has inspired illustrate the points I have been making more forcefully than I could ever have imagined being able to do myself,

7. See Jean-Pierre Dupuy, *La panique,* revised and augmented ed. (Paris: Les Empêcheurs de Penser en Rond/Seuil, 2003), 15–21.

for they demonstrate the inability of political and economic leaders to grasp the logic of self-exteriorization. The present crisis is one of indistinctness, as it might be said, in the sense that it is marked by a loss of the differences between levels that characterize hierarchy. And yet pundits and policymakers alike have hastened to multiply differences, notwithstanding that these reduce ultimately to a single distinction, between the good that must be preserved and the evil that must be eradicated, or in any case controlled, so that evil remains in the service of the good as a necessary evil. In other words, Dumont's rationalist interpretation of hierarchy has not been relinquished. Nevertheless the virtue of a crisis of such unprecedented scope is that it makes clear, at least to those who have the eyes to see it, that good and evil are profoundly related; indeed they have become identical with each other as a result of the crisis. If there is a way out, it will be found only by allowing evil once again to transcend itself and take on the appearance of the good.

What is at issue here is the impotence of orthodox economic analysis in the face of a crisis that blurs all the familiar distinctions of neoclassical theory. When an entire economic system reaches the point of behaving like a panic-stricken crowd, there is no alternative but to discard the prevailing doctrine. This was understood by an economist of genius, John Maynard Keynes, on the occasion of a crisis even more terrible than the present one. Not the rationalist Keynes, not the proto-cybernetician encountered in economics textbooks in the chapter on "Keynesian" economics, but the Keynes who perceived that, in times of market panic, mass psychology becomes the ruling force. Economic theory, blinded by its own pride, still fails to see this.

Commentators insist first upon distinguishing between the deliberate regulation imposed by the state and the uncontrolled self-regulation (or deregulation) that characterizes the market. The creative spontaneity of the market is conceded to be a necessary evil, one that must be restrained by the "visible hand" of regulation. At this juncture the apostles of regulation expose themselves to the same ridicule as the philosophy master in the hilarious third scene of act 2 of Molière's *Bourgeois Gentleman*. From the commanding heights of his magisterium, the philosophy master attempts to arbitrate between the competing claims of the music master, the dancing master, and the fencing master, each of whom demands that his art be recognized as the best one of all. But it is not long before he begins to squabble, and then to fight, with them, so that what had been a dispute among three parties swiftly escalates into a battle among four. No sooner has the philosophy master climbed up on his pedestal than he is knocked off it, having been swept up in a mimetic vortex of violence.

The challenge facing policymakers in a time of panic is to find an external fixed point that can be used to bring it under control. This is not always easily done. More than once one has seen unprecedented steps taken to reassure the markets, by injecting astronomical sums of money, produce exactly the opposite effect—the markets having concluded that only panic could explain why it should have been necessary to resort to such extreme measures. They did not believe for a moment in the advertised rationality of state intervention. To speak of reconstructing capitalism through market regulation is therefore a staggering piece of naiveté, for it supposes that the problem of finding an external point of support has *already* been solved.

Jean-Jacques Rousseau understood the paradox that apprentice regulators run up against today long before anyone else. The political problem, Rousseau observed, is to "put law over man,"[8] even though it is men who make the laws, as they themselves well know. Power in a democracy emanates from the people, and yet it is power only insofar as it is external to them. Rousseau shrewdly perceived the vicious circle in which any attempt at founding, or refounding, political institutions finds itself caught up: "[T]he effect would have to become the cause; the social spirit, which should be the result of the institution, would have to preside over the founding of the institution itself; and men would have to be prior to laws what they ought to become by means of laws."[9] In order to find a way out from the current economic crisis, then, the way out would already have had to have been found.

---

8. Jean-Jacques Rousseau, *Considerations on the Government of Poland and on Its Planned Reformation* (1772), ¶1; in Roger D. Masters and Christopher Kelly, eds., *The Collected Writings of Rousseau*, 13 vols. (Hanover, N.H.: University Press of New England, 1990–2010), 11: 170. See my reservations regarding this edition in chapter 5, n. 15, below.

9. Jean-Jacques Rousseau, *The Social Contract*, 2.7, in *The Collected Writings of Rousseau*, 4: 156.

It is not enough to proclaim oneself king in order actually to be one. A person who wants to be Napoleon is not therefore Napoleon. And yet, contrary to the logic of the *Social Contract,* Rousseau found the solution to the paradox of self-transcendence in his own personal experience as an outsider. As Michel Serres has pointed out,

When he was writing of the social pact, no contradiction bothered him; everything seemed crystal clear to him. It seemed transparent to go back to a first convention; it seemed evident to him that an act of association would produce a group ego or a public persona. Today, those plotting against me, those in league together, form, he says, an indissoluble body whose members can no longer be separated [from one another]. In the political sense, they form a republic. Rousseau sees that what he had foreseen is now constituted, but *he is [looking from] outside;* he sees a dispersed set form a unit, a unanimous gathering of forces—and it all seems obscure to him.

The truth is that he is right; the truth is that he made decisive progress in politics. . . . General will is rare and perhaps only theoretical. General hatred is frequent and is part of the practical world. . . . Not only does he see the formation of a social pact *from the outside,* not only does he notice the formation of a general will, but he also observes, through the darkness, that it is formed only through animosity, that it is formed only because he is its victim. . . . Union is produced through expulsion. And he is the one who is expelled.[10]

This victim is therefore an emissary victim, a scapegoat, whose expulsion from the community provides it with the external point of support it needs in order to put an end to crisis.

Indifferent to such considerations, if they are aware of them at all, analysts of the present economic crisis wheel out the usual hierarchical oppositions—the "real" economy versus the "financial" economy, the regulated market versus financial speculation, bullish speculation versus bearish speculation, and so on—as though they were following the model of theodicy described by Dumont, according to which good must *contain* evil while at the same time being its contrary. It is not a terribly arduous business to dispose of these oppositions, one by one; indeed, a moment's reflection is enough to make them collapse like a house of cards. Consider, for example, the hierarchical opposition between the real and the financial

10. Michel Serres, *Parasite,* trans. Lawrence R. Schehr (Baltimore: Johns Hopkins University Press, 1982), 118–19. The italics are mine. [Schehr's translation slightly modified.—Trans.]

economy. It proceeds from a feeble premise, namely, that money and credit constitute a necessary evil, redeemed only to the extent they serve the greater good of production, trade, and the consumption of wealth. Unless one seriously entertains the historically unsupported possibility of an economy founded entirely on barter, the inanity of this proposition is evident. Money can, of course, be regarded is a necessary evil, but only in the following way. In times of crisis, money is sought for its own sake, since its status as a *general equivalent* (in Marx's phrase) makes it the ultimate refuge from uncertainty. By virtue of this very status, however, the holding of money entails a substantial loss of information for the economic system as a whole—as Keynes, coming after Marx, saw very clearly. Mr. Henry Ford may very well pay high salaries to his workers so that they are able to buy his cars; but he does not pay them in vouchers that can be exchanged for Fords, he pays them in currency. Mr. Ford therefore has no guarantee that the purchasing power he distributes will be translated into an increased demand for his cars.

We may therefore accept that, in this sense, money may be an evil, even a necessary evil. And yet if there is evil, it must wholly contaminate the real economy. For it is this same money, the ultimate reserve instrument, that serves it as a unit of account and a means of payment. It is futile to place the real economy on a pedestal and to suppose that it looks down upon money, which is no more than its servant. Similarly, if credit is an evil, then plainly the real economy—once it ceases to be an economy of subsistence, in which production and consumption are simultaneous, and comes to be based instead on savings and investment (and therefore on intertemporal arbitrage)—cannot help but be infected by it as well.

The condescension shown toward the financial economy nevertheless feeds mainly on another, scarcely less pointless proposition. A financial economy comes into being when the activities of the market—whose existence, let us assume for the sake of argument, is tolerated in the real sphere—are extended to finance. These activities constitute what is called speculation, a term of opprobrium among us. It comes from the Latin *speculum,* meaning "mirror." Where, then, one might well wonder, are the mirrors of financial speculation? Curiously, the answer is to be found in a formula employed by David Hume in the *Treatise of Human Nature:*

"The minds of men are mirrors to one another."[11] Speculation consists in buying a good, not because one wishes to hold on to it indefinitely, but because one counts on being able to sell it to someone who desires it still more. The mirror is the gaze that another person casts on a good that one looks to acquire. In the world of finance, the relevant good is typically an accounting entry: a value, a share, a bond, a security, a currency. Yet the so-called real economy, even if it deals in goods and services having an undoubtedly material existence, exhibits essentially the same logic, for it is driven by what René Girard calls mimetic desire: we desire an object because the desire of another tells us that it is something to be desired.[12]

Long before Girard, a great philosopher (and, as it happens, a friend of Hume) had the same idea. His name was Adam Smith. He is still today considered by economists as the founding father of their discipline, even if, having never read him, they are wholly ignorant of his doctrines. In a key passage of his greatest work, *The Theory of Moral Sentiments,* Smith asks what wealth consists in. It is not what assures our material well-being, since a frugal life would provide for this satisfactorily enough. It is everything that is desired by what Smith calls the spectator, the person who observes us and whose regard we seek to attract.[13] Because both the financial and the real economy rest on a specular logic, the supposed ethical opposition between them cannot be taken seriously. If one condemns the first—something one is hardly obliged to do!—there is no reason not to condemn the second. Considering the economy as a whole, Smith himself speaks of "the corruption of our moral sentiments."[14]

11. David Hume, *A Treatise of Human Nature* (1739–40), ed. David Fate Norton and Mary J. Norton, 2.2.5 (Oxford: Oxford University Press, 2000), 236.

12. See René Girard, *Deceit, Desire, and the Novel: Self and Other in Literary Structure* (1961), trans. Yvonne Freccero (Baltimore: Johns Hopkins University Press, 1966).

13. "The man within the breast" (our conscience) and "the man without" (the spectator) are famously distinguished in Adam Smith, *The Theory of Moral Sentiments* (1759), 3.2.32, ed. Knud Haakonssen (Cambridge: Cambridge University Press, 2002), 152.

14. Ibid., 1.3.3.1, 72. This corruption, Smith says, has to do with the "disposition to admire, and almost to worship, the rich and the powerful, and to despise, or, at least, to neglect persons of poor and mean condition."

Those who regard the world of finance as a necessary evil will object, however, that one form of speculation is acceptable because it is consubstantial with the logic of the market: the premium granted to the person who is the first to discover a crucial piece of information that suggests an incorrect market valuation. Let us suppose that the market undervalues a particular security. The rational speculator will acquire the security in question in the hope of being able to resell it at a higher price, when the market will finally have discovered its true value. A sort of immanent justice is at work here, for the speculator will receive his premium only when the information that hitherto was known to him alone becomes accessible to everyone. Accordingly, he has no incentive to keep it for himself. Speculation therefore can be seen to be an essential ingredient of what in theory is responsible for the social utility of markets, which is to say their efficiency in processing information, having first collected it and then made it publicly available.

The difficulty is that a parasitical form of speculation inevitably comes to be grafted onto this positive form. If a speculator anticipates that the market is going to persist in its error and settle on a valuation that differs from what he knows to be the true worth of a security, it is on the basis of this mistaken valuation that he must decide to acquire the security. One cannot make money by going against the crowd. This is why the successful speculator is not the person who first correctly analyzes market fundamentals. Speculation instead becomes, in Keynes's phrase, "the activity of forecasting the psychology of the market." Accordingly, the successful speculator is the one who "guess[es] better than the crowd how the crowd will behave."[15] Like a snob, he gives the impression of being ahead of popular opinion only because he slavishly follows it.

In a situation of grave crisis characterized by radical uncertainty, however, it is impossible from within the financial system to determine whether speculation serves to disseminate objective information or whether, though it may point the market in a stable direction, it is wholly untethered from reality.[16] Between healthy speculation and parasitic speculation, undecidability intervenes. A regulated market, which is to say a market from which

---

15. John Maynard Keynes, *The General Theory of Employment, Interest, and Money* (London: Macmillan, 1936), 12.6, 157–58.

16. See André Orléan, "L'auto-référence dans la théorie keynésienne de la speculation," *Cahiers d'économie politique* 14–15 (1988): 229–42.

"bad" speculation has been banished, if that were actually possible, does not function any differently than a speculative market. The phenomenology is different, of course, but the underlying logic is the same.

This confusion of contraries includes the case of a market that itself collapses in confusion. The study of great financial crises, of the panic they provoke and the crash it invariably portends, shows that they do not come from out of the blue like some tragic and incomprehensible stroke of fate, an inexplicable catastrophe that suddenly brings an unbroken period of euphoric and exhilarating expansion to an end. One is tempted to say instead that such crises are programmed, that they are part of a single unfolding event—just as death is part of the course of life, only the day and the hour of its occurrence are unknown. Speculation—indeed, speculative mania—is usually identified with the ascendant phase, and panic with the phase of collapse,[17] but on further analysis it becomes clear that panic is already contained in the speculative phase and that the panic phase remains subject to the logic of speculation: the *same* mechanisms that cause the bubble to expand—to use the time-honored metaphor—also cause it to burst. It follows that to tolerate bullish speculation while banishing its bearish counterpart is no more reasonable than welcoming the bearer of good news while turning the bearer of bad news away.

Rationalist analysis of the crisis, in designating categories of necessary evil in order of increasing generality (bearish speculation, the speculative market, the financial economy), offers reassurance by assigning blame. Just so, it is very careful to keep a safe distance from the black hole in which all such distinctions are abolished and, as we shall see, human societies are brought into existence by self-transcendence.

When Satan Casts Out Satan

Friedrich Hayek, a great philosopher of society (and also, as it happens, a Nobel laureate in economics), is generally reviled by progressive thinkers, who see him only as an apologist for untrammeled economic competition. And yet Hayek was fundamentally correct on one point: the

17. See Charles P. Kindleberger, *Manias, Panics, and Crashes: A History of Financial Crises,* 4th ed. (New York: Wiley, 2000), 2, 15–16, 105–6.

self-regulating character of what he called "spontaneous social orders," one of the most sophisticated forms of which is the market. Even so, Hayek never quite understood that self-regulation operates by means of self-transcendence.[18] In times of both euphoria and panic, in both the material world and the immaterial sphere, the market is capable of producing its own external vantage point, its own external fulcrum, in the form of forces that seem to impose themselves on individual agents, whereas in fact they are a synergistic effect of the behavior of these same agents. Those who deny the market's ability to regulate itself are guilty of committing a category mistake: they confuse the market's capacity for self-exteriorization with the question of whether the consequences of this activity are good for human beings; in other words, they confuse ontology and ethics. They are perfectly free, of course, to disparage markets if they like. I will not dispute the justice of such a view here. My point is simply that, by neglecting the normative dimension of market economies, they fail to grasp an essential property of society.

Where self-transcendence is successfully achieved—by which I mean that it is deployed on a succession of levels sharing a common structure characterized by what Dumont calls the encompassing of the contrary—the level that is taken to be superior to the others and that is supposed to embody the good makes its undifferentiated origin manifest insofar as it preserves a paradoxical similarity with subordinate levels that are supposed to serve it as so many lesser evils. The same relation of difference *and* of identity that obtains between sacrifice and murder can be detected between the "productive" economy, on the one hand, and money and credit, on the other.

It is exactly this relation that rationalist and positivist thinkers have prohibited themselves from imagining. I have taken the example of economic crisis, because the world as we know it might one day fall apart without our understanding the least thing about the reasons for its collapse—but it is no more than that, one among a number of examples that I shall take up in the pages that follow. In all these cases, imagining the future of humanity requires a deliberate willingness to violate the rules and regulations of the Cartesian method, to renounce its ideal of knowledge founded on "clear and distinct ideas." Imagining the future now means trying to come as near as possible to that black hole in which *there*

---

18. See my critique in *Le sacrifice et l'envie: Le libéralisme aux prises avec la justice sociale* (Paris: Calmann-Lévy, 1992), 241–91.

are no longer any differences, in order to perceive the primordial chaos in which everything has its origin.

And what if this were also the condition of approaching God? By "God," I mean what all the divinities that human beings have made for themselves throughout history have in common—an exteriority that they have managed to project outside the sphere of human existence.

The arguments that I present in this book grow out of my struggle for more than thirty years now to come to grips with the thought of René Girard. I shall say nothing about it for the moment, except this. In reviving a long tradition of religious anthropology interrupted by the Second World War and the decades of structuralism and deconstructionist post-structuralism that followed, Girard renewed inquiry into the origins of culture. Like Durkheim, Mauss, Freud, Frazer, Hocart, and many other social theorists before him, he considers that culture arose in conjunction with the notion of the sacred. Girard's hypothesis (as he calls it) asserts that the sacred was produced by a mechanism of self-externalization, so that violence, in projecting itself beyond the domain of human control by means of ritual practices and systems of rules, prohibitions, and obligations, became self-limiting. On this view, the sacred is identified with a "good" form of institutionalized violence that holds in check "bad" anarchic violence.[19] The desacralization of the world that modernity brought about is built upon a kind of knowledge, or suspicion perhaps, that gradually insinuated itself in human thinking—the suspicion that good and bad violence are not opposites, but actually one and the same; that, at bottom, there is no difference between them. How, then, did this suspicion make its way into our minds? Girard's reply, which I shall consider in due course, poses in its turn a prior question that I am not quite sure how to answer: how can there be knowledge of self-transcendence without true transcendence?

Be that as it may, it cannot be denied that this suspicion, this knowledge, is now ours. We know that Satan casts out Satan, as the Bible says (Mark 3: 23–26); we know that evil is capable of self-transcendence, and, by virtue of just this, capable of containing itself within limits—and so,

19. See René Girard, *Violence and the Sacred* (1972), trans. Patrick Gregory (Baltimore: Johns Hopkins University Press, 1977).

too, of averting total destruction. The most striking illustration, which I shall discuss at length in the last chapter, is to be found in the history of the decades since the beginning of the Cold War. Throughout this period it has been as though the bomb protected us from the bomb—an astonishing paradox that some of the most brilliant minds have sought to explain, with only partial success. The very existence of nuclear weapons, it would appear, has prevented the world from disappearing in a nuclear holocaust. That evil should have contained evil is therefore a possibility, but plainly it is not a necessity, as the nuclear case shows with unimprovable clarity. The question is no longer: why has an atomic war not taken place since 1945? Now the question has become: when will it take place in the future?

If this much is admitted, it follows that the powerlessness of contemporary rationalism in its many forms to apprehend the nature of self-transcendence is identical with the denial that lies at its very heart: the refusal to accept that the ways of thinking it authorizes are rooted in our experience of the sacred.

I have cast this book in the form of a metaphysical and theological detective story, after the example of two masterpieces of the genre, to whose authors, it goes without saying, I do not dare compare myself: "The Approach to al-Mu'tasim," by Jorge Luis Borges,[20] and "The Sign of the Broken Sword," by G. K. Chesterton.[21] The objects of my investigation are indications, traces, signs. Taken together, they are the mark of the sacred that appears in texts, analyses, and arguments pretending to be founded on human reason alone, on scientific rationality and nothing else.

This mark of the sacred assumes any number of guises, which are so many deformations of the pure figure of self-transcendence as I have just tried to describe it. These deformations are due to error, of course, but not to just any error: it is because the various forms of rationalism I examine deny having any relationship at all to the sacred that they cannot help but reflect it; only they do so in a distorted fashion that is often illogical and self-contradictory. It may be wondered how the

20. Jorge Luis Borges, "The Approach to al-Mu'tasim" (1936), in *Collected Fictions*, trans. Andrew Hurley (New York: Penguin, 1998), 82–87.
21. G. K. Chesterton, "The Sign of the Broken Sword," in *The Innocence of Father Brown* (London: Cassell, 1911), 259–84.

sacred reveals itself when it structures a text in which it nowhere figures as a thematic element. The question already arises in connection with religious texts proper, such as myths. A mythic hero is expelled from a city, for example, for having destroyed the foundations of the political order. But the account of his expulsion transforms this event into the foundation of the very same political order. This paradoxical loop—how is it possible to have destroyed a social order that one creates by being expelled from it?—is the very signature of myth. Rousseau's political philosophy is based on precisely this same strange loop, as we have already seen, since the social contract, in order to be entered into, must already have been entered into.

Or again: in many mythic accounts, fate implacably unwinds until the moment of final catastrophe is reached, but in order for it to be fulfilled an accident must occur. The accident is not the same as fate; indeed, in a sense, it is its opposite. But it is the indispensable instrument of fate— a *supplement* of fate, in the sense that Derrida gives this term. The effectiveness of nuclear deterrence, for example, is a consequence of rational reliance on a paradoxical account of this type.

And yet another example, if one is really needed: is it better that one innocent man should die so that an entire people and nation will not perish? The high priest Caiaphas's decision to turn Jesus over to Pilate, or rather the revulsion at this decision that caused Christianity to branch off from Judaism, forms the core of the most influential moral and political doctrine of the twentieth century, the theory of justice developed by Rawls, which claims to depend on the resources of rationality alone.

In what follows I shall demonstrate the irreducibility of the paradoxical logic of the sacred by considering five very different spheres of contemporary rationality: transhumanism, which expresses mankind's urge to go beyond itself by means of science and technology; evolutionism, which uses Darwin's theory to account for the persistence and the insistence of religion; electoralism, or the introduction of numerical calculation into the rituals of politics; economism, which is to say the claim that economics is a normative science capable of resolving, among other things, the question of social justice; and catastrophism, whose morbid outlook informs the doctrine of nuclear deterrence—at once the most rational and the most insane idea that humanity has ever conceived.

One figure in particular has captured my imagination: the unfolding of self-transcendence in time. Baron Münchausen's feat finds its counterpart in this, when a community of people is pulled forward by an image of the future that it has projected in front of itself, an image that, once overtaken by events, becomes a part of reality. Humanity has sometimes managed to achieve this same feat, not only in its moments of greatest glory, but in the most tragic moments of its history as well. The present work was written in the shadow cast by the catastrophic future that seems today to be our destiny. This apocalyptic perspective makes it at once possible, urgent, and necessary that we grasp the most fundamental of human truths, namely, that it is the sacred that has made us who and what we are. Otherwise we shall be incapable of recognizing the desacralization of the world brought about by modernity for what it is: an unprecedented train of events that threatens to strip us of all protection against our own violence, and so to lead us directly to the final catastrophe. But this same train of events, if only we can fathom its true character in the time that is left to us, may also point the way to a radically different world than the one we know today, in which religion will have taken the place of the sacred.

I have also conceived the present work as a sort of logbook, in which I record the stages of my own intellectual development, the path by which I have come to think as I do today. This is why I have wished to begin with an account of my earliest influences, not omitting certain quite personal details. For the same reason I have chosen to end the book with an epilogue that takes the form of a confession, a baring of the soul. The figure of self-transcendence—or, as I should now say, bootstrapping—is illustrated not only by the computer; it is embodied in another marvel of engineering, the suspension bridge. Spanning the entrance to a bay, the roadway rises gracefully over the water, supported by cables suspended from high towers. The vertical thrust of the towers derives from their own weight: gravity has been converted into upward momentum. The most beautiful of the world's suspension bridges, the Golden Gate, watches over San Francisco Bay. It was there, in the immediate vicinity of the bridge, that two persons attached themselves to an image they had projected outside of themselves, an image that shattered and fell in pieces around them the moment they tried to make it a reality. Theirs was an impossible love, a tragedy of failed self-transcendence, swallowed up by the black hole of nothingness. The story of this love is told in Alfred Hitchcock's absolute masterpiece, *Vertigo.* Hitchcock's film is for me what Sophocles' tragedy *Oedipus Rex* was for Hölderlin and Girard: the womb from which I am issued. I pay tribute to it in conclusion.[22]

22. I owe the idea for this book to my editor and friend Benoît Chantre. It is true that my philosophical writings over the past fifteen years—touching on the philosophy of science and technology as well as moral and political philosophy, on social theory as well as literary theory, on metaphysics as well as epistemology—are apt to give the impression of having little to do with one another. Benoît discovered the Ariadne's thread that links them together. He made a selection from them and encouraged me to recast the various essays so as to bring out their common interest and purpose. I cannot adequately express my gratitude to him for his assistance.

1

Imagining the End

Staring at Catastrophe

It is my profound belief that humanity is on a suicidal course, headed straight for catastrophe. I speak of catastrophe in the singular, not to designate a single event, but a whole system of disruptions, discontinuities, and basic structural changes that are the consequence of exceeding critical thresholds. Feeding on one another and growing in strength, the calamities we are witnessing today herald an age of unprecedented violence. My heart sinks when I think of the future that awaits my children and their own children. Anyone who hopes that the present century will escape the horrors of the previous one will already have forgotten the inconceivable brutality of that gruesome September day in 2001. There is a widespread expectation that science and technology will come to our rescue, as they have always done in the past. When I was a child, we were taught in school that the misfortunes of humanity were all due to the fact that scientific progress had not been accompanied by a comparable advance in moral wisdom. Science is pure and noble, but human beings are still weighed down by evil and sin. The naiveté of this lesson beggars belief.

I owe to Ivan Illich, that great critic of industrial society and one of my mentors, the insight that humanity has always had to be on its guard against three types of threat, and not simply the two that immediately come to mind: the brute force of nature and the brutality of human beings—the earthquakes that reduce glorious cities to rubble and the barbarism that massacres, mutilates, and rapes their inhabitants in time of war. By learning more about nature, human beings have partially succeeded in taming it; by better understanding the mechanisms of hatred and vengeance, they have come to see that it is possible to live in peace with their enemies, and in this way to build lasting civilizations.

But there is a third front on which it is much more difficult to fight, for here the enemy is *ourselves.* We do not recognize this enemy, though it has our own features. Sometimes we suppose it to be the agent of a malign and treacherous Nature, sometimes of a malevolent and vengeful Nemesis. Yet the evil that besieges us from this direction is a consequence of our own faculty of action, which is to say our ability to irreversibly set in motion processes that are liable to turn against us, with lethal effect. As a great admirer of the work of Hannah Arendt, Illich was well aware that this faculty operates first of all upon human beings. Words and deeds, separately or in combination, create stories for which no single person can claim authorship, and that sometimes end in tragedy. It is from the primordial experience of action acquiring autonomy in relation to the intentions of actors that not only the idea of the sacred, but also religion, tragic drama, and politics—so many real and symbolic systems that serve to set limits to the capacity to act—were born. The wholly novel character of modern societies founded on science and technology derives from the fact that they are capable of unleashing irreversible processes *in and on nature itself.*

Fifty years ago, with extraordinary prescience, Arendt analyzed this transformation of action in her major work, *The Human Condition.*[1] The droughts, hurricanes, and tsunamis we are now witnessing—and indeed the weather itself (which has always served as a metonym for nature)—are increasingly the products of our behavior. We will not have *made* them, in the sense of fabrication, for this activity (called *poiesis* by the Greeks), unlike action *(praxis),* has not only a beginning but also an end, in both senses of the word: goal and terminus. Instead they will be the unanticipated results of a sequence of events that we have initiated, often without knowing it or intending it.

1. See Hannah Arendt, *The Human Condition* (Chicago: University of Chicago Press, 1958), 230–32.

One of the chief threats weighing upon the future of mankind, it is commonly said, is the energy crisis. The crisis is real: our civilization is founded on the proliferation of mechanical devices designed to satisfy our many needs, and soon there will not be enough fuel to keep them going. But in fact there is no energy shortage; indeed, the very phrase ought to be banned—as energetically as possible! It is quite true, of course, that fossil fuels (oil, gas, coal) are nearing exhaustion, and that they will have disappeared well before the end of the century if emerging powers such as China, India, and Brazil persist in blithely following the same path of development we have chosen. It is also true that alternative energies are not yet at hand. Dark clouds can already be seen gathering on the horizon, portents of a merciless war between the great commercial nations, which can be counted on to fight one another with desperate ferocity for possession of the last barrel of oil and the last ton of coal. Increasing pressure on prices, amplified by a major financial crisis, may well degenerate into widespread panic. Libertarian and other conservative economists, placing their faith in the efficiency of market mechanisms they trust to make whatever substitutions are necessary, discount the prospect of catastrophe: new reserves, as though by a miracle, will rapidly grow in number, for it will now be profitable to mine deposits that are not easily accessible, both on land and beneath the sea; energies that used not to be economical to produce, such as solar energy and biofuels, will suddenly become economical, and so on.

But this faith merely conceals the extreme gravity of the threat posed by climate change. Allow me to cite a figure that every citizen of the world, every person in a position to decide policy, even at a very modest level, ought to know and reflect upon. The technical advisors to the Intergovernmental Panel on Climate Change (IPCC) cannot say precisely what the average rise in global temperature will be between now and the end of the century. They do know, however, that half of this uncertainty results from an unknown, namely, which policies for reducing greenhouse-gas emissions will be adopted in the coming years and decades. This situation presents an interesting case of circular causation from the philosopher's point of view, since the policies that are adopted will themselves depend upon the way in which the seriousness of the threat is analyzed—and this analysis depends in part on the uncertainty that hampers forecasts of the extent of global warming.[2]

The same experts fear that climate change will have dreadful consequences. I do not wish to dwell on this point, for anyone who wishes to inform himself—and it would be either criminal or insane not to do so—is able to choose from among a large number of excellent studies. I should like simply to emphasize the following aspect of the matter: if the trends so far observed continue, the climate system will enter into a chaotic state that will cause a set of key variables to reach critical values (popularly known as tipping points). Exceeding these thresholds will trigger in turn a series of irreversible and catastrophic events, amplifying a self-reinforcing dynamic that may be likened to a plunge into the abyss. The deep circulation of the Atlantic may be altered, for example, bringing about a secular cooling trend in Europe that would have dramatic implications for agricultural production; or the permafrost that covers much of the Arctic regions may melt, releasing gigantic quantities of methane, one of the most dangerous greenhouse gases; or the Arctic ice cap may shrink further, causing sea levels to rise throughout the Northern Hemisphere. We do not know exactly where these thresholds lie. When they are discovered, it will be because they have already been exceeded, at which point it will be too late.

I now come to the figure that I promised to reveal a moment ago: *one-third*. If we wish to avoid the irremediable disaster that an increase of three degrees Celsius (fractionally more than five degrees Fahrenheit) in the average global temperature by the end of the century would represent, humanity must force itself not to extract from the earth more than one-third of its presently known carbon deposits, in the form of oil, gas, and coal.[3] *It is not scarcity that should concern us, then, but an overabundance of fossil resources:* we have three times too much. If more than a third of this supply is used up, the spontaneous dynamics of the market will produce an uncontrollable stampede in which the weakest will be trampled in a mad rush by governments and corporations and individuals to claim the last remaining resources for themselves.

2. See Jean Jouzel, Claude Lorius, and Dominique Raymond, *The White Planet: The Evolution and Future of Our Frozen World*, trans. Teresa Lavender Fagan (Princeton, N.J.: Princeton University Press, 2013).

3. See Henri Prévot, *Trop de pétrole! Énergie fossile et réchauffement climatique* (Paris: Seuil, 2007).

Popular opinion has begun to show signs of a growing awareness of the mounting peril, but there is little sense of urgency. Official reports such as the Stern Review, issued by the British government,[4] and films such as Al Gore's *An Inconvenient Truth* have shaken public complacency, the first by showing that it would be much less expensive to fight climate change than to let the world economy collapse under the effects of environmental degradation, the second by playing on emotions and fear. This joint appeal to the heart and the wallet notwithstanding, one often hears it said, by the highest government officials, that *two* dangers threaten the survival of the human race: the growing scarcity of fossil resources *and* a warming climate. The use of the conjunction here reveals a logical error: if the climate is becoming warmer, then resources are not scarce; they are overabundant. There is no better illustration why the various elements of what at the outset I called *the* catastrophe must not be considered in isolation from one another. In doing this, one risks concluding the opposite of the truth.

It is a remarkable fact that many—though by no means all—scientists are far more clear-sighted regarding these matters than the general public. It is remarkable because they courageously confront a truth that is ever so inconvenient for them: the civilization they have helped to create, based on the unrestrained development of science and technology, is in danger of dying. In January 2007, the theoretical physicist Stephen Hawking, renowned for his work in cosmology, and Martin Rees, Astronomer Royal of Great Britain, advanced the minute hand of the Doomsday Clock by two minutes. Three years later, it was pushed back by one minute. In January 2012, it was moved forward again by a minute, so that we are now only five minutes from midnight—the moment when humanity will have annihilated itself. The Doomsday Clock was established in 1947 by a group of physicists who were shocked, somewhat belatedly, by the dropping of atomic bombs on Hiroshima and Nagasaki. The clock was to be administered by the governing board of the *Bulletin of the Atomic Scientists,* a journal devoted to warning the public of the dangers posed by this new and incomparably powerful weapon of mass destruction. In the first year of its existence, at the beginning of the nuclear age, the hand of the clock was set at seven minutes

4. See Nicholas Stern, *The Economics of Climate Change: The Stern Review* (Cambridge: Cambridge University Press, 2007); originally published online, 30 October 2006, at www.hm-treasury.gov.uk/sternreview_index.htm.

before midnight. Since then it has been moved forward and pushed back twenty times. In 1953, when the United States and the Soviet Union tested thermonuclear devices within nine months of each other, the needle came closest to midnight, separated from it by only two minutes. In 1991, with the collapse of the Soviet Union and the end of the Cold War, it was pushed back to seventeen minutes, the earliest setting since the clock's inception; then advanced to seven minutes, in 2002, following the terrorist attacks of the previous year in New York and Washington.

We stand today five minutes from midnight, which is to say two minutes closer than in 1947. Three arguments are put forward to justify this sinister prognostication. First, there is the fact that humanity has entered into a second nuclear age, in which the dangers of continuing proliferation are now aggravated by terrorism. Additionally, the taboo against using the bomb that prevailed after Hiroshima and Nagasaki has begun to lose its force—a result of the passage of time and creeping forgetfulness. Finally, and for the first time in the history of the Doomsday Clock, a reason has been advanced that has nothing to do with the nuclear threat. It has to do instead with the risks associated with climate change.

Some of the greatest scientists of the age therefore recognize that humanity can do away with itself in one of two ways: either through internal violence—civil war on a global scale—or through destruction of the natural environment necessary to its survival. These two methods are evidently not independent of each other. The first tragic manifestations of a warming climate will not be a rise in the level of the oceans, the increasing frequency of heat waves and other extreme weather events, or the drying up of entire regions of the planet, but rather the conflicts and wars caused by the massive migrations that anticipation of these events will provoke. The Norwegian Nobel Committee laid emphasis on exactly this point in awarding the Nobel Peace Prize jointly to Al Gore and the IPCC in 2007.

The destruction of nature produces violence, and violence destroys nature in return. Human beings do not destroy nature because they hate it. They destroy it because, in hating one another, they fail to take due care to protect the third parties that are liable to be injured by their conflict—foremost among them the natural environment. Indifference and blindness kill many more living things than hatred alone.

Some scientists mention a third threat to the survival of humanity: the unrestrained competition to develop advanced technologies and to bring about their "convergence." It is remarkable that they should take notice of such a threat, for it is precisely on this technology race that the world is counting in order to be able to cope with the other threats. But what if, as we may well ask, the cure were to prove worse than the disease?

Scientists cannot avoid being the bearers of bad news: they have, as Martin Rees makes clear, special obligations.[5] Alas, their warnings have not been heard. Signs of the catastrophic future that awaits us, of the chaotic disruption of the climate to come and the unprecedented violence that will result from it, remain largely unheeded. The prophets of doom are mocked and jeered. In a world dominated by economic rivalry, the relationship to the future is conceived in terms of price movements that anticipate future scarcities. This is why imaginary energy shortages have overtaken the climate threat in the popular mind: the climate threat is too abstract to comprehend. Even when we see catastrophe staring us in the face, we do not believe what we know to be the case. In part this is because the willingness of a community to recognize the existence of a risk depends on the degree to which it is convinced that solutions exist.[6] Many, if not most, business executives and political leaders today understand that radical changes in our way of life are the price that must be paid for avoiding disaster; but because this price—amounting to a renunciation of "progress"—seems to them exorbitant, they inevitably succumb to what the philosopher Günther Anders called "blindness toward the Apocalypse."[7]

The problem, then, is that catastrophe is not believable: it is held to be possible only once it has occurred, and by that point it is too late. This

5. See Martin Rees, *Our Final Hour: A Scientist's Warning: How Terror, Error, and Environmental Disaster Threaten Humankind's Future in This Century—On Earth and Beyond* (New York: Basic Books, 2003), esp. 37–40 and 185–88.

6. This so-called inverse principle of risk evaluation is due to the economist David Fleming; see his article "The Economics of Taking Care: An Evaluation of the Precautionary Principle," in David Freestone and Ellen Hey, eds., *The Precautionary Principle and International Law* (The Hague: Kluwer, 1996), 147–67.

7. See Günther Anders, *Die Antiquiertheit des menschen,* 2 vols. (Munich: Beck, 1980).

obstacle can be overcome, I believe, only if an utterly new metaphysical conception is adopted of our relationship to time, which I have called enlightened doomsaying.[8] One cannot help but be struck by the fact that, in France at least, the technocracy is by and large much more alert to the seriousness of the problem than the general public. But its role is to propose solutions, not to play Cassandra. The admirably rigorous work of one senior civil servant in particular, Henri Prévot, has shown that if France were to commit itself to a program of cutting greenhouse-gas emissions by two-thirds in the next thirty or forty years, it would benefit from doing this, even if it were obliged to act alone; and, what is more, that such a program could be carried out without either excessive expenditures or major changes in the way people are accustomed to live today.[9] It nevertheless would require a drastic overhaul of the country's economic infrastructure, and therefore could succeed only if there were an unwavering political determination to put it into effect without delay—which brings us back once more to the question of the state of public opinion.

It is important to notice that Prévot's approach is wholly detached from moral and ethical considerations. It is guided solely by principles of instrumental rationality and efficiency: if we wish to survive, this is what needs to be done. Prévot denounces what he sees as the tendency of environmentalists to confuse two distinct things. In condemning the habits of modern industrial society in the name of a morality that is not universally shared, he says, environmentalists seek to impose a certain view of the world on their fellow citizens on the ground that any way of life that disagrees with the one they recommend will lead straight to disaster. Prévot rejects this claim, and accuses environmentalists of disingenuousness. Indeed it is quite possible that the ecological crisis will lead straight to what the social philosopher André Gorz called ecofascism, a moral order imposed in the name of survival.[10] What Prévot's attack on environmentalists implies is that we should not want survival at any price,

8. See Jean-Pierre Dupuy, *Pour un catastrophisme éclairé: Quand l'impossible est certain* (Paris: Seuil, 2002). An English translation is forthcoming.

9. See Prévot, *Trop de pétrole!*

10. Gorz sometimes speaks instead of "technofascism," echoing Ivan Illich's notion of technocratic fascism; see the discussion of this idea in André Gorz, *Ecology as Politics,* trans. Patsy Vigderman and Jonathan Cloud (Boston: South End Press, 1980), 14–17 and 77–91.

and especially not at the price of submitting ourselves to a new form of totalitarianism. The technological aspects of survival, in other words, cannot be separated from the ethical question.

Recent history leads us to expect that peoples and governments forced by global competition to struggle for survival will not hesitate to sacrifice their most precious values. The twentieth century demonstrated surpassingly well that when a society is overcome by fear and feels itself threatened in its very being, in its capacity to reproduce itself, the veneer that separates order from chaos, civilization from barbarism, can easily be stripped away. What use will it be for humanity to save itself if this means losing its very soul? For the panic that will grip the peoples of the earth if they discover too late that their existence hangs in the balance will sweep away all the barriers that for the moment protect civilization against falling back once more into barbarism. The resources of reason will be overwhelmed, and the values of law and justice obliterated. There exists a dual threat, then, whose elements must be analyzed in tandem: *the threat to survival* and *the threat to values*. It is essential that, in combatting the first threat, we do not inadvertently strengthen the second. Now that humanity is coming to understand that its survival is in danger, it is gradually becoming aware of its own unity, and begins to sense the duty that now falls on it to stem the advancing tide of barbarism. At stake in this moment of gravest crisis is nothing less than the human spirit and the meaning of human existence.

The Prévot plan calls for substantial reliance on nuclear energy. There is no better example of the potential conflict between the requirements of survival and the demands placed on values. The manner in which the catastrophe at Chernobyl was managed by international authorities and technical experts casts considerable doubt on whether the safety of this type of energy can be assured in ways that are compatible with the basic principles of an open, democratic, and just society.[11] If opacity, dissimulation, and deceit are the necessary conditions of safety, the energy/environment equation will obstinately resist solution—unless people choose to seek personal fulfillment by other means than unlimited economic growth.

The principal danger facing humanity, I believe, is the temptation of pride. The fatal conceit is believing that technology—which has severely

11. I have developed this argument in *Retour de Tchernobyl: Journal d'un homme en colère* (Paris: Seuil, 2006).

impaired all those traditional (that is, religious) systems that serve to curb the tendency to excess, itself inevitably a part of human action—will be able to assume the role that these systems once played when the capacity to act bore only upon other human beings, and not upon nature. To believe this is to remain the prisoner of a conception of technology that sees it as a rational activity subject to instrumental logic, to the calculus of means and ends. But today technology has much less to do with fabrication *(poiesis)* than with the power to act *(praxis),* which now means: the power to unleash irreversible processes; indeed, the power to generate "out-of-controlness."[12] In abandoning ourselves to scientistic optimism, counting on technology to rescue us from the very impasses into which it has led us, we run the risk of producing monsters that will devour us.

My recent work in philosophy of science considers this predicament in relation to advanced technologies whose convergence is now being aggressively promoted, the so-called nanotechnologies (which manipulate matter on the molecular and atomic scale) and biotechnologies (which manipulate genes and neurons, again with the assistance of techniques developed by computer scientists). I am interested primarily in the metaphysical foundations and the ethical implications of this fashionable new research paradigm, which now attracts billions of dollars in funding. Very quickly it has become the object of fierce competition on a global scale, on account of the stimulus it promises to give not only to basic scientific research, but also to industrial and military research. With the development of these novel technologies, mankind aims to go beyond biological processes by fabricating life itself. But note this, that anyone who wishes to fabricate—indeed, to *create*—life cannot help but seek to reproduce its essential property, the power to bring into existence something radically new. To the extent that the engineers of tomorrow dream of letting complex and irreversible forces loose in nature, they will not be apprentice

---

12. As the applied physicist Kevin Kelly revealingly remarked, "It took us a long time to realize that the power of a technology is proportional to its inherent out-of-controlness, its inherent ability to surprise and be generative. In fact, unless we can worry about a technology, it is not revolutionary enough." See Kelly's essay "Will Spiritual Robots Replace Humanity by 2100?" (15 March 2006), posted on his blog The Technium, at www.kk.org/thetechnium/archives/2006/03/will_spiritual.php.

sorcerers out of negligence or incompetence, but by design. The ultimate ambition is no longer mastery, but its opposite.[13]

Apocalypse Now

I believe that the present crisis is apocalyptic, in the etymological sense of the word: it *reveals* to us something fundamental about the human world. And this revelation, like the apocalypses of the Bible, from the seventh chapter of the book of Daniel to the synoptic Gospels (of Matthew, Mark, and Luke) and the book of revelation by John of Patmos, bears upon the violence of human beings. The violence of human beings, not of God.

Environmental ethics is often accused of being not only a morality, but also a sort of religion for warning that human beings, having gone beyond the sacred limits that nature, or God, had assigned them, are destined to be spectacularly punished for their transgression—just as the Greek goddess of retribution, Nemesis, was sent to punish man's hubris. But Nemesis has nothing to do with the Judeo-Christian tradition. And although there are indeed profound points of contact between the looming ecological catastrophe and apocalypse, the present struggle to avert calamity does not entail the sacralization of nature. Nor is apocalypse the same as divine punishment.

In the apocalypse according to Mark, one of Jesus's disciples points out the splendor of the Temple for him to admire. Jesus replies: "Do you see these great buildings? There will not be left here one stone upon another, that will not be thrown down." The other disciples ask when this will come to pass, and what signs will herald it. But Jesus refuses to let himself be carried away by millenarian fervor. He desacralizes both the Temple and the event of its destruction, denying that this moment has any divine significance: "And when you hear of wars and rumors of wars, *do not be alarmed;* this must take place, but the end is not yet. For nation will rise against nation, and kingdom against kingdom; there will be earthquakes in various places; there will be famines; this is but the beginning of the sufferings." And further on: "And then if any one says to you, 'Look, here is the Christ!' or 'Look, there he is!' do not believe it. False Christs

13. I take up this topic more fully in the following chapter.

and false prophets will arise and show signs and wonders, to lead astray, if possible, the elect." Thus Jesus concludes: "Take heed, watch; for you do not know when the time will come."[14]

The use of apocalyptic language to desacralize the apocalypse is a kind of ruse whose effect is to subvert the apocalypse from within. What I have called enlightened doomsaying is only the transposition of this ruse to our present crisis: to believe in fate is to prevent it from happening. The paradoxical rationality of such prophecy is utterly contrary to a fascination with catastrophe, for it obliges us instead to distance ourselves from it—a far cry from Rudolf Otto's definition of the sacred as *mysterium tremendum et fascinosum.*[15] One recalls the feeling of exaltation, even exultation, inspired by the tsunami of December 2004, and the extraordinary sense of solidarity that was experienced by people of all nations. Many believed that humanity had become one, that the end of the world was near. Similar sentiments had been expressed three years earlier, and still more forcefully, after the terrorist attacks of 11 September. The spectacle was sublime; there was talk of Armageddon. But the synoptic Gospels had demythologized this confused impulse in advance. God was not cruelly taking vengeance on mankind; the Savior had not yet triumphed over the wicked. Jesus said only this: take heed, watch!

Apocalypse, in the vulgar tradition, signals the end of the world. Revelation comes at the last moment, as in an ordinary detective novel. For Christians, however, the moment of catastrophe and revelation has *already* taken place, not at the end, but in the middle of history, with the killing of Christ, the Passion. The *meaning* of history belongs to a temporality that is not that of history, conceived as a succession of occurrences, but that of eternity. This annulment of occurring time is manifested in the most striking way imaginable by the fact that, in the apocalypses of the synoptic Gospels, Jesus prophesies a catastrophe to come, the destruction of the Temple by Titus in 70 CE—an event that for the authors of these accounts has *already* occurred—while at the same time alluding to the book of Daniel, so that past, present, and future are made to coincide.

---

14. Mark 13: 1–37. The emphasis is mine.

15. See Rudolf Otto, *The Idea of the Holy: An Inquiry into the Non-Rational Factor in the Idea of the Divine and Its Relation to the Rational,* 2nd ed., trans. John W. Harvey (New York: Oxford University Press, 1950).

From our vantage point, in occurring time, eternity can only be spoken of in the future perfect: when the history of this world comes to an end, it *will have become* eternity. At that point everything will come to have meaning; or, more precisely, everything will always and already have had meaning, even if it is necessary to wait until the end for this to be so. Until the end comes, those who await it can do only one thing: be vigilant, alert to what is going on around them, while being careful to avoid getting caught up in the fascination exerted by the great catastrophes of the age.

In this self-demystification of the apocalypse may be found all the elements of an effective campaign against ecological disaster. That the struggle must unavoidably be waged in secular terms is unimportant. There are, in any case, no sacred limits—no limits imposed by a divinized nature or by any other sacralizing authority. And yet liberty and autonomy exist only through and in self-limitation. These things can therefore be achieved only by means of our own free will. But beware the temptation of pride! If we maintain that humanity is responsible for all the evils that plague the world, natural catastrophes included (as Rousseau did after the Lisbon earthquake of 1755);[16] if we maintain that there is nothing apart from human will, and nothing that is not made by human beings, then we deny ourselves any possibility of transcendence—even secular transcendence, without which no human society could come into existence. In the chapters that follow I consider two forms of transcendence: chance and the future. With regard to the future, in keeping with Jesus's injunction of vigilance, enlightened doomsaying invites us to make an imaginative leap, to place ourselves by an act of mental projection in the moment following a future catastrophe and then, looking back toward the present time, to see catastrophe as our *fate*—only a fate that we may yet choose to avoid.

I have entered here into the religious aspect of ecology for a simple reason, that any consideration of last things—eschatology—is inevitably bound up with religion. But so long as we are careful not to confuse religion with the sacred, it becomes possible to devise a secular political strategy for preventing environmental catastrophe that does not fall into the error of moralism, much less the horror of fascism.

16. See my discussion in *Petite métaphysique des tsunamis* (Paris: Seuil, 2005), 31–54. An English translation of this work is forthcoming as well.

Illich and Girard

It has been my good fortune to have met two great thinkers, Ivan Illich and René Girard, whose penetrating and prophetic works have greatly influenced my own thinking. It seemed to me obvious that both men said things that were profound and true, and yet at the same time quite opposite. On the one hand, there is Illich's radical critique of industrial society; on the other, Girard's fundamental anthropology, which gives a persuasive and unsettling response to the question that ought to be the central preoccupation of the human sciences: how is it that modern society, of all human societies, should be the only one that is not rooted in the sacred?[17]

At the end of *Things Hidden Since the Foundation of the World,* Girard emphasizes the human need to escape from meaninglessness: "I hold that truth is not an empty word, or a mere 'effect' as people say nowadays. I hold that everything capable of diverting us from madness and death, from now on, is inextricably linked with this truth. . . . I [have] always cherished the hope that meaning and life were one."[18] With regard to the crisis now facing humanity, and to the choice facing humanity of which direction to take, Illich and Girard agree at least on this: we are heading in a direction that we imagine will lead us to a point lying between two extremes, a new Eden and a ruinous apocalypse. This movement may be likened to the flight of a panic-stricken crowd. Like Tocqueville before them, Illich and Girard are convinced that only the language of religion enables us to form a proper idea of the hidden forces at work in modernity. In the present age of globalization and the obsession with economic growth that drives it, it is instructive to recall Tocqueville's analysis of

17. In this connection, in addition to the works by Girard already cited, see three more: *Things Hidden Since the Foundation of the World* (1978), trans. Stephen Bann and Michael Metterer (Stanford, Calif.: Stanford University Press, 1987); *The Scapegoat* (1982), trans. Yvonne Freccero (Baltimore: Johns Hopkins University Press, 1986); and *Battling to the End: Conversations with Benoît Chantre* (2007), trans. Mary Baker (East Lansing: Michigan State University Press, 2010).

18. Girard, *Things Hidden Since the Foundation of the World,* 446–47. [The translation of *sens* as "meaning" at the end of this passage captures only one of the relevant senses of the French word, which also means "direction." Hence my interpolation in the sentence immediately following.—Trans.]

an equally unprecedented development, what he called the "equality of conditions." The tendency to equality, he observed, is "a providential fact which reflects its principal characteristics: it is universal, it is lasting, and it constantly eludes human interference; its development is served equally by every event and every human being"; indeed, as Tocqueville stressed, "all men have helped its progress with their efforts, both . . . those who fought on its behalf and those who were its declared opponents."[19]

Where Illich and Girard sharply diverge is with regard to the type of religious language that should be employed. For Illich, a former Roman Catholic priest who became one of the Church's harshest critics, it is the language of the sacred found in Greek mythology; for Girard, whose anthropology proceeds from a novel interpretation of Greek tragedy, it is the language of the Gospels. This splendid irony is only one of a number of surprising reversals to be found at the intersection of two compelling ways of looking at the world.

Illich died in December 2002. He and Girard scarcely knew each other's work. Neither one was influenced by the other. On recognizing the voice of truth in both these thinkers, I gradually came to see their writings as more complementary than contradictory. Illich, in spite of his bitter quarrel with the Church, remained a Christian, and he interpreted the role of Christianity in history in a similar fashion to Girard, albeit with significant differences of emphasis, that brought out their mutual affinity with other Christian thinkers, notably G. K. Chesterton. The modern world, they hold, is shot through and through with the gospel message. This is what accounts for its most original features—but it is a corrupt version of the message that does most of the work. Illich summed up this idea by the Latin formula *corruptio optimi quae est pessima* (the corruption of the best is the worst). Girard, for his part, is fond of quoting Chesterton himself: "The modern world is full of the old Christian virtues gone mad."

My first incursions into philosophy were the result of having come into contact with Ivan Illich. I had started out as an economist. My research at the time concerned the practice of medicine and the problem of escalating health-care costs, which even then were beginning to spiral out of control in France. In particular, I was interested in studying the

19. Alexis de Tocqueville, *Democracy in America*, 2 vols., trans. Gerald Bevan (London: Penguin, 2003), 1.1.15, 14.

role played by the prescription of medicines in structuring the relation-ship between doctors and patients. Though still young, I was already deeply troubled by questions of illness, suffering, and death, for reasons that had to do with my own family's medical history. The book report-ing the findings of my research team[20] caused a great stir and brought me a certain celebrity that I could have done without. Illich, who had already published his works on schooling and transport in relation to economic development, was now turning his attention to medicine. He learned of my research through the noted Catholic writer and intellectual Jean-Marie Domenach, who introduced me to him. A strong friendship grew up between us, no less personal than intellectual, and several times during the 1970s I traveled to Cuernavaca, the garden city located some sixty miles south of Mexico City where Illich had established a research center, the Centro Intercultural de Documentación (CIDOC). In 1975, we worked together on the French version of his great book on medicine, *Medical Nemesis*.[21] The third chapter, which lays out the general theory of counterproductivity, is mostly mine.

I have acknowledged the extent of my debt to Ivan Illich many times.[22] I shall limit myself here to mentioning an idea whose importance for enlightened doomsaying cannot be overstated: the invisibility of harm. Over the past ten past years, in thinking about the question of major catas-trophes—whether natural, industrial, or moral—from a philosophical standpoint, I have had occasion to consult the writings of three thinkers who, like Illich, were polyglot Jews having German as their native language: Hannah Arendt; her first husband, Günther Anders; and the person who brought them together, Hans Jonas. Unlike Illich, they were professional philosophers—all three of them students of Heidegger. In the writings of all

20. See Jean-Pierre Dupuy and Serge Karsenty, *L'invasion pharmaceutique*, 2nd ed. (Paris: Seuil, 1977).

21. See Ivan Illich, *Medical Nemesis: The Expropriation of Health* (Lon-don: Calder & Boyars, 1974; New York: Pantheon Books, 1976), translated by the author with the collaboration of Jean-Pierre Dupuy as *Némésis médicale: L'expropriation de la santé* (Paris: Seuil, 1975; 2nd ed., 1981).

22. To mention only two recent occasions: "Le détour et le sacrifice: Ivan Illich et René Girard," *Esprit* 274 (May 2001): 26–46, and "La médicalisation de la vie. Médecine et pouvoir: en hommage à Ivan Illich," *Esprit* 308 (October 2004): 26–39.

three, but especially in those of Anders, there are very strong, indeed deeply moving, resonances with Illich's thought. Probably this is why I have felt a particular need to go back and reread Illich in recent years.

Earlier I gave a first reason for believing that it is mistaken to speak of an energy shortage: we have too many fossil resources, not too few. A second reason is the one that Illich himself gave in his *Energy and Equity:* "The energy crisis focuses concern on the scarcity of fodder for these slaves"—the machines that help people produce the energy on which they believe they depend in order to live well. "I prefer to ask whether free men need them."[23] Illich's notion of the counterproductivity of the major institutions of industrialized society is a familiar one today, even if its author is seldom given due credit.[24] His critique, it should be noted, avoids the trap of moralism that so many environmentalists fall into. At least in his early works, Illich argues on grounds of instrumental rationality and efficiency. If you want to waste less time in getting from here to there, beyond a certain point, a certain critical threshold, you should stop using motorized transport. Is health something whose value has no price for you? Again, beyond a certain point, you should turn away from conventional medicine. Note that Illich's "critical threshold" is the equivalent, in the social and political domain, of the idea of a tipping point in the physical sciences: once the threshold has been exceeded, it is inevitable that medicine destroys health, that transport immobilizes those who use it, that education makes students stupid, that telecommunications make people deaf and mute, and so on. Wild charges? Not if one defines use-value as Illich does, which is to say not only in physical terms, but also in all its cultural and symbolic dimensions. It is at this point that the invisibility of harm intervenes.

Why do we remain blind to the fact that more than a quarter of our waking lives is taken up by transportation? This startling figure is arrived at by adding to the time actually spent in getting from place to place the

23. Ivan Illich, *Energy and Equity* (London: Calder & Boyars, 1974; New York: Harper & Row, 1974), 4.

24. On counterproductivity in technological development, see the second of Illich's seven short books on industrial society, *Tools for Conviviality* (London: Calder & Boyars, 1973; New York: Harper & Row, 1973). The first was *Deschooling Society* (London: Calder & Boyars, 1970; New York: Harper & Row, 1971).

time spent working in order to pay for the means of getting from place to place. The answer is that industrial transport conceals this absurdity from us by substituting working time for traveling time in our implicit economic calculations. Even though the French word for work *(travail)* and the English word "travel" have the same etymological root,[25] we are accustomed to think of work as labor, that is, as a benefit rather than a cost, an end rather than a means. Why, in the domain of medicine, do we not see that the promise of immortality conveyed by nanobiotechnologies is not only false, but actually works to undermine the structural conditions of health in the broadest sense? Because we have not understood that health is not only the silence of our organs, as it were; it is above all the ability, nourished by a shared culture and tradition, of free men and women to confront suffering and mortality—and, more generally, the finitude of the human condition—by incorporating these things in a common spiritual history and, in doing this, giving them meaning. No such thing is possible if suffering and mortality are regarded merely as problems awaiting a technological solution.

My research on the aftermath of the nuclear accident at Chernobyl abruptly brought me face to face with the invisibility of harm. This invisibility is physical, to begin with, since the first impression one has on visiting the immense contaminated area that stretches from Ukraine northward to Belarus is one of absence: the absence of whole villages that have been razed and of persons who have been displaced; the absence of life in the towns that are still standing, but destined to remain uninhabited for the next twenty thousand years. There is also the invisibility of the harm itself—tasteless and odorless radiation. Finally, and more insidiously, there is a kind of statistical invisibility that explains why the number of deaths is reckoned to be between only one and fifty. Since the radioactive exposure was spread out in time and distributed over a vast population, it is impossible to assert with confidence that a person who dies from cancer or leukemia has died as a result of the accident at Chernobyl. The most one can say is that the prior probability of dying from cancer or leukemia was very slightly increased as a result of the accident. Due to their statistical invisibility, the deaths caused

---

25. Both derive from the Latin *trepalium*, a three-pronged instrument of torture; the related English word "travail" was originally identical with the modern word "travel," signifying a laborious journey.

by the catastrophe cannot be *named*. Even so, they can reasonably be estimated to be in the range of tens of thousands.[26] The official position is that no one died, or almost no one. This is an ethical crime.

The mission of the International Atomic Energy Agency (IAEA) in Vienna is "to accelerate and enlarge the contribution of atomic energy to peace, health, and prosperity throughout the world."[27] What is frightening is that we have more to fear today from well-intentioned international nucleocrats than from wicked ones. In every bureaucracy that takes it upon itself to save the world—whether this salvation is called "health,"[28] "mobility," "education," or "information"—Illich saw the mark of the mother of all such priesthoods: the Catholic Church. He was not afraid to invert the definition of the devil that Goethe gives in *Faust,* describing Mephistopheles instead as that which ever seeks good and ever does evil. Illich's insight that evil acquires a power that is independent of the intentions of those who commit it strikingly echoes the arguments made by Arendt and Anders in relation to Auschwitz and Hiroshima, respectively.[29] The shocking implication of these arguments, whose power to disrupt the categories we continue to use in judging the world still makes itself felt today, is that an immense evil may be caused by an absence of malignity; that a monstrous responsibility may go hand in hand with an absence of bad intentions.

Only a madman or a crackpot, disregarding all the conventions of scholarship in the humanities and social sciences, could make the following outrageous claims today. That the history of humanity, considered in its entirety, and in spite—or rather because—of its sound and fury, has a meaning. That this meaning is accessible to us, and that although a science of mankind now exists, it is not mankind that has made it. That this science was given to mankind by divine revelation. That the truth of mankind is

26. My own estimate is about 40,000; see Dupuy, *Retour de Tchernobyl,* 58–59.

27. The Statute of the IAEA, Article II, Objectives; see www.iaea.org/About/statute.html.

28. As a polygot who worked in ten languages, Illich was able to appreciate that the same word, *salud,* is used in Spanish for both "salvation" and "health."

29. See my discussion in *Petite métaphysique des tsunamis,* 70–90.

religious in nature. That of all religions, only one possesses full knowledge of the human world, and therefore encompasses the knowledge of all other religions. Finally, that this religion is Christianity, insofar as it is founded on the Gospels, which is to say on the accounts of the death and the resurrection of Jesus Christ.

This madman is René Girard. The superiority of Christianity, he insists, may be seen above all in the light of its intellectual power. Since the eighteenth century the religion of the Crucified Christ has been considered to be a spent force, and Christians themselves have been vilified as swine or ridiculed as imbeciles. Lift your heads up, Girard tells them, because your faith gives you a faculty of reason that is infinitely superior to that of all the human sciences combined—but do not lift up your heads too high, because this reason is not yours: it has been given to you, and it exceeds your own understanding.

Even the most sympathetic readers of the books that followed *Things Hidden Since the Foundation of the World* (first published in French in 1978, then in English nine years later) felt that Girard's system was complete and henceforth could only go around in circles, mirroring its own obsessive leitmotif—the recurrence of murder, over and over again throughout human history. But they were wrong to feel this way, because they failed to grasp the supreme originality of the hypothesis that Girard advances. In its biblical simplicity it does remain imperturbable and unchanging, that is quite true. Nothing is more human, Girard holds, than the propensity to make gods by making victims. When a delirious crowd discharges its unanimous hatred on a single innocent person, it becomes a machine for creating the sacred, that is, for generating transcendence. It expels its own violence by ascribing it to a radical otherness that can only be divine, since the victim who embodies this spirit is both infinitely bad—for having sparked a crisis (or so it is believed) that threatens to tear society apart—and infinitely good—for having restored order and peace through his own violent expulsion.

The scapegoat mechanism itself is singular and unique. But the outward forms it assumes are as many and various as human cultures and institutions themselves, all of which arise from a mistaken interpretation of the founding event. Myths are documents of persecution composed from the point of view of the persecutors. While Nietzsche and pre-structuralist anthropologists were right to regard the Passion of Christ as just another instance of collective murder, they failed to grasp the one thing that decisively distinguishes the gospel account from all primitive religions, namely, that for the first time the innocence of the victim is *revealed*. The things hidden since the foundation of the world can therefore now be seen. This is the predicament of the modern world, tested by a knowledge that gives it a single choice, between making still more victims (though from now on without the excuse of ignorance) and renouncing the sacrifice of innocents.

One of Girard's former students remarked to him that, in both his work and his life, he seems to have felt that he did not belong: "In Avignon, you felt uneasy among your friends; as a European in the [United States], you experienced the feeling of being a foreigner; at the beginning of your career, you didn't belong to the field of literary criticism, and then later you shifted to anthropological studies." To this Girard replied, "[I]t is true that I tend not to belong to specific environments or fields, but on the other hand, *I cannot be considered an outsider in the classical sense of the term.* I never felt [I was] an *outcast,* as many intellectuals like to represent themselves."[30] This way of describing his own situation appears very odd at first sight, for it suggests that Girard himself escaped the attraction of mimetic desire—contrary to the theory that bears his name, which he himself says admits of no exception. But the contradiction is illusory. Noting that the romantic distinction between the authentic and the inauthentic is based on the refusal of an "observer [to] acknowledge the fact that he himself is implicated in his observation," Girard emphasizes that apprehending the truth of mimetic theory requires an intellectual conversion "in which you accept that you are part of the mimetic mechanism which rules human relationships." The main thing, he says, is being aware of one's own mimetic desire.[31] There is good reason, then, to suppose that the inventor of mimetic theory is himself a hyper-mimetic individual who underwent exactly this conversion; and also that a necessary, though not sufficient, condition of being converted is exactly that sense of *unrootedness* (though not of being an outsider) that he felt as an exile from his own land. The similarity with Simone Weil's situation springs to mind.

30. René Girard, with Pierpaolo Antonello and João Cezar de Castro Rocha, *Evolution and Conversion: Dialogues on the Origins of Culture* (London: Continuum, 2008), 26. My italics added to emphasis in the original.

31. Ibid., 45.

In one of his most profound essays, Girard analyzes Albert Camus's *The Stranger* in terms of self-exclusion.[32] Meursault is a sullen loner, a sulker. Even though no one pays any attention to him, he wants to believe that he is the object of universal persecution. His only wish is to be left alone, free to lead a solitary and marginal life. This self-deception can only succeed, however, if others share his distorted view of reality. He therefore feels obliged to communicate his refusal to communicate—a strange paradox of *bad faith* that can be resolved only by means of an incomprehensible act. Meursault kills the Arab with extreme detachment, as if by negligence or inadvertence—just as a sullen child might burn down a house by setting fire to the curtains. In one sense this act is unimportant. Meursault wants himself and others to believe that he is being punished, not because of the act he committed, but because he is a stranger to the world, someone who did not cry at his mother's funeral. This is why he committed the act as though he did not commit it: he does not feel any more responsible for it than for a stroke of luck or a manifestation of fate; and yet had he not killed the Arab, he would never have been expelled from society. Still today, many—perhaps most—readers of *The Stranger* nevertheless mistake Meursault for an innocent victim, almost a Christ figure, wrongly condemned by stupid and corrupt judges.

Meursault's bad faith reflects Camus's own resentment, which blurs the distinction between self-sacrifice that aims at the good of all and self-sacrifice that aims at killing innocent people by killing oneself. It is this caricatural and monstrous inversion of the Christian message that Girard sees at work in the various elements that together constitute what is commonly called globalization. Speaking of the new forms of inequality and of violence that have emerged throughout the world since the publication of Camus's novel, Girard notes that everywhere

there is a reliance on ancestral traditions to explain phenomena that, to the contrary, are rooted quite obviously in the loss of these traditions—a loss that has remained uncompensated until the present day. The hatred of the West and of everything that it represents arises not because its spirit is really foreign to peoples [in other parts of

32. See René Girard, "Camus's Stranger Retried," *PMLA* 79 (December 1964): 519–33; reprinted in Girard, *"To Double Business Bound": Essays on Literature, Mimesis, and Anthropology* (Baltimore: Johns Hopkins University Press, 1978), 9–35.

the world], nor because they are really opposed to the "progress" that we embody, but because the *competitive spirit* is as familiar to them as it is to ourselves. Far from turning away from the West, they cannot prevent themselves from imitating it, from adopting its values without admitting it to themselves. They are no less consumed than we are by the ideology of individual and collective success.[33]

It is for this reason that we have entered into what Girard calls an era of essential violence, when hierarchies are toppled and the old distinctions vanish. *There are no longer any differences:* the more the perpetrators of violence seek to set themselves apart from their adversaries, the more they resemble one another.

Globalization—a cultural "valley of death," as it may well be called[34]—is therefore less an economic or legal or political phenomenon than it is a religious phenomenon. So long as we remain blind to the obviousness of this fact, we will be powerless to prevent globalization from leading us to catastrophe.

The Education of a Prophet of Doom

Girard's theory may be thought of as an inverted pyramid, balanced on the mimetic hypothesis. Everything arises from this, the idea that our own desires are not our own, that we desire what others tell us by their own desires is desirable. From this it follows that those whom we take as our models automatically become our rivals. Human violence is not the manifestation of an innate aggressiveness; it is the result of a peculiar deficiency, a lack of being that inevitably brings us into conflict with those whom we believe will be able to remedy it. But the apparent simplicity of the theory is misleading. Many people, on encountering it for the first time, have difficulty grasping the extraordinary morphogenetic power of the mimetic hypothesis. I have devoted considerable effort to clarifying this aspect of Girard's thinking, which falls under the head of logic and epistemology and suggests points of contact with the most advanced theories in the physical and biological sciences.

33. René Girard, *Celui par qui le scandale arrive* (Paris: Desclée de Brouwer, 2001), 23–24. The emphasis is mine. An English translation is forthcoming from Michigan State University Press.
34. Girard, *Things Hidden Since the Foundation of the World*, 447.

In 1915, Einstein had a brilliant idea that removed the apparently insuperable obstacles that Newtonian physics had run up against. He saw that gravitation was not a force as Newton understood it, but a consequence of the "curved" geometry of space-time. The idea that one body might exert an influence on another at a distance seemed to Einstein to belong more to magic than to science; indeed it seemed to verge on belief in a diabolical causality that causes us to attribute the misfortune that befalls a person or a community to the malicious designs of a wicked being. Newtonian mechanics was therefore heir to the logic of the scapegoat. In a single stroke Einstein found a way out from this traditional universe and opened up radically new perspectives on the physical world. The shock was immense; its effects are still felt today. Why, then, should what we readily praise in a genius of the natural sciences go unrecognized in a genius of the human sciences—*in an Einstein of the moral world?*

To put the same question another way: how is it that a theory that is often accused of being overly simple, if not actually simplistic, should prove to be so difficult to understand—and lend itself to so many misunderstandings? This brings us back to the inexhaustible debate about the "two cultures."[35] Today, more than ever, the tendency of our educational system to divide the world into two camps, scientists and humanists, threatens to drive us straight over the cliff. I was listening on the radio not long ago to a very lively and sophisticated discussion of contemporary culture in France when one of the guests admitted to priding himself on not having more than a high-school knowledge of mathematics and science—at which point the others burst out laughing and congratulated each other on sharing his ignorance. To see how shocking this is, or how shocking it *should* seem to us, imagine someone saying: "Well, I don't know if Victor Hugo lived before or after the French Revolution, but that doesn't stop me from living my life!"

The widespread lack of culture today and the inability of science and technology to cultivate the mind—to prepare young people for a lifetime of learning, to give them a passion for all the things that are summed up in the French phrase *culture générale*—are two aspects of the

35. See C. P. Snow, *The Two Cultures* (Cambridge: Cambridge University Press, 1960).

same phenomenon. Nothing can be done about this problem if we remain determined to ignore it. The crisis of the humanities is usually attributed to the growing influence of science and technology, but in fact these fields attract fewer and fewer students in Western countries. Before long, at the present rate, there will be no scientists and engineers in Europe and the United States; they will all be in India, China, and Brazil, even if yet for a certain time they will have been trained in American universities by professors from their own countries. Whereas science and technology will affect our lives and our thinking to a greater degree than ever before, there will be fewer skilled workers to produce the goods on which we depend, and still fewer thinkers able to work out where science and technology are leading us.

Given the immense challenges and dangers that confront humanity, only a shared cultural sensibility can save us—so long as scientific and technological literacy forms an integral part of this sensibility, which is not the case today. It seems very odd that reasonable people in the twenty-first century should not wish to acquire a basic understanding of science and technology. We need to go straight to the heart of the problem. A cultured person cannot aspire to anything more than mere bourgeois respectability if he has not learned to cherish liberty above all other things. The freedom to speak and act as we will is our most precious resource. Yet it is also the source of the most terrible evils, for the possibilities of action have now been so enlarged that humanity is free to exert its will in and on nature itself, not only in and on human society. In France, a least since Sartre, philosophy and intellectual life have for the most part remained unacquainted with this transformation of human action, whose scope has come to include the power to profoundly modify the natural world. Most thinkers are happy to advertise their ignorance of the very fields in which this power will henceforth be most decisively exercised. Condemned to impotence by their own lack of culture, they have forfeited their traditional role. The main questions of public policy must therefore be reformulated, and examined with the aid of a revitalized moral and political philosophy that assigns a central place to nature and technology.

The question of immigration is a topic of much debate in both Europe and the United States today, and rightly so. But in trying to agree upon criteria that will make it possible to achieve an "optimum" level of immigration, planners and politicians in advanced industrial countries are rather like the tourists lying on the beach in Thailand who saw only at the last moment that a gigantic wave was about to crash over them. They take no notice of the hundreds of millions of wretchedly poor people who will be chased from their homelands in the near future by drought, rising seas, hurricanes and storms, and who will seek refuge in our lands, this time not from oppressive regimes, but from the devastation of whole regions of the world brought about by our own thoughtlessness and irresponsibility. These waves of humanity will make a mockery of our poor attempts to calculate optimum population inflows. In France, as elsewhere, public policy must be considered in the perspective, not of some glorious revolution remaining to be completed, but of a catastrophe needing to be repelled while there is still time.

The reason why uncultured scientists, technocrats, and engineers are a danger to public safety follows from the fact that this imminent catastrophe imperils the very existence of human civilization. From now on we must keep our eyes fixed on what used to be an unthinkable prospect, the self-destruction of humanity, with the aim, not of rendering it impossible, which would be a contradiction, but of delaying its occurrence as long as possible. We now find ourselves living under a suspended sentence. Anyone who believes that science and technology will manage to provide a solution to problems created by science and technology, as they have always done until now, does not believe in the reality of the future. Theirs is a corollary of the belief that the future is as indeterminate as our free will: there can be no science of the future, for the future is something we deliberately design. The fatal conceit of modern society is exactly this view of the future as a branching, tree-like structure—a catalogue of possible futures from which humanity is free to select, and put into effect, the one that it finds the most agreeable.

This kind of free-market metaphysics largely explains why we do not believe in catastrophe, even when it is staring us in the face. For if the future is not real, neither is the prospect of future catastrophe. Believing that it can be avoided, we do not believe that it really threatens us. It is this sophism that I have sought to demolish by applying the method of enlightened doomsaying—a ruse that consists in pretending we are the victims of fate, while keeping in mind that we are the sole cause of what happens to us.

It has become fashionable to say that we now live in a "risk society."[36] But a risk is something that one *takes*. Our current predicament more closely resembles a stone that falls from the sky on our head—a fatality of sorts—even though we threw the stone up in the air ourselves. The appeal to fate is quite obviously a fiction. Isn't all metaphysics fictitious? Of course it is. But all that is demanded of metaphysics is that it be both rational and useful. Indeed, it is our very familiarity with literary fiction that makes this double game, the ruse of enlightened doomsaying, altogether natural. As we are reading a story, a part of us knows perfectly well that the author was free to end his tale as he pleased; and yet we experience the unfolding of events as though it were dictated by an implacable necessity that directly imposes itself on the author. Paul Valéry once described this paradoxical mixture of freedom and necessity as the "natural growth of an artificial flower."[37]

Catastrophe, in Aristotelian aesthetics, is the tragic dénouement of a drama, the end of an inexorable sequence of events that retrospectively gives it meaning. It is this closing off of time that enlightened doomsaying invites us to contemplate in connection with human history. It requires a skill very similar to the one involved in making up and understanding stories, and there is no better preparation for acquiring this skill than a classical literary education. To make sense of what is happening today, one has to imagine the effects of our technological intervention in the world and on ourselves. For this purpose an appreciation of the art of storytelling is indispensable. It would be a great step forward if every engineer, every technocrat, and every business executive were to read at least one novel and see at least one film a week.

If scientists were well acquainted with the humanities and humanists were well versed in science, there would be (in Michel Serres's phrase) neither uncultivated savants nor cultivated ignoramuses. But this could come about only if science and technology were considered a part of what every informed citizen should know, and, conversely, if the humanities

36. See Ulrich Beck, *Risk Society: Towards a New Modernity* (New York: Sage Publications, 1992).

37. "Croissance naturelle d'une fleur artificielle"—thus Valéry's image of the way in which his poem "La jeune parque" (1917) took shape over the course of four years' unremitting labor; from a 1928 letter to André Fontainas, quoted in *Œuvres*, ed. Jean Hytier, 2 vols. (Paris: Gallimard, 1957–60), 1: 1632.

were considered a part of the basic knowledge of scientists. But the problem is not just scientists' lack of general culture. It is their lack of *scientific* culture. Science itself, as we shall see in the next chapter, has increasingly become an unreflective activity, diverted from its philosophical and historical sources and crippled by an institutionalized blindness that threatens to engulf us in chaos.

The debilitating character of specialization is largely responsible for this alarming state of affairs. Scientific, technological, and industrial rivalry now occurs on a global scale, and any company or research laboratory that is not prepared to compete on these terms is bound to perish. The best way to protect oneself, in science no less than in business, is to specialize to the highest possible degree. The consequence of this is that each researcher knows an enormous amount about an ever smaller area of his field. In the whole world he may have at most a dozen or so peers, who are also rivals. There is no point wasting valuable time to learn the history of his discipline if science, as most scientists believe, progresses asymptotically toward the truth and the only relevant results are the most recent. Examine the bibliographic references of a typical scientific article and you will have the impression that science began three years ago. But in order for any intellectual pursuit to become a public activity, a part of general culture, it must at least be able to turn its gaze upon itself, and also to accept that not everything lies within its field of competence. Hypercompetitive—which is to say hyperspecialized—science can hardly contribute anything of value to a generally shared sensibility that might, in its turn, shape society's capacity to act upon itself for the good.

Another reason why science in its current form cannot hope to be part of a generally shared sensibility is more difficult for non-scientists to grasp. It has to do with the fact that scientific discoveries are evaluated primarily with an eye to the things they promise to make possible. The main question asked of a discovery is: Does it have any practical application? Scientists therefore have an instinctive distrust of everything that belongs to the domain of interpretation, which they gladly leave to historians and philosophers of science. Disagreement over how to interpret quantum mechanics has persisted for a hundred years now, but that does not prevent physicists from effectively applying Schrödinger's equation. The fact that the metaphor of the genome as a computer program has been demonstrably false since the earliest days of molecular biology has not stopped biologists from developing powerful technologies for modifying living organisms.

Competition can only aggravate this tendency. There is no point arguing about the theoretical implications of a discovery, much less about the meaning and purpose of what one is doing in the laboratory, when what matters is developing profitable applications more quickly than one's rivals. Nevertheless, it is during the years of a scientist's formal education that the disastrous effects of competition first make themselves felt. I trust I shall be forgiven for mentioning my own personal experience in this connection, and the reasons why I decided against becoming a physicist. Before entering the École Polytechnique in Paris, I was fascinated by the *ideas* of physics—that is, the controversies and the paradoxes to which the interpretation of theories gives rise. I felt that I had a *vocation,* a calling to be a physicist. The course of instruction at the École promptly disabused me of this notion. Mathematical formulas were the only things that mattered. Why? Because as a matter of tradition and principle, students were forced to vie with one another for the highest ranking in their class. Grading performance on the basis of responses to questions about the meaning of physical theories and experimentation is inevitably a subjective, inexact, and therefore unsatisfactory business; dexterity in manipulating equations and formal models, on the other hand, furnishes an objective criterion for assessment. And so I abandoned physics for economics, in large part because of its status as the queen of the social sciences—a title that, as I came to discover, it hardly deserved! Economic theory was consumed by a desire for respectability, which it believed could be achieved only by imitating the "hard" sciences. A typical examination in economics in a top school in France at the time employed as few words of the vernacular language as possible, relying almost exclusively on mathematical symbols. In transforming a social science into a branch of applied mathematics, it created a perversion, against which students have only recently begun to rebel.[38]

We will not succeed in making science a part of the general culture of society by encouraging competition among scientists at every stage

38. See chapter 5 below, pp. 156–57.

of their careers. Indeed, as the great mathematician Benoît Mandelbrot remarked, "Science would be ruined if (like sports) it were to put competition above everything else, and if it were to clarify the rules of competition by withdrawing entirely into narrowly defined specialties. The rare scholars who are nomads-by-choice are essential to the intellectual welfare of the settled disciplines."[39] I would go further: if the underlying structural conditions of scientific training and practice are not changed, there will be no chance of reviving an ancient tradition of cultivating the mind and soul, dormant since the eighteenth century, when science and technology were equal partners with the humanities in an endless and mutually enriching conversation.

The course of my career, like most people's careers, has been shaped by a great many encounters and influences. But perhaps more than others, mine gives the impression of restless curiosity, for I have been no more able to give up humanism for science than science for humanism.

It was on account of Illich that I became a philosopher. On the one hand, this obliged me to renounce my years of training for the technocracy, which until then had seemed to be my destiny; but it also led me to reject what I considered to be a certain irrationalism—the flirtation with Greek mythology—in Illich's rhetoric (though not, mind you, in his thought). Elsewhere I have recounted how, in Illich's company or through him, I came to know three pioneers of the theory of complex self-organizing systems: Heinz von Foerster, Henri Atlan, and Francisco Varela.[40] A marginal branch of cognitive science in the 1970s, it has subsequently redirected inquiry throughout the social and physical sciences. In the meantime, the philosophical implications of this research inspired me to join Jean-Marie Domenach in establishing a research institute at the École Polytechnique, where we were both teaching. Since 1981, the history of the Centre de Recherche en Épistemologie Appliquée (CREA) has coincided with my own career.

39. Appended by Mandelbrot to his entry in *Who's Who* and reproduced in Alan Lindsay Mackay, ed., *A Dictionary of Scientific Quotations* (Philadelphia: A. Hilger, 1991), 163.

40. See Jean-Pierre Dupuy, *Ordres et désordres: Enquête sur un nouveau paradigme,* 2nd ed. (Paris: Seuil, 1990), 11–28.

CREA turned out to be, among other things, the cradle of cognitive science in France. Contrary to a common opinion, I was never a promoter of cognitive science in its standard form, much less a zealot. Indeed, the truth is quite opposite: the main part of my work in the history and philosophy of science has been devoted to criticizing a materialist, mechanist, and reductionist paradigm that aims at conquering an entire intellectual continent, the social sciences in their broadest sense.[41] My present inquiry into the philosophical foundations of nanotechnologies represents the culmination of this effort. Today, with the incipient convergence of nanotechnologies, biotechnologies, information technologies, and cognitive science ("nano-bio-info-cogno" in the conventional shorthand), the ideas of self-organization and complexity—which were no more than ideas when we first began to explore them in the 1980s—are now, for better or for worse, in the process of acquiring physical reality. I take up this topic in detail in the following chapter.

The concept of self-organization was also the point of departure for my studies in the philosophy of economics and politics, as well as social and moral philosophy, which occupied the other half of my time during the 1980s and 1990s. It provided me with both the reason and the occasion to reexamine the classical liberal tradition that sprang from the Scottish Enlightenment, under the influence of David Hume, Adam Smith, and Adam Ferguson, and received its highest expression two centuries later in the social philosophy of Friedrich Hayek. Among French political philosophers I have always been a bit of an outsider for taking an interest in this tradition, which in France is usually thought to be too close to economic theory to be admitted to the kingdom of philosophy—an absurdity in my view.[42]

In economic philosophy, I have collaborated with the economists André Orléan and Olivier Favereau in constructing a new paradigm, the

41. See Jean-Pierre Dupuy, *The Mechanization of the Mind,* trans. M. B. DeBevoise (Princeton, N.J.: Princeton University Press, 2000); reissued with a new preface as *On the Origins of Cognitive Science* (Cambridge, Mass.: MIT Press, 2008). See also my book *Les savants croient-ils en leurs théories? Une lecture philosophique de l'histoire des sciences cognitives* (Paris: INRA Éditions, 2000).

42. I have developed this argument in a series of works: *Introduction aux sciences sociales: Logique des phénomènes collectifs* (Paris: Éllipses, 1992); *Libéralisme et justice sociale* (Paris: Hachette, 1997); *Éthique et philosophie de l'action* (Paris: Éllipses, 1999).

economics of conventions (named for the notion of convention introduced by Hume in the *Treatise of Human Nature*), a form of cooperative behavior that is distinct from both market self-regulation and state regulation. This led me to explore the possibilities for cross-fertilization between cognitive science and the other social sciences, particularly with regard to the role of symbolic exchange and the omnipresence of religion in human societies.

In moral philosophy, the challenge of founding a Kantian-style ethics by relying on instrumental rationality alone is one that the analytic tradition (which today expresses itself mainly in English) has tried to meet in various ways. I have drawn up a systematic inventory of these,[43] with particular attention to John Rawls's *A Theory of Justice*, the French translation of which I sponsored in 1987.[44] It was at CREA that the study of Rawls in France began to develop over the course of the following decade.

Finally, my ongoing research in philosophy of action prompted me to examine the philosophical foundations of rational choice theory and game theory, which in turn made it necessary to revisit the question of free will and determinism, one of the oldest questions in metaphysics. The utter inadequacy of a probabilistic framework for confronting uncertainty in human affairs led me to develop the philosophical attitude of enlightened doomsaying I mentioned earlier.[45]

I have visited many different philosophical lands over the past four decades, but I confess that I have looked at them more with the eyes of an anthropologist than of a native. From cognitive science to political philosophy, from economic theory to rational metaphysics, I have always treated the products of these fields of research—the works that I studied, commented on, criticized, and sometimes myself helped to bring into the world—as symptoms of some more general way of thinking, not as

43. See Jean-Pierre Dupuy, *Le Sacrifice et l'envie: Le libéralisme aux prises avec la justice sociale* (Paris: Calmann-Lévy, 1992).

44. See John Rawls, *A Theory of Justice* (Cambridge, Mass.: Belknap Press of Harvard University Press, 1971), trans. Catherine Audard as *Théorie de la justice* (Paris: Seuil, 1987).

45. See section 2 of Jean-Pierre Dupuy, "The Precautionary Principle and Enlightened Doomsaying: Rational Choice Before the Apocalypse," *Occasion: Interdisciplinary Studies in the Humanities* 1 (October 2009).

self-contained bodies of knowledge having an intrinsic value. I am not a deconstructionist, at least not in the sense that Derrida has given this term. My relation to texts is nevertheless much the same, since I am interested chiefly in detecting flaws, defects, contradictions, and paradoxes—not in order to declare these texts worthless, but to make them say much more than what they seem to say, taken in isolation from others, deprived of context, closed in upon themselves for the sake of an illusory consistency.

There were friendships lost along the way. After the shock of 11 September 2001, I ceased to take seriously large parts of social and political philosophy in which I used to be interested. In a book that expressed my anger and frustration, I lashed out at Rawls's work and its obsessive concern with "a possible world, populated by reasonable zombies to whom the tragedy of the human condition is completely foreign. But this world is not ours—alas, perhaps. The naïve, pompous, academic, and sometimes ridiculous irenicism of the arguments developed in *A Theory of Justice* strike me today as a sin against the human spirit. Not to see evil for what it is is to make oneself a party to it."[46] Not all of my colleagues forgave me for this. Some spoke of me as a traitor.

As an anthropologist of the most abstract productions of the human mind, I know now that I have a single purpose: to find hidden there the mark of the sacred.

---

46. Jean-Pierre Dupuy, *Avions-nous oublié le mal? Penser la politique après le 11 septembre* (Paris: Bayard, 2002), 79.

2

Science

A THEOLOGY IN SPITE OF ITSELF

The Purported Neutrality of Science

Anyone who wishes to think intelligently about the political dimension of science owes it to himself to read a pair of lectures delivered by Max Weber, the first at the height of the First World War and the second immediately afterward. They have long been available in both French and English in one volume.[1] The first lecture, *Wissenschaft als Beruf* (Science as a Vocation, 1917), is generally remembered for its enunciation of the principle of axiological neutrality, according to which science is "value-free." About what Weber called the war of the gods—the implacable and eternal struggle between different value systems—science therefore has nothing to say. The second lecture, given two years later under the title *Politik als Beruf* (Politics as a Vocation, 1919), insisted on the importance of distinguishing between an ethic of responsibility, which concerns those who are charged with protecting the interests of the nation, and an ethic of conviction, which

---

1. See Max Weber, *Le savant et le politique,* trans. J. Freund, with a preface by Raymond Aron (Paris: Plon, 1959); and *The Vocation Lectures: Science as a Vocation, Politics as a Vocation,* ed. David S. Owen and Tracy B. Strong, trans. Rodney Livingstone (Indianapolis: Hackett, 2004). [These lectures first appeared in English shortly after the French version, as part of the collection of Weber's essays edited by Hans Gerth and C. Wright Mills, *From Max Weber* (New York: Oxford University Press, 1961), which the Livingstone translation claims to correct and supersede.—Trans.]

concerns everyone on a personal level. Taking the two lectures together, though only by oversimplifying to an outrageous degree, the lesson can be drawn that science is morally neutral and that public policy in scientific and technological matters is for politicians alone to decide.

No matter how far Weber may himself have believed these claims, often ascribed to him still today, they were utterly discredited by other German thinkers in the years leading up to the Second World War. In the wake of this catastrophe, still more cataclysmic than the first, it was no longer possible to assert the neutrality of science or to absolve it of all responsibility in relation to politics. Science does indeed decide, but in the same way that a collective and anonymous mechanism, a subjectless process, decides—blindly and thoughtlessly. This is the point of Heidegger's aphorism "Science does not think."[2] Far from being value-free, science has a purpose, namely, to fulfill the promise of Western metaphysics. Another of Heidegger's aphorisms has remained no less famous: "Cybernetics is the metaphysics of the atomic age."[3] It was in cybernetics, the precursor of cognitive science, that Heidegger saw the apotheosis of the Cartesian ambition to make man like God, the master and possessor of nature.

One is not obliged to follow Heidegger, of course, and I shall not do so here. But it should be noted that Weber's reasoning on this point is more subtle and complex than is generally realized, particularly with regard to the role of science in bringing about the "disenchantment" of the world:

Let us begin by making clear what is meant in practice by this intellectual process of rationalization through science and a science-based technology. Does it mean, for example, that each one of us sitting here in this lecture room has a greater knowledge of the conditions determining our lives than an Indian or a Hottentot? Hardly. Unless we happen to be physicists, those of us who travel by streetcar have not the faintest idea how that streetcar works. Nor have we any need to know it. It is enough for us to know that we can "count on" the behavior of the streetcar. We can base our own behavior on it. But we have no idea how to build a streetcar so it will move. . . . Thus the growing process of intellectualization and rationalization does *not* imply a growing understanding of the conditions under which we live. It means something

2. Martin Heidegger, "What Calls for Thinking?" (1954), trans. Fred D. Wieck and J. Glenn Gray, in *Basic Writings*, ed. David Farrell Krell (New York: Harper & Row, 1977), 349.

3. This remark occurs in a posthumously published interview with Martin Heidegger, "Nur noch ein Gott kan uns retten," *Der Spiegel*, no. 23 (31 May 1976): 193–219.

quite different. It is the knowledge *or the conviction that if only we wished to understand them we could do so at any time. It means that in principle, then, we are not ruled by mysterious, unpredictable forces,* but that, on the contrary, we can in principle *control everything by means of calculation.* That in turn means the disenchantment of the world. Unlike the savage for whom such forces existed, we need no longer have recourse to magic to control the spirits or to pray to them. Instead, technology and calculation achieve our ends. This is the primary meaning of the process of intellectualization.[4]

Disenchantment need not, then, be the same thing as knowledge and mastery. For the very great majority of the citizens of societies ruled by science and technology, there is neither knowledge nor mastery.[5] But disenchantment, which is to say the supplanting by rational explanation of a magical way of apprehending the world, is paradoxically itself both a belief and an act of faith.

The mistaken claim that science and technology are no more than neutral instruments in the service of a will that is wholly political in nature is indissociable from what I call the theological-scientific problem. What Spinoza called the theological-political problem arises from the question of whether people can live together and resolve their problems as fully *autonomous* agents, which is to say without recourse to religious (or any other form of) transcendence. This is the guiding question of modern political philosophy, which has not yet succeeded in giving a positive reply to it. I should like to pose two questions of my own, which together make up the theological-scientific problem. The first asks whether a purely immanent science is possible, which is to say a science that limits itself to stating facts while remaining indifferent to values. The second asks whether science can, or indeed must, aim at being a purely operational, or functional, form of knowledge—having renounced once and for all the task, which it leaves to philosophy, of giving meaning to the world.

4. Weber, *The Vocation Lectures,* 12–13. The italics I have added to the third and fourth sentences following the ellipsis reinforce and expand the emphasis already given to them by Weber in the original German text.

5. Better, perhaps, to speak of revelation: a November 2003 study commissioned by the National Science Foundation concluded that a good half of American adults do not know how long it takes the earth to revolve around the sun (or do not understand the question), and that the same people believe in miracles and ghosts and place their trust in astrology. Other studies reveal a similar situation in France.

The Theological-Scientific Problem

The philosopher of science Dominique Lecourt recently published a fascinating book that poses questions very similar to the ones I raise here, but responds to them in a quite different way.[6] Lecourt lays emphasis on the clash between two variants of scientific theology: catastrophism and what he calls techno-prophetological optimism. Although they are opposite to each other, these tendencies issue from a single religious source, which, he says, assigns a salvational and millenarian mission to technology. Lecourt assigns himself the philosophical task of "reconceiving technology *as such,* setting aside the initial theological basis for its development, which remains, in the eyes of some, its ultimate justification, and for others, by contrast, the principal ground for its condemnation."[7] Reconceiving technology and science "as such," which is to say in purely positivist or scientistic terms, stripped of all metaphysics and ideology, is exactly what I claim to be both impossible and, in our present predicament, futile.

Lecourt numbers me among the champions of the first camp, the "biocatastrophists," apparently on the basis of nothing more than the title of one of my books.[8] This must be regarded as a doubtful privilege, considering the misguided prejudice that Lecourt reproaches doomsayers for cultivating. He accuses them of hating science, of stirring up public opinion against scientists and discouraging the young from pursuing a scientific career; of being technophobes and irrationalists; and, in extreme cases, of resorting to terrorism and targeted assassinations in order to achieve their ends.[9] Lecourt notes in passing that many "prestigious figures" are nonetheless to be found in this camp, among them eminent

6. Dominique Lecourt, *Humain, posthumain: La technique et la vie* (Paris: Presses universitaires de France, 2003).

7. Ibid., 14.

8. Lecourt no doubt has in mind my 2002 book on enlightened doomsaying, *Pour un catastrophisme éclairé,* which he seems not to have read, or at least not carefully.

9. Lecourt devotes an entire appendix to the case of the American mathematician Theodore Kaczynski, the "Unabomber" terrorist, who killed or wounded some two dozen scientists over a period of almost twenty years before finally being apprehended by the FBI in 1996.

scientists, spiritual authorities, and political leaders.[10] But it does not occur to him for a moment that if so many eminent scientists since Hiroshima have issued cries of alarm, they have done so with good and sufficient reason. He cannot imagine that one can, as I do, place love of science and the desire for knowledge in the first rank of those values that make civilized life possible; that one can not only have a passion for practicing and teaching science, but also be fascinated by technology and committed to its rational development for humane purposes—while at the same time recognizing that science and technology jointly constitute one of the chief dangers confronting the human race today.

One of the first serious warnings came to us from Great Britain. Its author, Martin Rees, whom we met earlier as one of the keepers of the Doomsday Clock, is above all suspicion of irrationalism or hatred of science or technophobia, occupying as he does the chair once occupied by Isaac Newton at Cambridge. Rees gives humanity only a 50 percent chance of surviving until the end of the present century.[11] I shall not go into detail here regarding the reasons he advances in support of this calculation. Whether it is a question of predatory human behaviors that are now destroying bio-diversity and climatic equilibria; of the proliferation of nuclear technology; of the advances of genetic engineering and, soon, of nanotechnologies; or of the risk that these products of human ingenuity will escape human control, either by error or by terror—on all these dangers there exists an immense literature and a very precise understanding. Contrary to what many people suppose, it is not scientific uncertainty that is the cause of our inaction. We know, but we have not yet managed to believe what we know.

Rees is certainly not alone in speaking of the possible extinction of the human race. The signs of impending disaster accumulate, and among scientists, at least, awareness of the threat continues to grow; among politicians, alas, the sense of urgency is rather less keen. One thinks in particular of the warning issued almost a decade ago now by Bill Joy, a co-inventor of the Java programming language that supports much of the Internet's functions and one of the most brilliant living computer scientists. In a very widely noted and discussed essay that appeared in the April

10. Lecourt, *Humain, posthumain*, 2.
11. See Rees, *Our Final Hour*, 7–8.

2000 issue of *Wired* magazine, "Why the Future Doesn't Need Us," Joy developed an argument summarized by the article's subtitle: "Our most powerful 21st-century technologies—robotics, genetic engineering, and nanotech—are threatening to make humans an endangered species." One recalls, too, that the late Gérard Mégie, a former president of the Centre Nationale de la Recherche Scientifique (CNRS) in France and a foremost expert on the physical chemistry of the earth's upper atmosphere, who helped to identify the role of aerosols and other man-made chlorinated products in opening a hole in the stratospheric ozone layer, warned before his death in 2004 that if we do not dramatically change our way of life, we are bound to meet with catastrophe. It is not by chance, after all, that the minute hand on the Doomsday Clock is closer to midnight today than it was at the beginning of the Cold War.

One recalls, finally, the frank words spoken by Jacques Chirac to his fellow world leaders at the Johannesburg World Summit on Sustainable Development in the summer of 2002: "Our house is on fire, but we look the other way." The French Constitution, as a consequence of the reform sponsored by Chirac two years later, now incorporates in its preamble a Charter for the Environment. In a number of speeches, he pleaded that our first responsibility toward future generations is to protect them against major ecological risks, and therefore to put an end to the general degradation that is taking place before our eyes. This could only be done, he argued, by forging a new relationship between human beings and nature on the basis of a radical change in our mode of production and consumption.

It will be objected that what is at issue here is not science and technology *as such,* but what society does with the products of science and technology. Quite so. Nevertheless, science and technology cannot disown their share of responsibility for what society does. They are an integral part of an entire civilization that today finds itself in crisis—the crisis of an incipiently global society, a society that is giving birth to itself at the very moment when it has come to realize that its own survival hangs in the balance.

The modern notion of progress suffers from a crippling contradiction. Development in all its forms—scientific, technological, economic, and political—is imagined to be universal; indeed, no other possibility is entertained. In their most autistic fantasies, secular progressives imagine that the history of humanity could have led only to this outcome, which constitutes the end of history. It is an end that, in a sense, atones for all the trial and error that has so laboriously preceded it and made it intelligible. And yet secularists know that the universalization of progress, both in space (equality among peoples) and in time (the sustainability of development), will one day inevitably run up against internal and external obstacles, if only because the atmosphere of our planet can no longer support it.

Modern society must therefore decide which it considers to be essential: the ethical requirement of equality, which carries with it certain absolute obligations, or else the mode of development it has embraced until now. Either the developed countries have to retreat into themselves, seeking protection behind every possible sort of shield against whatever fresh assaults the outcasts of the world will devise, each one more cruel and abominable than the last; or they have to invent another way of relating to the world and to nature, to inanimate things and living beings alike, which will have the property of being generalizable on a global scale. If the latter option is preferred, science and technology cannot help but play an essential role in bringing about a metamorphosis that has yet to be worked out in all of its details.

Why We Need the Future

Remaking science and technology in the image of a certain positivist ideal, uncontaminated by human values, is no longer possible. The time has come when we must take up the hard question of the moral responsibility of science and challenge an idea that has too readily been accepted, to the point of becoming a cliché, namely, that it is to future generations that we are answerable for our actions.

The customary reliance on the language of rights, duties, and responsibilities in thinking about what is commonly called our solidarity with those who come after us raises considerable conceptual difficulties, which Western philosophy has on the whole proved to be incapable of resolving. There is no more eloquent testimony to this state of affairs than the quandaries into which John Rawls was led in his crowning work, *A*

Theory of Justice (1971),[12] an attempt both to summarize and remedy the defects of modern moral and political philosophy. Having formulated and rigorously established the principles of justice that must govern the basic institutions of any true democratic society, Rawls is obliged to conclude that these principles do not apply to the question of intergenerational justice, to which he offers only a vague and ill-considered reply. The source of the difficulty, quite obviously, is the irreversibility of time. Whereas a theory of justice that rests on contract is bound to uphold the principle of reciprocity, there can be no reciprocity among successive generations: those who come later receive something from those who came before, but can give nothing to them in return.

The problem is actually deeper than this, however. In the Western perspective of linear time and its companion, progress, inherited from the Enlightenment, future generations are supposed to be happier and wiser than their predecessors. But because Rawls's theory of justice embodies the fundamental moral intuition that priority should be given to the weakest members of society,[13] the obstacle is plain to see: the present generation, though it is worse off than the ones that come after it, is the only one that can give something to others.[14] This is why likening the forward march of humanity to the construction of a house that only the last generation would be able to live in struck Kant as deeply enigmatic. And yet he could not bring himself to dismiss what seems to be not only a ruse of both nature and history, but in a sense the height of instrumental rationality itself—the idea that prior generations should make sacrifices for the ones that come last.[15]

The situation we face today is very different, since our main worry is to avoid ultimate catastrophe. Is this to say that we must substitute for the ideal of progress one of regression and decline? There is no simple answer. Opposing progress to decline is quite pointless, for wholly contrary statements about the age in which we live are equally true—for example, that

12. See chapter 1, note 44 above.

13. See the discussion in chapter 5.

14. See the section entitled "The Problem of Justice Between Generations" in Rawls, *A Theory of Justice*, §44, 284–93.

15. See Immanuel Kant, "Idea for a Universal History from a Cosmopolitan Point of View" (1784), in *On History*, ed. and trans. Lewis White Beck (Indianapolis: Bobbs-Merrill, 1963), 11–26.

it is at once the most exhilarating and the most frightening of all the ages of man. While recognizing the possibility of a supreme calamity, humanity must at the same time accept the daunting responsibility of doing everything it can to avert it. Rawls's error is to say that, at the table of social contract, all generations are equal; that is, there is no generation whose claims have more weight than those of others. But evidently generations are *not* equal from the moral point of view: ours and the ones that will follow us have a considerably greater moral burden than previous ones, of whom it may be said today that, unlike us, they did not know what they were doing. We are the first to experience the emergence of humanity as a quasi-subject; the first to grasp that it is fated to destroy itself unless avoiding this destiny is agreed to be an absolute necessity.

No, our responsibility is owed not to future generations, to a class of anonymous beings whose existence is merely potential, and in whose well-being we shall never be persuaded that we have the slightest reason to take an interest so long as our moral responsibility is conceived in terms of an abstract need to assure distributive justice between generations. It is to the fate of mankind that we are answerable, and therefore to ourselves, here and now. Recall Dante's words, in Canto X of the *Inferno*: "[W]herefore you can comprehend that all our knowledge will be dead from that moment when the door of the future will be closed."[16] If we are the cause of this door's closing, the very meaning of human history will both forever and in retrospect be destroyed.

The conceptual resources needed to face up to our current predicament will only be found, I believe, if we begin by looking outside the rationalist tradition. Native American wisdom has handed down a very fine maxim: "The Earth is loaned to us by our children." This saying expresses a cyclical conception of time that has long been foreign to the Western mind. Yet it stands to gain still greater force in the context of a linear temporality. Notwithstanding that our "children"—the children of our children, their children, and so on indefinitely far into the future— have neither physical nor juridical existence, the maxim implicitly enjoins us to imagine, by reversing the direction of time, that they are the ones

16. Dante Alighieri, *The Divine Comedy*, 2 vols., 2nd ed., trans. Charles S. Singleton, Bollingen Series LXXX (Princeton, N.J.: Princeton University Press, 1977), 1: 105.

who bring "the Earth" to us—everything, that is, that we value and that is not of our own making. We do not own nature. We have the usufruct of it, the right to enjoy its fruits and its blessings. From whom or what have we received it? From the future! Should someone object that the future has no reality, he will only have pointed out the stumbling block that every philosophy of impending catastrophe encounters. The problem is that we do not sufficiently appreciate the reality of the future.

Notice, too, that this maxim does more than simply reverse time. It reconfigures it as a continuous loop. When we project ourselves into the future and look back upon the present in which we live, the imaginative act of splitting apart and then reuniting the present and the future has the same logical form as conscience. Through this act it becomes possible to establish a reciprocity between present and future. The future may have no need of us, but we very much need the future—for it is what gives meaning to everything we do.

When Technologies Converge

How, then, do we account for the fact that science has become so risky an enterprise that some of the world's most distinguished scientists consider it to constitute the chief threat to the survival of humanity? This question must now be regarded as taking precedence above all others. Many philosophers reply to it by saying that Descartes's dream—of putting man in the place of God, as the master and possessor of nature—turned into a nightmare, with the result that mastery is now itself in urgent need of being mastered. I fear that they have not the least understanding of what is really at issue. They fail to see that the technology now taking shape at the intersection of a great many fields *aims precisely at non-mastery*. I repeat: the engineer of tomorrow will be an apprentice sorcerer not by negligence or incompetence; he will be one *deliberately*. He will begin by imagining and designing complex organisms in the form of mathematical models, and will then try to determine, by systematically exploring the landscape of their functional properties, which behaviors they are capable of supporting. In adopting a "bottom-up" approach of this kind, he will be more an explorer and an experimenter than a builder; his success will be measured more by the extent to which these creatures surprise him than by their agreement with a set of preestablished criteria and specifications. Fields such as artificial life, genetic algorithms, robotics, and distributed artificial intelligence already display this character. In the years ahead the aspiration to non-mastery threatens to reach fruition with the demiurgic manipulation of matter on the atomic and molecular scale by nanotechnologies. Moreover, to the extent that the scientist is now likelier to be someone who, rather than seeking to discover a reality independent of the mind, investigates instead the properties of his own inventions (more as a researcher in artificial intelligence, one might say, than as a neurophysiologist), the roles of engineer and scientist will come to be confused and, ultimately, conflated with each other. Nature itself will become what humans have made of it, by unleashing in it processes over which, *by design,* there is no mastery.

In 2004, a group of European nanotech research centers was formed under the name Nano2Life—short for "Bringing Nanotechnology to Life." The ambiguity of this expression is a masterpiece of the rhetorical style increasingly favored by scientists today. It may be interpreted to mean, innocently enough, bringing nanotechnologies into existence, or bringing nanotechnologies and the life sciences together. But one cannot help but detect in it the unmistakable mark of the demiurge, the urge to fabricate life by means of technology. As I say, anyone who wishes to fabricate—indeed, *to create*—life cannot help but wish to reproduce its essential property, namely, the capacity of a living creature to create in its turn something that is utterly new.

This desire is to be realized through a process of technological convergence. The phrase derives from an official American document that two years earlier, in June 2002, announced a vast interdisciplinary initiative, generously supported by federal funding, called Converging Technologies for Improving Human Performance.[17] This program is better known by the acronym NBIC, for the convergence it envisages will bring together research

17. This report was jointly sponsored by the National Science Foundation and the U.S. Department of Commerce. See Mihail C. Roco and William Sims Bainbridge, eds., *Converging Technologies for Improving Human Performance: Nanotechnology, Biotechnology, Information Technology, and Cognitive Science* (Washington, D.C.: National Science Foundation, 2002). The report is also available through the World Technology Evaluation Center (WTEC) website: www.wtec.org/ConvergingTechnologies/Report/NBIC_report.pdf.

in nanotechnology, biotechnology, information technology, and cognitive science. Assessing the many implications—economic, social, political, military, cultural, ethical, and metaphysical—of these technologies, so far as their development may be foreseen, obliges us to consider the problem of risk. It goes without saying that any normative evaluation of converging technologies must give risk its rightful place, neither more nor less. Amidst the confusion that presently passes for reasoned debate, however, risk takes up all the available space. Striking the proper balance requires a recognition of two things: first, that risk is only one type of effect among many others, and certainly not the most important or the most interesting; second, that the calculation of risk, which is the only method of evaluation contemplated,[18] is unsuited to a proper understanding of the majority of such effects.

I have proposed a typology of the effects that the development of NBIC may be expected to produce, with a view to showing that *these effects are for the most part not reducible to risk.*[19] The concept of risk, as it is usually understood, is distorted by the dominant economism of our age, which I examine in a later chapter.[20] For the moment it is enough to observe that risk is generally supposed to involve three elements: the possibility of harm, conventionally indicated in mathematical treatments of the topic by a minus sign; the degree of probability that this harm will occur; and the population of individuals who are liable to be affected by the harm and whose "utilities" furnish a basis for estimating the scale of their injury. It will readily be seen that the effects I discuss in the next section are not in fact risks, for they satisfy none of these three conditions. The National Science Foundation claims, not implausibly, that NBIC will change the course of civilization. But it would be a very clever person indeed who could say whether such an outcome would be a good or a bad thing, who could estimate its likelihood with precision, or who could accurately reckon its consequences by summing individual utilities over entire populations. Critics who dare to point this out naturally find themselves relegated at once to the obscurantist hell of Deep Ecology. And yet

18. This method goes by various names: economic calculation, cost-benefit analysis, and so on; the latest is "the precautionary principle."

19. See Jean-Pierre Dupuy, "Some Pitfalls in the Philosophical Foundations of Nanoethics," *Journal of Medicine and Philosophy* 32 (2007): 237–61.

20. See chapter 5, especially 152–57, 165–68, and 173–74.

one may dissent from fundamentalist environmentalism, and accept the anthropocentric view of man as the measure of all things, without therefore falling into the naïve errors of methodological individualism associated with the economic calculation of risk. Between these two positions, there is a ample room for a rigorous and original normative approach to be developed.

Beyond the Obsession with Risk

The development of nanotech in the near and medium term poses risks to health, the environment, security, personal privacy, and many other things. The greatest risk for a country today, however, is not to have moved quickly to position itself in the race for nanotech dominance, whether in science and technology, industry and commerce, or the projection of military power. And yet the very suddenness with which this international competition has started up, and the sense of inevitability that accompanies it, have worked to discourage serious reflection, and sometimes actually to preempt it. It is essential that we think through the consequences of this imminent revolution, which may be grouped under five heads: ontological, epistemic, ethical, metaphysical, and anthropological.

Consequences for Man's Relation to Nature: Ontological Effects

The current—and so far, as I say, quite uncritical—debate regarding the transformation of humanity's relationship to nature under the influence of new technologies assumes the following form. On the one hand, there are the claims of Deep Ecology, which treats nature as an immutable model of equilibrium and harmony, and man as an irresponsible and dangerous predator; on the other, there is the modern humanist ambition of liberating human beings from nature and making them masters and possessors not only of the world, but also of themselves. Whereas "transgression" is reviled in the one case, in the other it is demanded. Between these extremes one finds a series of intermediate positions, variants to one degree or another of the argument, defensively pressed by many scientists, that since mankind is a part of nature, human interventions must themselves be natural, and that new technologies are only accelerating processes that have always been at work. A reasonable policy, on this view, would be to restrict human action upon nature to interventions that do not imperil either the well-being or the survival of humanity.

This debate misses the essential point. Behind every scientific and technological paradigm there is what Karl Popper called a metaphysical research program—a set of non-testable propositions that are assumed to be true without any attempt having been made to challenge them. These propositions constitute a theoretical framework that not only limits the type of questions one may ask but also serves as the primary inspiration for such questions. The metaphysical research program of NBIC is shot through by an enormous paradox. The assumptions involved are plainly thought to be monist: whereas the scholastics held that everything in the universe proceeds from the same *substance,* today it is said that nature, life, and the mind are all governed by the same *principles of organization.* Thus the project of "naturalizing the mind"—the watchword of cognitive science—is seen to be a matter of restoring the mind and, more generally, life to their full and proper place within the natural world. And yet the principles of organization that are supposed to be common to everything existing in the universe are mechanistic principles; in other words, a machine that processes information according to fixed rules (an algorithm, in mathematical parlance) is taken to be the sole model for all the things there are in the world. Chronologically, and contrary to the received version of events, it was the mind that was first likened to an algorithm (in the model devised by Warren McCulloch and Walter Pitts in 1943); life's turn came a few years later with the birth of molecular biology (through the work of Max Delbrück's "phage group" at Caltech in 1949), and subsequently with the popularization of the idea that the laws of physics are "recursive" (which is to say calculable by the algorithm known as a Turing machine). In this way the naturalization of the mind gradually came to be identified with the mechanization of the mind.[21]

Here, as in many other cases, it is the literature of scientific propaganda that inadvertently expresses the underlying motivation, for in its boundless philosophical naïveté it is not inclined to exercise rhetorical caution. The futurologist Damien Broderick, for example, has given a revealing

---

21. I have developed this theme at length in *The Mechanization of the Mind;* see esp. 43–69.

account of the history of biological evolution. In the beginning, he says, "[g]enetic algorithms in planetary numbers lurched about on the surface of the earth and under the sea"; now, eons later, "the entire [accumulated] living ecology of the planet . . . represents a colossal quantity of compressed, schematic information."[22] In this telling, the prokaryotic and eukaryotic cells that formed the basis of life have been converted into products of the human mind, genetic algorithms, even though these algorithms first appeared only toward the end of the twentieth century. Life is regarded as a digest, or summary, of *information*—the blueprint for the *fabrication* of living beings themselves. The materialist monism of modern science has suddenly become a spiritualist monism: if the mind is identical with nature, it is because nature is interpreted as if it were a creation of the mind. One is reminded of the great Swiss clown Grock, a magnificent concert performer who used to walk out on stage to his Steinway and then, on discovering that the bench was too far from the piano, began with great difficulty to drag the piano toward the bench. The piano is nature, and the bench the mind. Recasting nature in such a way as to make it seem as though the mind is its creator makes it possible in turn to say that the mind has been moved closer to nature. An oxymoronic expression perfectly captures the oddity of this situation: nature has become *artificial nature.*

Inevitably, then, the next step is to ask whether the mind might not be able to take over from nature, carrying out its work more efficiently and more intelligently. Broderick approvingly mentions the possibility "that nanosystems, designed by human minds, will bypass all this *Darwinian wandering,* and leap straight to design success."[23] The irony that science, which in America has had to engage in an epic struggle to root out every

---

22. Damien Broderick, *The Spike: How Our Lives Are Being Transformed by Rapidly Advancing Technologies* (New York: Forge, 2001), 116. A genetic algorithm is a computer program designed to solve a given optimization problem through a process of natural selection, in the Darwinian sense, that operates on a population of programs constituting a universe of possible solutions to the problem. Even though not directly conceived by a human mind, since it is the result of a mechanism that mimics biological evolution, a genetic algorithm is an intellectual construction that nevertheless requires a human artifact, the computer, in order to display behavior that can be interpreted, which is to say given meaning.

23. Broderick, *The Spike,* 118. The emphasis is mine.

trace of creationism (including its most recent avatar, "intelligent design") from public education, should now revert to a logic of design in the form of the nanotechnology program—the only difference being that now it is mankind that assumes the role of demiurge—is exquisite.

Consequences for Human Knowledge: Epistemic Effects

At the dawn of the modern age, in *The New Science* (1725), Giambattista Vico famously enunciated a fundamental principle: *Verum et factum convertuntur* ("the true and the made are convertible"). This meant that human beings can rationally know only that of which they are the cause, that which they have fabricated themselves. Originally the doctrine of *verum factum* was interpreted negatively: we shall never be able to know nature as God does, for God created it and we can only observe it. Soon, however, the principle acquired a positive value more in keeping with the growing assertiveness of modern subjectivism. What man makes he can rationally know, demonstratively and deductively, despite the finiteness of his understanding. By this criterion of knowing, in decreasing order of perfection, mathematics ranked first, followed not by the sciences of nature, however, but by the moral and political sciences. Vico, as Hannah Arendt remarked, was responsible for the idea that history is "the only sphere where man [can] obtain certain knowledge, precisely because he deal[s] here only with the products of human activity."[24] Nevertheless, the science of nature itself was guided from the beginning by the conviction that one can know only by making, or rather only by remaking. Thus it was that "from the onset [the scientist] approached [nature] from the standpoint of the One who made it."[25] This explains not only the insistence on the how of processes, rather than on the being of things, but also, and especially, the privileged role reserved for scientific experimentation and modeling. "The use of the experiment for the purpose of knowledge was already the consequence of the conviction that one can know only what he has made himself, for this conviction meant that one might learn about those things man did not make by figuring out and imitating the processes through which they had come into being."[26]

24. Arendt, *The Human Condition*, 298.
25. Ibid., 295.
26. Ibid. See also Dupuy, *The Mechanization of the Mind*, 27–42.

With NBIC, the principle of *verum factum* has found its ultimate expression. It is no longer only in performing experiments on nature, no longer only in modeling it, that human beings henceforth will know nature; it is in remaking nature. For just this reason, however, it is no longer nature they will know, but that which they themselves will have made. Henceforth the very idea of nature, as something given outside of oneself, will appear to be old-fashioned. With NBIC, the distinction between knowing and making will lose all its meaning, as well as anything that still today separates the scientist from the engineer.[27]

More than fifty years ago, in 1958, Arendt had already identified the ethical problem in all of this with stunning acuity. If knowledge becomes pure know-how, because it coincides precisely with the making of things, then there will be no interest in what until now has been called thought:

[I]t could be that we, who are earth-bound creatures and have begun to act as though we were dwellers of the universe, will forever be unable to understand, that is, to think and speak about the things which nevertheless we are able to do. . . . If it should turn out to be true that knowledge (in the modern sense of know-how) and thought have parted company for good, then we would indeed become the helpless slaves, not so much of our machines as of our know-how, *thoughtless* creatures at the mercy of every gadget which is technically possible, no matter how murderous it is.[28]

Note that the word I have italicized, *thoughtless,* is exactly the same adjective that Arendt was to apply to Adolf Eichmann a few years later. The link between this condition and the possibility of monstrous crime is a constant feature of her thought.

Consequences for Normative Judgment: Ethical Effects

In treating nature as an artifact, human beings give themselves the power to act on it to a degree that no technology or science until now has ever dreamed possible. Mankind may hope not only to manipulate this artificial nature at will, but even to fabricate it to suit human desires and

27. Already today one notices in the case of biotechnologies that the distinction between discovery and invention, on which patent law rests, is more and more difficult to discern, as disagreements over the patentability of living organisms attests.

28. Arendt, *The Human Condition,* 3. The emphasis is mine.

aims. Nanotech opens up a vast continent over which moral norms will have to be instituted if this enterprise is to be given meaning and purpose. If human beings are to decide, not what they can do, but what they *ought* to do, a fully elaborated ethics—infinitely more demanding than the one that today is slowly taking shape as part of an effort to limit both the pace of development and the unintended consequences of genetic engineering—will be necessary. This will require in turn an immense act of will and application of conscience.

Whoever uses the words "ethics," "will," and "conscience," as I have just done, looks forward to the triumph of the human subject. But what meaning could this have in a conception of the world that treats nature, including mankind, as a computational machine? In the name of what, or whom, will human beings who have made machines of themselves be able to exert their immense power over nature and themselves? In the name of a meaning that they pretend is only apparent or phenomenal? In that case their will and their choices can only be left to dangle over the void. The unlimited extension of the field of ethics will be expressed by a negation of ethics, in the same manner that the knowledge of nature, now converted into an object of human fabrication, will be expressed by a negation of both nature and of knowledge.

It is instructive to examine what the proponents of NBIC convergence imagine to be the state of mind of those whom they take to be their adversaries, or in any case their critics. These enemies of the new science, they say, insist that human beings do not have the right to usurp powers reserved to God alone; that *playing God* is forbidden (a taboo, it is often claimed, that is specifically Judeo-Christian). But this allegation wholly misconstrues the teaching of the Talmud as well as that of Christian theology. In conflating these doctrines with the ancient Greek conception of the sacred—according to which the gods, jealous of men who have committed the sin of pride, *hubris,* send the goddess of vengeance, Nemesis, to punish them—it forgets that the Bible depicts man as co-creator of the world with God. The biophysicist and talmudic scholar Henri Atlan forcefully makes this point with regard to the golem literature of Jewish tradition. Nowhere in it, Atlan observes, at least not to begin with, "do we find a negative judgment about the science and creative activity of human beings, 'in the image of God'; in this it differs starkly from the Faust legend. Quite the contrary: it is in and through creative activity that human beings achieve their fullest humanity, in an *imitatio Dei* that associates them with God in an ongoing and ever-more-perfect process of creation."[29]

Christianity, as Chesterton, Girard, and Illich have argued, was the womb of Western modernity—a modernity that betrayed and corrupted its message. Illich, in particular, saw that "[w]hat Jesus calls the Kingdom of God stands above and beyond any ethical rule and can disrupt the everyday world in completely unpredictable ways. But Illich also recognize[d] in this declaration of freedom from limits an extreme volatility. For should this freedom ever itself become the subject of a rule, then the limit-less would invade human life in a truly terrifying way."[30] This insight, in combination with Weber's analysis of the disenchantment—or desacralization—of the world, helps to explain why Christianity, or at least what modernity was to make of it, became the driving force behind the progressive elimination of all taboos, all prohibitions, all limits.

In the meantime science itself has taken over from the religions of the Bible in bringing about this desacralization, by stripping nature of its prescriptive or normative value. It is therefore perfectly futile to set science in opposition to the Judeo-Christian tradition on this point. Kant ratified the devaluation of nature by transforming it into a world without intentions or reasons, inhabited solely by causes, and by enforcing a strict separation between this natural world and the human world, a domain of freedom in which reasons for acting fall under the jurisdiction of moral law. Where, then, is the ethical problem located, if in fact there is one here? Clearly it does not lie in the transgression of this or that taboo sanctioned by nature or the sacred, since the joint evolution of religion and science has removed any *heteronomous* foundation for the very concept of moral limitation, and hence of transgression.

29. Henri Atlan, *The Sparks of Randomness,* vol. 1: *Spermatic Knowledge,* trans. Lenn J. Schramm (Stanford, Calif.: Stanford University Press, 2011), 30–31.

30. From David Cayley's introduction to Ivan Illich, *The Rivers North of the Future: The Testament of Ivan Illich as Told to David Caley* (Toronto: House of Anansi Press, 2005), 31; see also Jean-Pierre Dupuy, "Detour and Sacrifice: Ivan Illich and René Girard," in Lee Hoinacki and Carl Mitcham, eds., *The Challenges of Ivan Illich: A Collective Reflection* (Albany: State University of New York Press, 2002), 189–204.

But that is precisely the problem. For there can be no free and autonomous human society that does not rest on some principle of self-limitation. Rousseau, and Kant after him, identified liberty with autonomy and defined it as obedience to a law that one imposes on oneself. Rousseau proved unable to carry out this program, and ended up giving human laws the same exteriority and the same inflexibility as the laws of nature. But in a society that aspires to fashion and fabricate nature according to its own desires and needs, the very idea of an external source of authority no longer has any meaning. Traditionally, nature was defined as all that which is external to the human world, unaffected by its longings, its conflicts, its various depravities. But if nature becomes identified in our dreams with what we make of it, plainly there can no longer be any such exteriority: sooner or later, everything in the world will reflect what human beings have done or not done, what they have wanted or not wanted.

The ethical problem is evidently not restricted to specific questions that bear, for example, on the "enhancement" of this or that cognitive capacity through the application of various technologies. I do not mean that these questions are not important, or that we should not give them our full attention. But they must always be placed in the religious context that I have just described—the gradual turning away from the sacred that we see in the world today.

Consequences for Fundamental Categories of Thought: Metaphysical Effects

We may join Henri Atlan in holding that the mechanistic metaphors of information theory on which cognitive science and molecular biology are built are both scientifically false and philosophically feeble,[31] and yet concede that they radically enlarge the scope of human action on, and mastery over, the natural and living worlds. In that case, however, the very successes enjoyed by new technologies will prevent anyone from seeing that the mechanistic conception of nature and life is an illusion. It is hardly an exaggeration, then, to speak of metaphysical effects. The most troubling of these is surely the blurring of the fundamental categories that

---

31. See Henri Atlan, *La fin du «tout génétique»? Vers de nouveaux paradigmes en biologie* (Paris: INRA Éditions, 1999).

humanity, for as long as it has existed, has used to make sense of the cosmos. The nonliving natural world, the living world, and the man-made world are now well on their way to being merged into one.

In the meantime, attempts to make life from scratch have been organized as a formal scientific discipline under the seemingly innocuous name of synthetic biology. In June 2007, the occasion of the first Kavli Futures Symposium at the University of Greenland in Ilulissat, leading researchers from around the world gathered to promote the convergence of work in synthetic biology and nanotechnology and to take stock of the most recent advances in the manufacture of artificial cells. Their call for a global effort to further "the construction or redesign of biological systems components that do not naturally exist" evoked memories of the statement that was issued in Asilomar, California more than thirty years earlier, in 1975, by the pioneers of biotechnology. Like their predecessors, the founders of synthetic biology drew attention not only to the splendid things that would soon be achieved, but also to the dangers that might arise from them. Accordingly, they invited society to prepare itself for the consequences, while laying down rules of ethical conduct for themselves.[32] We know what became of the charter drawn up at Asilomar: the hope that scientists might succeed in regulating their own research was shattered only a few years later. The dynamics of technological advance and the greed of the marketplace refused to suffer any limitation.

Only a week before the symposium in Ilulissat, a spokesman for the Action Group on Erosion, Technology and Concentration (ETC), an environmental lobby based in Ottawa that had expanded its campaign against genetically modified foods to include emerging nanotechnologies, greeted the announcement of a feat of genetic engineering by the J. Craig Venter Institute in Rockville, Maryland, with the memorable words, "For the first time, God has competition." In the event, ETC had misinterpreted the nature of the achievement.[33] But if the Ilulissat statement is to be believed, the actual synthesis of an organism equipped with an artificial

32. The Ilulissat Statement, Kavli Futures Symposium, "The Merging of Bio and Nano: Towards Cyborg Cells," 11–15 June 2007, Ilulissat, Greenland.

33. Carole Lartigue's JCVI team had succeeded in "simply" transferring the genome of one bacterium, *Mycoplasma mycoides,* to another, *Mycoplasma capricolum,* and showing that the cells of the recipient organism could function with the new genome. In effect, one species had been converted into another.

genome ("a free-living organism that can grow and replicate") will become a reality in the next few years. Whatever the actual timetable may turn out to be, the process of fabricating DNA is now better understood with every passing day, and the moment when it will be possible to create an artificial cell using artificial DNA is surely not far off.[34]

It is not clear, however, whether such an achievement will really amount to *creating* life. In order to assert this much, one must suppose that between life and non-life there is an absolute distinction, a critical threshold, so that whoever crosses it will have transgressed a taboo, like the prophet Jeremiah in the Old Testament or Rabbi Löw of Prague of Jewish legend, who dared to create an artificial man, a *golem*. In the view of its promoters and some of its admirers, notably the physicist and science writer Philip Ball,[35] synthetic biology has managed to demonstrate that no threshold of this type exists: between the dust of the earth and the creature that God formed from it, there is no break in continuity that permits us to say (quoting Genesis 2: 7) that He breathed into man's nostrils the breath of life. And even in the event that synthetic biology should turn out to be incapable of fabricating an artificial cell, these researchers contend, it would still have had the virtue of fatally undermining a prescientific notion of life.

Nanotechnologies are typically defined with reference to the scale of the phenomena over which they promise to exert control—a scale that is described in very vague terms, since it extends from a tenth of a nanometer to a tenth of a micron.[36] Nevertheless, over this entire gamut, the essential distinction between life and non-life loses all meaning. It is meaningless to say, for example, that a DNA molecule is a living thing: it is only at the level of cellular metabolism that it plays its well-known role in the organization of life. The lack of precision in defining nanotechnologies is therefore only apparent. Their distinguishing characteristic on the metaphysical level, with which I am now concerned, is bound up with a deliberate attempt to abolish the basic difference that the phenomenon of life introduces into the material world.

34. With JCVI's announcement in the 20 May 2010 issue of *Science* of the creation of an artificial bacterium, the age of synthetic biology has now arrived.—Trans.

35. See Philip Ball, "Meanings of 'life': Synthetic Biology Provides a Welcome Antidote to Chronic Vitalism," *Nature* 447 (28 June 2007): 1031–32.

36. A nanometer is one billionth part of a meter; a micron, one millionth.

Once again, we find that science oscillates between two opposed attitudes: on the one hand, vainglory, an excessive and often indecent pride; and on the other, when it becomes necessary to silence critics, a false humility that assumes the form of denying one has done anything out of the ordinary, anything that departs from the usual business of normal science. As a philosopher, I am more troubled by the false humility, for in truth it is this, and not the vainglory, that constitutes the height of pride. I am less disturbed by a science that claims to be the equal of God than by a science that nullifies and abolishes one of the most fundamental distinctions known to humanity since the moment it first came into existence: the distinction between that which lives and that which does not; or, to speak more bluntly, between life and death.

Let me propose an analogy that is more profound, I believe, than one may at first be inclined to suspect. With the rise of terrorism in recent years, specifically in the form of suicide attacks, violence on a global scale has taken a radically new turn. In the past, the persecutor expressed his attachment to life, because he killed in order to affirm and assert the primacy of his own way of living. But when the persecutor assumes the role of victim, killing himself in order to maximize the number of people killed around him, all distinctions are blurred, all possibility of reasoned dissuasion is lost, all hope of controlling violence is doomed to impotence. If science is allowed, in its turn, to continue along this same path in denying the crucial difference that life introduces in the world, it will, I predict, prove itself to be capable of a violence that is no less horrifying.

Consequences for the Human Condition: Anthropological Effects

The human condition is inescapably a mixture of that which has been given to mankind and that which mankind has fabricated. Until recently, human beings had to a large extent been able to fashion that which fashions them and to condition that which conditions them, while at the same time preserving a precarious equilibrium between the given and the fabricated. After the Second World War, however, three German philosophers driven out of their native land by the rise of Nazism—Hannah Arendt, Günther Anders, and Hans Jonas—prophesied the coming of a revolt against the age-old conditions of human existence. With extraordinary prescience, Arendt wrote these words:

The human artifice of the world separates human existence from all mere animal environment, but life itself is outside this artificial world, and through life man remains related to all other living organisms. For some time now, a great many scientific endeavors have been directed toward making life also "artificial," toward cutting the last tie through which even man belongs among the children of nature. . . . This future man, whom the scientists tell us they will produce in no more than a hundred years, seems to be possessed by *a rebellion against human existence as it has been given,* a free gift from nowhere (secularly speaking), which he wishes to exchange, as it were, for something he has made himself.[37]

She wrote these words in 1958—long before the first great achievements of genetic engineering, before the idea of nanotechnology was even conceived. One is reminded that ideas and dreams precede their realization, and that philosophy comes before science.

The dream of doing away with death, or, at a minimum, of extending life indefinitely, is explicit in many of the documents cataloguing the benefits that NBIC convergence will confer, whether they belong to the official literature of government-sponsored research or to science fiction. One of the scenarios contemplated by the 2002 National Science Foundation report baldly proclaims: "No death!"[38] And a recent bestseller by the influential futurist Ray Kurzweil, *Fantastic Voyage,* carries a subtitle that magnificently summarizes its purpose: live long enough to live forever.[39] I do not wish here to debate the scientific validity of an attempt to keep people alive until technology has developed to the point it can make them effectively immortal. This project may very well be, at bottom, an intellectual fraud, but the dream itself is quite real. Obviously it is far older than the nanotech program itself, and the underlying metaphysics of this program can only make the dream grow stronger.

"I view disease and death at any age," Kurzweil has remarked, "as a calamity, as problems to be overcome."[40] Let us pause to reflect upon this remarkable idea for a moment: death and disease *as problems to be overcome.* Human beings have always wondered what it would be like to live

37. Arendt, *The Human Condition,* 2–3. The emphasis is mine.

38. Roco and Bainbridge, eds., *Converging Technologies for Improving Human Performance,* 169.

39. Ray Kurzweil and Terry Grossman, *Fantastic Voyage: Live Long Enough to Live Forever* (New York: Rodale Press, 2004).

40. From the front cover of ibid.

forever, of course, even if not everyone has actually wished immortality for himself. But it is only very recently that death has been considered as a problem that science and technology could solve, which is to say, make disappear. The scale of the rupture this represents, by comparison with the way in which the human condition and, more specifically, human mortality have been understood until now, cannot be underestimated. I think of a speech Ivan Illich gave almost twenty years ago. It concludes with an exhortation that reveals the unbridgeable abyss separating his philosophy from Kurzweil's dream:

I do not believe that countries need a national "health" policy, something given to their citizens. Rather, [their citizens] need the courageous virtue to face certain truths:

- we will never eliminate pain;
- we will never cure all disorders;
- we will certainly die.

Therefore, as sensible creatures, we must face the fact that the pursuit of health may be a sickening disorder. There are no scientific, technological solutions. There is the daily task of accepting the fragility and contingency of the human situation. There are reasonable limits which must be placed on conventional "health" care. We urgently need to define anew what duties belong to us as persons, what pertains to our communities, what we relinquish to the state.

Yes, we suffer pain, we become ill, we die. But we also hope, laugh, celebrate; we know the joy of caring for one another; often we are healed and we recover by many means. We do not have to pursue the flattening out of human experience.

I invite all to shift their gaze, their thoughts, from worrying about health care to cultivating the art of living. And, today, with equal importance, to the art of suffering, the art of dying.[41]

Myself, I do not believe that the role of ethics is primarily to say where good and evil lie. Its main point is to force us to ask unsettling questions about aspects of the human condition that ordinarily we do not think of calling into question. Illich's position may well be considered reactionary. But there is one aspect of it, manifested not only by the way in which he lived, but also by the way in which he chose to die, whose logic cannot be

41. Ivan Illich, "Health as One's Own Responsibility—No, Thank You!" This essay, based on a lecture Illich gave in Hannover, Germany on 14 September 1990, subsequently edited by Lee Hoinacki and translated by Jutta Mason, is available at www.davidtinapple.com./illich/1990_health_responsibility.PDF.

escaped. Health, considered from a structural or symbolic point of view, is the ability to confront with full awareness, and in an autonomous way, not only the dangers of the world around us but also a series of more intimate threats, known now and always to every one of us in the form of pain, sickness, and death. People in traditional societies found the source of this strength in their culture, which enabled them to come to terms with their mortality. The sacred was indispensable to this purpose.

Modernity was born amidst the rubble of traditional symbolic systems, in which it could sense the presence only of the irrational and the arbitrary. But in its urge to do away with these systems once and for all, to utterly demystify the world, modernity failed to see that traditional systems, by setting limits to the human condition, endowed it with meaning; in replacing the sacred by reason and science, it lost sight of the fact that the very finiteness of life is what makes it worth living. The growth of medicine went hand in hand with the spread of the belief that the complete suppression of pain and disability and the indefinite postponement of death are desirable things that could be made possible by the unlimited development of medical technology. But one cannot give meaning to what one seeks to abolish. Once certain critical thresholds have been crossed, the machine and its myths will inexorably destroy the structural conditions of health. When the finiteness of the human condition is perceived as a reason for alienation, and not as a source of value, something infinitely precious is given up in exchange for the pursuit of a puerile fantasy.

The Matrix of the Transhumanists

Few readers will have heard of William Sims Bainbridge, a fascinating and, it must be said, rather disturbing character. Looking at his curriculum vitae,[42] one notices at once that he is an active member of an international movement known as "transhumanism."[43] The aim of technological convergence, transhumanists maintain, is to hasten the transition to the next stage

42. See http: //mysite.verizon.net/wsbainbridge.

43. The World Transhumanist Association's principal organ, of which Bainbridge is a consulting editor, changed its name in 2004 from the *Journal of Transhumanism* to the apparently more dignified *Journal of Evolution and Technology*. See www.jetpress.org/index.html. The WTA itself changed its name four years later to Humanity+.

of biological evolution. Biotechnologies take the products of biological evolution as given and limit themselves to using or reproducing them in the service of human ends. The nanobiotechnological program is far more ambitious. It proceeds from the premise that nature, whose designs have for the most part been left to chance, is a poor engineer, replacing what worked tolerably well in the past with more or less unreliable variants. The human mind, assisted by computer science and cognitive technologies whose capacities for intelligence and imagination will soon exceed its own, can be counted on to do much better. Indeed, it will soon succeed in transcending itself.

In a July 2003 address to the World Transhumanist Association (subsequently renamed Humanity+), Bainbridge sketched the outlines of the incipient *transition*—whence the term "transhumanist"—to a posthuman stage of evolution in which machines will have replaced human beings, as well as the obstacles that are likely to be encountered along the way. The cyber-posthumanity that is now emerging will lead on to immortality once it becomes possible to transfer the brain's informational content, and "therefore" the mind and the personality of an individual, into computer memories. For this reason, Bainbridge advised his audience, neither the established religions, whose stock in trade is the fear of death, nor the scientific-technological establishment and the other basic institutions of society—all of them deeply conservative, not to say reactionary—will allow transhumanism to go forward unopposed. Bainbridge concluded his talk by calling upon "citizens of the future" in all countries to organize themselves in "clandestine groups" and, if necessary, to enter into resistance and rebellion against a social order based on the propagation of death.[44]

Dominique Lecourt, in the spirit of Habermas and Latour before him, misses no opportunity to heap ridicule on these techno-prophets of a brave new world. They must not be taken seriously, he says, not least because their preaching calls forth in response the equally baseless doomsaying of the technophobes. Lecourt nonetheless credits the techno-prophets with a line of intellectual descent: they are the direct heirs of

44. The quoted phrases are taken from a paper entitled "Challenge and Response" that Bainbridge read before the World Transhumanist Association on 9 July 2003. The paper was subsequently posted on the Association's website, www. transhumanism.com/articles_more.php?id=P697040C. This site is no longer active, however, and the reference to the paper that formerly appeared in Bainbridge's online curriculum vitae has now, unsurprisingly perhaps, been removed.

medieval Christian theology, which regarded technology as an instrument of redemption and salvation. This, I believe, is a serious error of analysis and judgment alike, for three reasons. The first of these is connected with the fact that these prophets are not crying out in a wilderness. Bainbridge himself is a program director at the National Science Foundation in Arlington, Virginia. Together with Mihail Roco, he was responsible for overseeing the National Nanotechnology Initiative (NNI), announced in July 2000 and expanded two years later to include biotechnology, information technology, and cognitive science, which rains more than $1.5 billion of taxpayer money annually on both civilian and military research institutions. Tellingly, Bainbridge is not a scientist in the usual sense of the word; he is a sociologist, specializing in the study of religious sects—and therefore well qualified to evaluate the type of resistance that the religious mind is likely to mount against research on convergent technologies. It has not been sufficiently appreciated that more than a few of those who are widely considered to be far-sighted guides to the future condition of humanity occupy positions of considerable political power.[45]

45. Formerly co-director of Human-Centered Computing at the National Science Foundation, Bainbridge is currently responsible for Information and Intelligent Systems (IIS) programs and continues to serve as a senior fellow at the Institute for Ethics and Emerging Technologies (IEET), based in Hartford, Connecticut. But he is part of a much broader network of influence. In the summer of 2003, the U.S. Defense Department's research and development arm, DARPA (incontestably one of the world's most inventive think tanks, to which we owe, among other things, the Internet), organized a speculative market in which wagers ("idea futures") regarding the likelihood of political instability, for example, or a terrorist attack, a major international crisis, or even the assassination of a particular Middle Eastern leader could be traded. In the event the Policy Analysis Market (PAM), as it was called, provoked widespread outrage and was rapidly abandoned; but its conceptual foundation, which is to say the capacity of markets to anticipate crises, has been vigorously defended by leading economists. When I discovered that the principal architect of the project, the economist Robin Hanson, is, along with Bainbridge, a consulting editor of the journal of the World Transhumanist Association, I was, I confess, unable to suppress a shudder. One trembles at the thought that other major institutions in the United States and elsewhere, in addition to the National Science Foundation and the Pentagon, have been infiltrated by transhumanism. [Bainbridge's professional biography has been updated by the author.—Trans.]

The second reason that leads me to disagree with Lecourt follows immediately from this state of affairs. It is peculiar, to say the least, to see transhumanism as evidence of the persistence of religion when religion is its declared enemy. And if the organization and rhetoric of transhumanism make one irresistibly think of a sect, the paradox is only apparent: it is the same paradox as the one that, in France, transforms upholders of secularist ideals into guardians of a republican religion. For transhumanists, the supreme being is not a divinity: the creator capable of creating a creature in his own image, of endowing it with autonomy, and of consenting to be dispossessed by his own creation is man. It was Dostoyevsky who warned that if God is dead, men would then be gods for one another. No theology, be it Jewish or Christian, will have anything whatever to do with the deification of man, for this is the supreme sin—the sin of idolatry. Transhumanism is the perfect ideology for a world without God.

The third and final reason is the most important of all. Transhumanist ideology stands in complete contradiction to the metaphysics that underlies the NBIC program. As in the case of cognitive science, the metaphysics of technological convergence assumes the form of a non-reductionist materialist monism: mind and matter are one and the same, both coming under the head of algorithmic computation. The non-reductionist character of this monism may be seen in the importance accorded to the idea of complexity by nanoscience and in the bottom-up approach adopted by nanotechnologies, where each level of organization causes another, higher level to emerge by self-transcendence, or bootstrapping. Movement in the opposite direction does not occur, however, for the encompassing level cannot be reduced to the encompassed level. Transhumanist ideology, on the other hand, is unashamedly dualist: minds are peeled away from their material substrate more easily than the skin of an orange; they migrate from "wetware" (the neuronal system) to "hardware" (the hard disk of future computers) without the least difficulty—grist for the mill of popular American culture in films such as *The Matrix*. By drowning ideology and metaphysics together in the opaque seas of religion, thinkers like Lecourt make it impossible even to see that the two things may be at odds with each other, as in this case, much less to inquire into the reasons for this contradiction.

The argument I have been making here will be clearer if we examine the differences in logical status among the following five propositions:

(1) $ih \, du/dt = -h2/2m \, \Delta u + Vu$

This is Schrödinger's equation, one of the crowning achievements of scientific thought, indeed of the human mind itself. I deliberately introduce it as a sequence of uninterpreted symbols, for the main thing to grasp is that it is a purely syntactical statement in which the operators act blindly, albeit in a well-ordered fashion, on a set of algebraic signs.

(2) "It from Bit"

This proposition, due to the physicist John Archibald Wheeler, very concisely expresses one possible interpretation of quantum mechanics: information ("bit") precedes and begets existence ("it"—a shorthand for that which is). In other words, quantum theory—and physics as a whole—is deducible from a certain theory of information.

(3) Integers can be broken down into their prime factors by means of quantum computation.

This discovery, announced in 2002 at the Massachusetts Institute of Technology, represents a prodigious technical accomplishment that heralds a revolution in information technology whose consequences will be staggering.[46] In the quantum world, information is not associated with a binary choice "0 *or* 1"; it is embodied in the *superposition* of the two states—"0 *and* 1," both at the same time. Quantum computation promises to improve computing speeds by a factor of more than a million.

There exist many other possible interpretations of quantum mechanics than the one expressed by (2), which remains controversial. But this has not prevented scientists from reaching agreement about (1); nor has it prevented (3) from becoming a reality, a fact of technological life. Taken together, these first three propositions illustrate one of the aspects of the thoughtlessness that characterizes science. At any given stage of historical development, a scientific result commands universal assent only insofar as it is expressed by means of a purely mathematical syntax, unencumbered

46. See Jeffrey H. Shapiro and Osamu Hirota, eds., *Quantum Communication, Measurement, and Computing,* Proceedings of the Sixth International Conference held at MIT in July 2002 (Princeton, N.J.: Rinton Press, 2003).

by any interpretive apparatus; and yet this syntax is all that is needed for a result to have practical effect on the world, often amounting to a very considerable power over it. Science therefore permits us to act on reality by means of technology without our really knowing what we are doing.

We now come to the last two propositions, which illustrate respectively what I mean by metaphysical and ideological claims:

(4) Consciousness is reducible to quantum computation.

(5) Science and technology should be used to accelerate the transition to the next stage of biological evolution, marked by the advent of conscious machines expressly designed to replace human beings.

The fourth proposition (urged by researchers at the Center for Consciousness Studies, University of Arizona at Tucson, and elsewhere) may one day be acknowledged as an element of the metaphysical research program of NBIC. It is owing to faith in the truth of such claims that research has been undertaken in new directions in recent years—research that may lead, in the best case, to results and interpretations such as the ones expressed by the first three propositions.

The fifth proposition comes under the head of ideology. Its difference from the preceding one needs to be clearly understood. Propositions such as (4), even though they are "unscientific" in Popper's sense of the term, are indispensable to science. They give an impetus to research, a reason for pursuing it, and, above all, meaning to its findings. Ideological propositions, on the other hand, grow on the compost of science like parasites: they cannot do without science, but science can do very well without them. The question nevertheless arises whether this parasitism may yet play a role, perhaps a very important one, in shaping the direction of scientific investigation. In that case we are faced with a second dimension of scientific thoughtlessness: research depends for its existence on ideology. NBIC itself is a perfect example of the difference between metaphysics and ideology. To the extent that ideology does in fact influence science, it is not principally in the world of ideas that the causal relation operates, but through social and institutional channels.

There can be no contradiction whatever, then, in avowing a love for science, in expressing admiration for technological prowess, in admitting the need one feels as a philosopher to absorb and reflect upon scientific ideas, while at the same defending the view that science, on account of its fundamentally unreflective character, is more than ever likely to loose blind forces upon the world that may lead to disaster.

The Responsibility of Science

The promoters of nanoscience and nanotechnology are many, powerful, and influential: scientists and engineers, excited by the prospect of hitherto unimagined breakthroughs; manufacturers and business executives, attracted by the promise of gigantic markets; governments, alarmed by the thought of falling behind in a very rapidly evolving industrial, economic, and military contest in which jobs, growth, and future defense capabilities are at stake;[47] and, finally, the vast and anonymous collective subject constituted by the headlong rush of technology itself, which is to say the precipitous embrace of technology by all those who still believe that technology, and technology alone, is capable of containing its own undesirable and unintended consequences.

It is therefore altogether unsurprising that the benefits for humanity of the scientific and technological revolution that is now under way should everywhere be praised in hyperbolic terms. The 2002 report prepared under the aegis of the National Science Foundation and the U.S. Department of Commerce, which I have already referred to more than once, is unsurpassed in this regard. It envisages nothing less than the eventual unification of the sciences and technology, universal material and spiritual well-being, world peace, peaceful and mutually advantageous interaction among humans and intelligent machines, the complete disappearance of obstacles to communication among the earth's peoples (particularly ones arising from the diversity of languages), access to inexhaustible supplies of energy, and the end of concerns about dire environmental degradation. The report goes so far as to speculate that "it may be that humanity would become like a single, distributed and interconnected 'brain' based

47. I shall say nothing further here of the military aspects—official secrecy in this connection, as one might expect, is maximal—except that the competition over NBIC in which America, the East Asian powers (China, Taiwan, and Japan), and, belatedly, Europe are now engaged, at a cost of billions of dollars, has already to a large extent assumed the form of an arms race.

in new core pathways of society."[48] William Sims Bainbridge, one of the two authors of the report's executive summary,[49] prudently refrains from discussing the program of the World Transhumanist Association in this document.

By vastly overstating the promise of technological convergence, however, its advocates invite retaliation from opponents in the form of no less overblown countercharges. If the maximalist nanotechnological program is taken seriously, one cannot help but be frightened by the unprecedented *risks* that it seems to carry.[50] Michael Crichton's 2002 novel *Prey*,[51] alerted credulous readers to the horrors of a "grey goo" scenario, also known as global ecophagy, in which the runaway self-replication of nanorobots following a programming accident threatens to destroy all or part of the biosphere by depleting the carbon supply these machines rely on in order to survive. But this risk can really only frighten someone who believes in the possibility of such machines. One has only to deny this premise in order to dismiss the scenario with a shrug of the shoulders as a pseudo-risk.

The scientific community today is the prisoner of the sort of studied ambiguity it has often practiced in the past. When it needs to sell a new product, the most grandiose perspectives are paraded before legislators; but when skeptics raise the question of risks, these claims are retracted, or at least soft-pedaled, and the aims for which funding is sought are said to be modest. Thus the genome is advertised as containing the essence of the living being—but DNA is only a molecule like any other (and, what is more, it is not even alive). Thanks to genetically modified organisms, it will be possible once and for all to solve the problem of hunger—but

48. Roco and Bainbridge, "Converging Technologies for Improving Human Performance," 20.

49. See, in particular, the two final sections of the editors' introduction to the report, dealing with prospects for current research and policy recommendations, ibid., 16–28.

50. See the report of the ETC Group (which previously had taken on the multinational agro-chemical company Monsanto over the issue of genetically modified foods), "The Big Down: Atomtech—Technologies Converging at the Nano-scale," 29 January 2003, accessible via : www.etcgroup.org/en/node/171. ETC's call for a global moratorium on nanotechnological research, renewed in 2006, has evidently gone unheeded.

51. Michael Crichton, *Prey* (New York: HarperCollins, 2002).

human societies have practiced genetic engineering since Neolithic times. Nanobiotechnologies will bring cures for cancer and AIDS—but this is simply another case of science going about its business in the usual way, doing what it has always done. And so on. By permitting itself to engage in this sort of doubletalk, science shows that it is not equal to its responsibilities.

At the present moment there is an unspoken fear among representatives of the nanotech lobby that its efforts may yet meet with an even more complete failure than the one experienced by genetic engineering. In the wake of the Asilomar Conference in 1975, the scientific community confidently imagined that it would be able by itself to regulate the course of future research in the general interest. Within thirty years, however, unrestrained competition had produced a public-relations disaster, with the result that the least biotechnological achievement now looks like a monstrosity in the eyes of ordinary citizens. Today nanotechnologists seek to steer clear of the same fate by doing a better job of selling their product, taking care to reassure skeptics and to persuade doubters of the acceptability of nanoresearch. It must be said that there is something obscene about the vocabulary of advertising when it comes from the mouths of scientists.

What is to be done? It would be naïve to believe that a moratorium on research can be imposed, and still less realistic, in the short term at least, to imagine that a statutory framework for regulation could be enacted, since this must be global in scope if it is to have any meaningful effect. The forces and dynamics presently at work would dispose of any such initiative in short order. The most that can be hoped for is that the forward march of nanotechnologies may be accompanied, if not actually anticipated, by studies of their possible impact and an attitude of constant vigilance no less interdisciplinary than nanoscience itself. Introducing a dimension of self-reflexivity to scientific and technological change, in real time, would be a landmark event in the history of humanity. The quickening pace of events makes this unavoidable if disaster is to be averted.

In no case can science be permitted to evade its responsibilities. Obviously this does not mean that it should be given a monopoly over deciding policy. No sane scientist would wish such a thing. It means that science must be obliged to forswear its splendid isolation from public deliberations about the common good. In a modern democracy, the power to decide must be shared. This, however, entails a corresponding obligation that most scientists adamantly refuse to bear. Their training and their sense of professional self-interest lead them instinctively to take cover behind the myth of the neutrality of science. If society will only allow them to work in peace, steadily and harmlessly adding to its stock of knowledge, then society will be able to set its own course for the future. However defensible this view may have been in the past, it is wholly inadmissible today.

The conditions under which science and society might one day act in concert, on the basis of a shared responsibility for human survival, have not yet come about. One of these conditions, perhaps the chief one, requires of each partner a complete change in its way of thinking. Together they must aim, as I have already urged, to make science a part of everyone's basic education; indeed, a part of the culture of society. *Understanding* science is something entirely different than being told about it. The indifference, or, more often, incomprehension, with which media accounts of scientific research are met on the whole is due to exactly this confusion between information and learning. Plainly the way in which science is taught, not only in elementary and secondary schools, but also at the university level, must be completely reconsidered. Introducing the history and philosophy of science into the standard curriculum would be a welcome first step, but it is far from being sufficient: students who go on to become scientists, having acquired the habit of thinking critically about science, must see this as an integral part of their professional training. The majority of scientists today are no more educated in this respect than the man in the street. The reason for this has to do, as I say, with the specialization of the scientific profession. Max Weber perfectly intuited the problem almost a century ago. In his 1917 lecture on science as a vocation, Weber uttered these terrible words:

At the present time, that inner vocation, in contrast to the external organization *[Betrieb]* of science as a profession, is determined in the first instance by the fact that science has entered a stage of specialization that has no precedent and that will continue for all time. Not just outwardly, but above all inwardly, the position is that only through rigorous specialization can the individual experience the certain satisfaction that he has achieved something perfect in the realm of learning. . . .

Nowadays, a really definitive and valuable achievement is always the product of specialization. And anyone who lacks the ability to don blinkers . . . should keep well away from science. He will never be able to submit to what we may call the "experience" of science.[52]

One must nevertheless hope that Weber's analysis, on this point as on others, will be refuted by the future. Blinkered scientists are a luxury that society today can no longer afford, now that its survival is at stake. Society needs scientists who will have been trained in *thoughtfulness*—scientists who will be under no illusions about the ideological dross that debases their research; who will also be more aware than scientists today that their research inevitably rests on a series of metaphysical decisions. As for God, may they feel free to do without this hypothesis if it so pleases them.

52. Weber, *The Vocation Lectures*, 7–8.

3

Religion

NATURAL VERSUS SUPERNATURAL

In examining the question of advanced technologies, we have seen how true it is that myth is dense in science, to recall Michel Serres's profound insight.[1] Mankind dreams science before doing it. There is no science without metaphysics—as Karl Popper showed long ago, and before him Émile Meyerson.[2]

I now turn to the following question: is it possible to imagine a science concerned with the universal phenomenon of religion in human societies that is nonetheless completely freed of any connection with religion, in the manner of astronomy, for example, which developed by detaching itself from the belief that the stars exert an influence on human beings, and therefore, in particular, on astronomers? Newtonian mechanics was still plainly dependent on astrology, with its notion of action at a distance. In chapter 1, I likened the work of René Girard to the Einsteinian

1. See Michel Serres, *Feux et signaux de brume: Zola* (Paris: Grasset, 1975), 49. Serres knows his mathematics. The term "dense" is to be understood here in the sense it has in set theory, where one says, for example, that the set of rational numbers is *dense* in the set of the reals. This means that in the vicinity of any real number (the square root of 2, say), no matter how small this interval may be, one will always find at least one rational number (that is, a number that is expressible in the form of a fraction).

2. "Man does metaphysics the same way he breathes, without trying and, above all, without suspecting it." See Émile Meyerson, *De l'explication dans les sciences* (Paris: Payot, 1927), 509–63.

revolution in physics. Yet Girard admits that his theory of religion is completely dependent on religion, from which it derives its claims to knowledge. Here we find the object of a science acting upon the science itself. The challenge this presents to the dominant positivism of the modern age can scarcely be underestimated. When scientists purport to treat religion in the same way that they treat heat or electricity, there is every reason to suspect that they are constructing monuments to their own stupidity.

Looking In the Wrong Place

One can speak of religion only by immersing oneself in it, by bringing to bear not only all the resources of the intellect but also the whole emotional range of one's being—in other words, by engaging one's convictions and beliefs as fully as possible. Our being is indissolubly bound up with religion, no less than it is bound up with society and history, even when we examine these things critically or seek to demystify them. As Pascal famously said to those who doubt God's existence, "[I]l faut parier; cela n'est pas volontaire, vous êtes embarqué." There is no escaping uncertainty: whether we like it or not, we have to place our bets.

This is why is it is useless to speak of religion in the third person, adopting the sort of disinterested attitude that is appropriate to a scientific investigation on the positivist model. Those who do speak this way typically find that they cannot avoid betraying the hatred they feel toward religion. It is altogether natural, then, that they should hold it at arm's length, holding their noses against the stench it gives off—not out of a concern for scientific objectivity, but because of the stinking abuse and ridicule they themselves have heaped upon it. Understanding the least thing about religion in this case is quite obviously impossible.

Do I exaggerate? The literature I wish to examine, a rather unappetizing one it must be said, is a by-product of attempts made by cognitivists in biology, psychology, and anthropology to account for religion in terms of evolutionary theory. Religion stands revealed instead as their stumbling block, their *skándalon.* To be fair, these scholars have grasped the fact that they can realize their ambition of conquering the vast continent of the social sciences (including philosophy) only on the condition that they succeed first of all in explaining the universal presence of religion in human societies. The ethologist and evolutionary biologist Richard Dawkins argues that religious beliefs are irrational, nonsensical, and pathological; that they spread like a virus, infecting the brains they attack; that they teem like parasites, vermin, and cockroaches, infesting human populations; and that we should be ashamed of holding them. Pascal's Wager is the wager of a coward, we are told. As for the Gospels, the only thing that separates them from *The Da Vinci Code* is that this is a modern fiction, whereas they are an ancient fiction.[3] The cognitive anthropologist Pascal Boyer, even if he has a less vulgar way of putting things, will not be outdone when it comes to ironic derision and facile humiliation. Rituals are nothing more than cognitive "gadgets." More than this, because there is "something dramatically flawed *in principle* about religion as a way of knowing things," it is unsurprising that the Church should have lost the war of ideas: in its long competition with science to explain "what happens in the world . . . [e]very battle has been lost and conclusively so."[4]

Cognitivism is not the only doctrine to have expounded crude idiocies in the matter of religion, of course; nor has religion been attacked solely by those who lack intelligence or education.[5] Voltaire saw in religion a conspiracy of priests, and Freud a neurosis; Bertrand Russell, for his part, thought nothing of making the slanderous charge that the "immense majority of intellectually eminent men disbelieve in Christian religion, but they conceal the fact in public, because they are afraid of losing their

3. See Richard Dawkins, *The God Delusion* (Boston: Houghton Mifflin, 2006), 188–89, 104, 97.

4. Pascal Boyer, *Religion Explained: The Evolutionary Origins of Religious Thought* (New York: Basic Books, 2001), 255, 321, 320; emphasis in the original.

5. A number of well-known scholars and intellectuals have denounced religion in recent years. Having read very carefully, pencil in hand, the nearly eight hundred pages that make up the books by Dawkins and Boyer, I have not thought it necessary to examine four others that, so far as one can tell, are identical in spirit: Scott Atran, *In Gods We Trust: The Evolutionary Landscape of Religion* (Oxford: Oxford University Press, 2004); Sam Harris, *The End of Faith: Religion, Terror, and the Future of Reason* (New York: Norton, 2004); Daniel Dennett, *Breaking the Spell: Religion as a Natural Phenomenon* (New York: Viking, 2006), and, perhaps most famously of all, Christopher Hitchens, *God Is Not Great: How Religion Poisons Everything* (New York: Twelve, 2007). It may be that I am guilty of negligence. The chance that any of these books redeems the ones by Dawkins and Boyer seems to me remote, however.

incomes."[6] Let me clearly state my own interest in this matter at the outset. I consider myself intellectually a Christian. Note that I do not say I am a Christian intellectual, like Gabriel Marcel or G. K. Chesterton, who writes in the light of his faith. By "intellectually a Christian" I mean that I have come to believe that Christianity constitutes *a body of knowledge about the human world,* one that is not only superior to all the human sciences combined, but that is also their principal source of inspiration. And yet I do not belong to any of the denominations that compose Christianity. I might with equal justice say that I am also intellectually a Jew, to the extent that I believe Judaism made Christianity possible. It was my collaboration with thinkers such as Ivan Illich, and later René Girard, that led me to this *epistemological* conversion to Christianity.

I believe that the Christian message, as it is expressed in the Gospels, is a human science—without which no other human science would be possible. Because Christianity deals with the human world, it bears upon all the religions that have contributed to the history of humanity. What is more, the body of knowledge that Christianity represents is fatal for all these religions. If Christianity is a body of knowledge about the religions of mankind that, by the very fact of explaining them, destroys them as well, this can only be because Christianity is not a religion like the others. Indeed, one might even say that it is not a religion at all; that it is the religion of the end of religions. Many thinkers in the Western tradition have said something similar, from Kant to Hegel and Weber and, nearer our own time, Louis Dumont and Marcel Gauchet.

If they are right, one sees at once that cognitive approaches to religion are profoundly misconceived. Like Nietzsche, though without the smallest spark of his genius, Dawkins and Boyer both take malicious pleasure in treating Christianity as a religion like any other. It is much more degrading for Christianity, in their view, than for any other faith, to be reduced to the common run of religions. Boyer recounts a personal anecdote that Dawkins finds especially revealing, so much so that he quotes from it and then devotes almost a page to commenting on it. The challenge these authors have set for themselves is to understand how human

6. Bertrand Russell, "Freedom Versus Authority in Education," in *Skeptical Essays* (London: George Allen and Unwin, 1928); quoted in Dawkins, *The God Delusion,* 97.

beings, people like you and me, can believe unbelievable things, such as the existence of a mountain that is alive and feeds on animals that are sacrificed to it. Explaining this challenge, and his method of meeting it, to a prominent Catholic theologian, Boyer was "dumbfounded" when the divine turned to him and said: "'That is what makes anthropology so fascinating and so difficult too. You have to explain *how people can believe such nonsense.*'"[7]

Fearing that the reader will fail to understand why, Dawkins hastens to list the nonsensical beliefs that a Christian is supposed to entertain, none of them any less absurd than stories of flying witches who cast spells on their victims or invisible dragons that wear cologne. First there is the belief in a man born of a virgin mother without the aid of a human father. This same fatherless man, it is claimed, brought back another man from the dead. Both the fatherless man and his heavenly father (who are one and the same) know your innermost thoughts and everything you do, whether for good or evil, and they will reward or punish you after you die. As for the fatherless man's virgin mother, she never died—and her body rose directly up into heaven. And then there is the business of the bread and the wine, which, so long as they have been blessed by a person who has been ordained as a priest (and who must have testicles),[8] are transformed into the body and blood of the fatherless man.[9]

One thinks of the dictum mistakenly attributed to Tertullian: *Credo quia absurdum est.* The striking thing about Dawkins's grotesque catalogue is that it omits something at the heart of the Gospels—something that, despite its extreme familiarity, nonetheless constitutes the central article of Christian faith: the Passion. This fatherless man, God become man, was put to death under the most horrible conditions imaginable, rejected on all sides (even by his own disciples), accused of crimes he did not commit. Nietzsche understood this, at least, and summed up the essence of Christianity in the formula: "God is dead. God remains dead.

7. Boyer, *Religion Explained*, 297 (italics in the original); quoted in Dawkins, *The God Delusion*, 178.

8. I doubt that Dawkins displays such coarseness in discussing other subjects. It may be that he imagines himself to be freed from all rules of decency by the justice of his campaign against the ignominy that attaches to religious belief.

9. Readers may satisfy themselves that I have invented nothing by consulting Dawkins, *The God Delusion*, 178–79.

And we have killed him."[10] One must be blind not to know this, or else fantastically blinkered, if one lives in a Christian land, in the sight of the thousands of crosses that dot the landscape. It is *this* that is incredible— not that supernatural beings engage in improbable exploits. It is incredible that a religion—if in fact Christianity is a religion—should choose for its god the victim—the human, all-too-human victim—of a collective lynching. Still today in Mexico, in Oaxaca, one can see the crosses that the missionaries who brought the Gospel there had designed to convert the native peoples, Mixtecs and Zapotecs: simple wooden crosses with the face of Christ at the center; that is, a head without a body—and there-fore without the body of a victim of torture. The Franciscan missionaries sought to avoid portraying their god as a pitiable being, lest he be thought inferior to local deities for seeming to be nothing more than a defeated man, oozing blood.

It is this story, the Passion, that the West, and then the whole world, committed to memory, and that shaped the world in return. Whatever else it may be, it is not the sort of fantastic tale that spread solely because of its counterintuitive nature—because, owing to its shocking contradic-tion of common sense, it was easily memorized and transmitted. On the contrary, it is a purely human story in which it is very easy to recognize oneself, for everyone at one time or another has been the innocent victim of the wrath of others or a party to such an offense. From this one of two things follows: either cognitivists include Christianity in what they call religion, in which case their explanation does not hold; or they exclude Christianity, in which case their explanation fails to achieve its purpose.

Religion as Collective Effervescence

The second fundamental error committed by cognitivists, which causes them to lose their way at the very start, is to believe that religion is above all a system of ideas, beliefs, and concepts. On this view, two ques-tions naturally arise. First, how can such evidently absurd ideas actually be conceived and maintained in a person's mind? Second, how can they then spread, like an epidemic, passing from the mind of one person to another?

10. From aphorism 125 ("The Madman") in Friedrich Nietzsche, *The Gay Science,* trans. Walter Kaufmann (New York: Vintage, 1974), 181.

What cognitivists altogether forget is that religion is first and foremost an *activity* that is practiced collectively, in the company of others, and that it is in this active, social context that religious ideas are formed simultaneously in the mind of each person. Dawkins sees ritual as the product of myth,[11] and as something still more enigmatically ridiculous than myth itself. "Why do humans fast, kneel, genuflect, self-flagellate, nod maniacally towards a wall, crusade, or otherwise indulge in costly practices that can consume life and, in extreme cases, terminate it?" he asks, apparently sincerely—and pathetically, in view of his confessed incomprehension.[12]

For the theory of evolution, which serves as the theoretical basis for cognitive psychology and anthropology, explaining ritual presents an even more formidable challenge than accounting for the origin of religious ideas. Indeed, Darwinian selection acts in the same way as Occam's razor: hating wastefulness, it eliminates the superfluous and, like a utilitarian judge, ruthlessly punishes everything that strays from the optimum. How could the bizarre extravagance of religious practices have been allowed to pass through its selective filter? That cognitivists should find no satisfactory response to a question that arises only because they have approached the problem the wrong way around comes as no surprise. Their failure is a consequence of this very mistake. Already in *The Elementary Forms of Religious Life* (1912), Durkheim had identified the same misapprehension:

11. See Dawkins, *The God Delusion*, 173–74.

12. Ibid., 166. Boyer, for his part, takes up the question of ritual only on page 229 of a book whose text runs to 330 pages. As it turns out, he has nothing to say about it: "[R]itual is not an activity for which we can demonstrate some specific disposition or a special adaptive advantage;" or again: "[W]e have no evidence for a special 'ritual system' in the mind, at least not so far" (p. 234). It is as if, in seeking to explain human phenomena by reference to the theory of general relativity, one were to say: until now we have not been able to find in the brain of the modern individual a black hole that would account for the universality of selfishness. Nevertheless, there is one point of interest. Boyer, unlike Dawkins, does not explain ritual in terms of beliefs nor, for that matter, beliefs in terms of ritual; for him it is a basic fact of social life that people perform rituals—make use of "cognitive gadgets," whose origin is poorly understood—and invent entities called "gods" in order to fill a "causal gap" (pp. 234–35, 261–62). I shall come back to Boyer's account below, at pp. 98–105.

Most often, the theorists who have endeavoured to express religion in rational terms have seen it, above all, as a system of ideas that correspond to a definite object. This object has been conceived in different ways: nature, the infinite, the unknowable, the ideal, and so on. But these differences are unimportant. In all cases, it was ideas and beliefs that were considered the essential element of religion. As for rites, they seem from this point of view to be merely an external, contingent, and material expression of these inner states that were singled out as [the only ones] having intrinsic value. This conception is so widespread that, for the most part, debates about religion revolve around the question of knowing whether it can be reconciled with science or not, that is, if there is a place next to scientific knowledge for another form of thought that would be specifically religious.[13]

Durkheim's explanation of religion and of the preponderant place that ritual plays in it is well known. The reality to which mythologies and religious experience refer, without knowing it, he says, is society:

Society can make its influence felt only if it is in action, and it is in action only if the individuals who compose it are assembled and act in common. It is through common action that it becomes conscious of itself and affirms itself; it is above all an active cooperation. . . . Therefore, action dominates religious life for the very reason that society is its source.[14]

This explanation is not itself without serious problems, to which I shall return. But one cannot help but be impressed by the force of conviction one finds in a passage such as the following:

A philosophy can indeed be elaborated in the silence of inner meditation, but not a faith. For faith is above all warmth, life, enthusiasm, the exaltation of all mental activity, the transport of the individual beyond himself. Now, without leaving the self, how could one add to the energies he has? How could he surpass himself with his forces alone? The only source of heat where we might warm

13. Émile Durkheim, *The Elementary Forms of Religious Life,* ed. Mark S. Cladis, trans. Carol Cosman (Oxford: Oxford University Press, 2001), 311. [The Cosman translation is an abridged version based on the corrected edition of *Les formes élémentaires de la vie religieuse* published in Paris in 1991 by Livre de Poche and incorporates additional corrections supplied by Dominique Merllié. In addition to the French edition, I have also consulted the integral version of Durkheim's text edited and translated by Karen E. Fields (New York: Free Press, 1995). —Trans.]

14. Ibid., 313.

ourselves morally is that formed by the society of our peers; the only moral forces with which we might sustain and increase our own are those [lent to us by] others. . . . [B]eliefs work only when they are shared. One can certainly maintain them for a time through wholly personal effort; but they are neither born nor acquired in this way. It is even doubtful that they can be preserved under these conditions. In fact, the man who has real faith has an irrepressible need to spread it; to do this, he leaves his isolation, approaches others, and seeks to convince them, and it is the ardour of their convictions that sustains his own. His faith would quickly [wilt] if it remained alone.[15]

In the light of this remarkable passage, it becomes clear that the laboratory experiments conducted by cognitivist researchers to make religious beliefs grow in the mind of an isolated individual have as much chance of succeeding as the attempt to make roses grow on Mars.

Dawkins and Boyer find it the height of absurdity that believers should prostrate themselves before an inanimate statue and address prayers to it—unlike Molière's Don Juan, who refused to yield to "the awesome mystery of a statue that walks and talks."[16] It is instructive that Boyer should see in this behavior, not a ritual act, but a religious concept. Like every religious concept, it combines a particular ontological category—in this case an "artificial object," from which all sorts of propositions can be inferred (for example, that the object was made by someone, that it is not found in several places at the same time, and so on)—with the violation of at least one of these inferences (the artificial object hears the requests addressed to it and may, if it wishes, grant them). It is this combination of an inference-bearing ontological category with a counterintuitive feature, Boyer claims, that characterizes every religious concept, and that constitutes one of the necessary conditions for it to be able to reproduce itself and successfully pass through the filter of Darwinian selection.

The distressing thing about this is that Boyer does not make the least effort to look beyond what he takes to be "supernatural" phenomena, which is to say phenomena that are not reducible to the intuitions of ordinary physics and psychology—the distinctive mark of religious *ideas* in his view (he does not think to look for purely human experiences, so human that all of us share them, even when they are transfigured by the

---

15. Ibid., 320. [Cosman's version very slightly modified.—Trans.]

16. Molière, *Don Juan: Comedy in Five Acts, 1665*, act 5, scene 2, trans. Richard Wilbur (San Diego: Harcourt, 2001), 134.

effect of the emotions one feels in those moments of *collective effervescence* that, according to Durkheim, are the very condition of religion itself). Only a very small effort of imagination is needed to produce plausible hypotheses. Durkheim himself proposes this one:

[T]he fact that collective feelings are attached in this way to foreign things is not purely a matter of convention; it tangibly embodies a real feature of social phenomena, namely their transcendence of individual consciousness. Indeed, we know that social phenomena arise not in the individual but in the group. Whatever part we play in their creation, each of us receives them *from the outside*. When we imagine them as emanating from a material object, we are not entirely wrong about their nature. Although they do not come from the specific thing to which we attribute them, they do originate *outside us*. If the moral force that sustains the worshipper does not come from the idol he worships, from the emblem he venerates, it is none the less external to him and he feels this. *The objectivity of the symbol merely expresses this exteriority.*[17]

The original sin of cognitivism, if I may be permitted such a phrase, was to assign itself the heroic task of producing a rational explanation for the apparent irrationality of religious phenomena. It does not for one moment occur to either Dawkins or Boyer that this irrationality may in fact conceal a great wisdom, a subtle body of knowledge about the human and social world. Dawkins frankly acknowledges his puzzlement. Quoting the philosopher of science Kim Sterelny, he asks how people can be *so smart and so dumb* at the same time. Sterelny's personal observations drew Dawkins's attention to aboriginal peoples in Australia and Papua New Guinea who have a detailed knowledge of their natural environment—a knowledge that is indispensable to their survival under very difficult conditions—and who, Dawkins says, "clutter their minds with beliefs that are palpably false and for which the word 'useless' is a generous understatement." After all, these are people who for countless generations have succumbed to profoundly destructive obsessions with female menstrual pollution, magic, and witchcraft. Why should they go on in this way, Dawkins asks, go on being chronically tormented by the fears they experience and (in Sterelny's phrase) *"by the violence that accompanies those fears"*?[18]

17. Durkheim, *The Elementary Forms of Religious Life*, 176; the emphasis is mine.

18. Dawkins, *The God Delusion*, 165–66; again, my emphasis.

Astonishingly, Dawkins fails to see that the answer to this question is contained in the question itself. Aboriginal peoples have every reason to fear internecine violence—a violence that threatens to destroy social order, and much more efficiently than any cyclone or tsunami could do. It is true that this violence is the product of religious beliefs and behaviors; but it is equally true that these same things constitute a rampart against violence.[19] The relation to violence constitutes the central enigma of religion: how can it actually be both remedy and poison? This coincidence was built into the very language of the ancient Greeks, who had only one word for these two opposed notions: *phármakon*—a word that itself derives from *pharmakós,* one who is sacrificed as an atonement for others. In other words, a scapegoat.

Sacrifice and Murder

The psychotherapist Bernard Lempert, in a profound and disturbing analysis of the sacrificial mind,[20] reports an atrocity that occurred in Kosovo in the spring of 1999 during the Feast of Sacrifice. On the day of Eid al-Adha, Serbian police burst into a Kosovar home. The Muslim ceremony performed on this, the second of the two Eid holidays, commemorates Abraham's failed sacrifice of his son, Ishmael, interrupted by the angel of the Lord: the throat of a ram is cut in memory of the animal substituted at the last moment by the angel for the human victim. The policemen asked if the family had carried out the sacrifice. No, they replied, we are too poor for that. The policemen then seized the son of the household, a young man seventeen years of age, saying "He is fattened enough for the sacrifice," and slit his throat in front of his parents.

This act was all the more vile as it cynically exploited religious feeling. To be sure, it was not a religious act; it was a murder, pure and simple. Nevertheless, its perpetrators knew a great deal about religion, much more in any case than all the world's cognitive anthropologists put together,

19. Boyer has an unwitting moment of lucidity, whose illumination might have shown him the way out from the impasse in which he had landed himself, when he writes: "From the anthropologist's viewpoint it seems plausible that . . . rituals create the need they are supposed to fulfil" *(Religion Explained,* 20).

20. Bernard Lempert, *Critique de la pensée sacrificielle* (Paris: Seuil, 2000).

which enabled them to ape a ritual form in a particularly dreadful way. The murderers knew that the sacrificial ritual rested on the substitution of victims. The non-sacrifice of Ishmael (or of Isaac in the Judeo-Christian tradition) marks an exceptional moment in the history of religion—the passage from human sacrifice to animal sacrifice. By usurping the blood-stained clothes of the sacrificer, and by substituting a human victim for an animal victim, the Serbian policemen not only brought about a barbaric regression; they also exposed the disconcerting kinship of violence and the sacred.

It is easy to mistake two things here. The first error consists in not seeing that sacrifice rests upon a murder—a relationship that all religious thought works to conceal. The second, and converse, error consists in simply asserting the identity of sacrifice and murder (as the atrocity committed by the Serbian policemen did) without taking into account the difference between the two acts—a difference that lies at the very source of civilization. The history of humanity is the history of a kind of evolution peculiar to sacrificial systems, by which civilization made a dramatic advance in replacing the human victim by a stand-in—first an animal, then certain plants, and finally abstract symbolic entities. It is in this sense that the history of humanity is a story of symbolization.

Not all the cognitivists' intuitions are false, however, and it is this that gives the matter its special fascination. Despite having set off down the wrong path, their thinking is illuminated by the religious mind itself, however much they may regret this. Extending his definition of religious concepts, according to which a particular ontological category is combined with a feature or characteristic behavior that comes into conflict with the inferences usually derived from this category (a mountain that feeds on the flesh of animals, for example), Boyer writes: *"[R]eligious concepts invariably include information that contradicts certain expectations* arising from the category activated."[21] Let us take the category of murder. This is a category that is familiar to us from the origin of the world, at least if one credits the great mythologies of the planet, which all begin by a murder:

21. Boyer, *Religion Explained,* 65; emphasis in the original. [The English text has been slightly modified, following the edition published simultaneously in France as *Et l'homme créa les dieux: Comment expliquer la religion* (Paris: Robert Laffont, 2001); the corresponding passage is found on p. 95.—Trans.]

Oedipus killing Laius, Romulus killing Remus, Cain killing Abel, and so on. Now consider the subcategory of collective murder, where a crazed mob carries out the lynching of a particular person. We are immediately capable of drawing a multitude of commonsensical inferences, for example, that the victim suffered horribly and finally died. If we consider the same scene in a sacred context, which is to say (as the etymology indicates) a rite of sacrifice, we find that certain inferences are violated. The victim (for example, a child who is burned at the stake) does not suffer; more precisely, the ritual is performed in such a way as to encourage belief in an absence of suffering. The mother caresses the child so that he does not moan, witnesses do not weep or cry out for fear of compromising the dignity of the ceremony, and so on. Nor does the victim consider himself a victim, since his mother has handed him over to the priest, and since he has been made to understand that his sacrifice is necessary to appease the wrath of the god.[22]

In this regard, Durkheim notes: "[T]he sacred character [cloaked by] a thing is not implied by its intrinsic features, it is *added to them*. The world of the religious is not a particular aspect of empirical nature: it is *superimposed* on it."[23] The features that the sacrificial rite *adds* to the sordid reality of the murder are a shock to intuitive understanding. In exchange for a modest "cognitive effort" on the part of those who are witnesses to the rite, they arouse rich "mental inferences," to use the jargon of the cognitivists, who say that such ceremonies "maximize relevance."[24] One

22. Diodorus Siculus tells of a ritual sacrifice of a similar kind performed in 310 BCE by the Carthaginians: see François Decret, *Carthage ou l'Empire de la mer*, 2nd ed. (Paris: Seuil, 1977), 143–44; also Bernard Lempert, *Critique de la pensée sacrificielle*, 169–71.

23. Durkheim, *The Elementary Forms of Religious Life*, 174 (translation slightly modified).

24. I shall be forgiven, I trust, for pointing out that what Boyer calls "relevance"—the maximization of which is defined as a minimization of cognitive cost *and* a maximization of inferential effects—is a meaningless notion, because it commits the fallacy of double maximization: generally speaking, it is not possible to maximize or minimize two functions at the same time. The only way to salvage this concept would be to convert the costs and the effects into a common measure and then to decide, for example, whether or not the incremental increase of an inferential effect is worth the corresponding increase in cognitive cost. It is not clear, however, on what psychological foundations such a *cognitive economics* could rest.

might more naturally say that they capture the imagination. But is this really what makes them into something supernatural, something whose elements will be memorized and transmitted to millions of minds, thus constituting a religion, as Boyer supposes? Are we not dealing instead with a ruse, with a quite human—indeed all-too-human—exercise in collective self-deception in which everyone pretends that no violence has occurred? It is enough that only a few people (the parents of the sacrificed child, for example) refuse to be fooled in order for the violence that the sacrificial rite is meant to contain to start up again with renewed vigor.

It will be objected that here I am speaking of ritual and not of religious ideas or beliefs. But myth does not do anything other than what ritual does: in order to contain social violence, the violence of religion must be transfigured—although this means violating the physical and psychological intuitions that constitute common sense. In Euripides' *Iphigenia in Aulis,* Iphigenia accepts her sacrifice, which is to say the slaughter that she is made to undergo, but the horror of her fate is covered up. A messenger reports:

> . . . Oh, then I stood with my head
> Bowed, and a great anguish smote my heart—
> But suddenly a miracle came to pass.
> . . . .
> . . . [A]fter, with no man knowing where or how,
> The maiden vanished from the earth.
> Then the priest with a great voice cried aloud
> And the whole army echoed him—this when
> They saw a portent which a god had sent
> But no man had foreknown. Though our eyes saw,
> It was a sight incredible, for a
> Panting hind lay there on the earth. . . .[25]

This was indeed a miracle, a sight that could not be believed: a young girl transformed into a doe. But who today, apart from cognitivists, will believe that the supernatural had anything whatever to do with this?[26]

25. Euripides, *Iphigenia in Aulis,* 1579–88, in *The Complete Greek Tragedies,* ed. David Grene and Richmond Lattimore, 4 vols. (Chicago: University of Chicago Press, 1992), 4: 385.

26. Here I follow Lempert's analysis in *Critique de la pensée sacrificielle,* 174–85.

Who, apart from the naïve or the deliberately cruel, is still taken in by the vulgar duplicities through which religion hides from itself its dual relation to violence? For religion *contains* violence, in the compound sense of blocking it while at the same time harboring it within itself.

Or consider the rite of capital punishment. This is not a religious ritual in the strict sense, even if the two things have many features in common.[27] The natural facts are not any less horrible than in the case of a collective murder. Nevertheless, the ritual and its interpretation superimpose on the brutality of these facts certain features that run contrary to intuition, or, I should say, rational naturalistic intuition. Neither the executioner nor the witnesses to the scene will have put the condemned person to death, for example. The extreme meticulousness with which the macabre sequence of events unfolds is intended to emphasize exactly this point. Instead it is the entire nation that delivers the fatal blow. Boyer would no doubt protest that no one has ever seen a nation place a noose around anyone's neck. No, of course not. But is it actually a supernatural property that makes the act a quasi-religious ritual, and the nation a quasi-sacred transcendental entity? If control over the ritual is suddenly lost—say, because the executioner insults the person about to be hanged, as recently happened in Iraq when Saddam Hussein was put to death—the fragile distinction between a death sentence and an act of vengeance dissolves and it suddenly becomes clear to all that the whole point of the ritual is to say: "This is not an act of vengeance!" There is nothing supernatural in any of this. It is human, all too human.

Let us move still further away from religious ritual and consider the central political ritual of every democracy, voting. In the next chapter I shall examine this activity in some detail. For the moment it will suffice to note the following paradox. No potential voter is unaware that his voice risks going unheard in the immense clamor that surrounds the summoning of the people to the polls. Indeed, this is why many people stay away, out of a sense that their votes do not matter. Yet every voter knows perfectly well that the outcome of an election is determined by counting all the votes cast, and that in this sense every vote matters. To resolve the paradox, one has only to adopt a symbolic mode of thought, which in the

27. See François Tricaud, *L'accusation: Recherche sur les figures de l'agression éthique* (Paris: Dalloz, 1977).

case of national elections we do spontaneously. We interpret the results of an election, even (or perhaps especially) when the outcome is in doubt, as a manifestation of the considered choice of a collective subject: the people, the electorate, or the like. From the perspective of the strict naturalism insisted upon by cognitivists, the collective subject that is appealed to in this instance is a pure fiction, a supernatural entity no less undiscoverable than a ravenous mountain or a dragon that is everywhere and at every moment present. Yet the assumption of a collective subject causes the paradox to vanish on the moral level, which in this case involves the question of responsibility. An election need only be sufficiently close that repeated and conflicting tabulations of the ballots cast fail to yield an unambiguous result for the crucial purpose of the collective subject, now threatened with dissolution, to be revealed, together with the function of the electoral procedure that underlies it. Like many religious rituals, the rite of voting involves two phases: a rivalry is first established, and then transcended in such a way as to bring forth an overarching consensus—the "will of the people"—that will guarantee social order.

Sacrificial Thought and the Confusion of Categories

On 11 September 2001, New Yorkers—and, in sympathy with them, the vast majority of Americans—spontaneously looked upon the place where the twin towers were struck down by the terrorists that day as a sacred space. There is no doubt that they did this unreflectively, for on many occasions afterward they asked themselves what had prompted them to take this view. Was it because they saw in the event a manifestation of divine purpose? But surely no god, at least no god recognized by most Americans, would have sanctioned such an abomination. Were they inspired by the martyrdom undergone by the victims in defense of American values ("democracy, pluralism, and productivity," as one Internet discussion group summarized them), which the terrorists are often said to have hated above all else? But many of the victims were not American, and no doubt at least some of them did not share all of these values, having been chosen, as it were, at random—or, rather, blindly. This is a question that I regularly pose to my students in the United States, and I have still to this day not received an answer that *they themselves* are satisfied with.

Henri Hubert and Marcel Mauss, in their famous essay on the nature and function of sacrifice,[28] came up against the following paradox: it is criminal to have killed the victim, because he is sacred; but he cannot be sacred if he has not been killed. "If sacrifice resembles criminal violence," René Girard later observed, "we may say that there is, inversely, hardly any form of violence that cannot be described in terms of sacrifice—as Greek tragedy clearly reveals. . . . [S]acrifice and murder would not lend themselves to this game of reciprocal substitution if they were not in some way related."[29] Accordingly, the answer to the question posed a moment ago is simply this: what renders the site of the terrorist act sacred is the very violence that was committed there. To call the annihilation of the European Jews a "holocaust" responds to the same logic, and the same impulse.

It was during a trip to Japan, in 1958, that the German philosopher Günther Anders learned of the appearance of a new book by his rival Karl Jaspers, *The Atomic Bomb and the Future of Man*.[30] Stigmatizing the sort of pacifism associated with Gandhi and shared by Anders, Jaspers objected that the "radical 'no' to the atomic bomb includes the willingness to submit to totalitarianism," and warned that "[o]ne must not conceal from oneself the possibility of having in the near future to decide between totalitarian domination and the atomic bomb." Anders was outraged above all by the use that Jaspers made of the words "sacrifice," "victim," and "sacrificial victim."[31] In order to prevent any form of totalitarianism from taking over the planet, Jaspers argued, it would be necessary to use

28. Henri Hubert and Marcel Mauss, *Essai sur la nature et la fonction du sacrifice* (Paris: F. Alcan, 1899), originally published in *Année sociologique* 2 (1898): 29–138. Translated by W. D. Halls as *Sacrifice: Its Nature and Function* (Chicago: University of Chicago Press, 1964).

29. Girard, *Violence and the Sacred*, 1.

30. Karl Jaspers, *Die Atombombe und die Zukunft des Menschen: Politisches Bewusstsein in unserer Zeit* (Zurich: Artemis V, 1958); published in English as *The Atom Bomb and the Future of Man,* trans. E. B. Ashton (Chicago: University of Chicago Press, 1961).

31. See the French edition of Jaspers's book, *La bombe atomique et l'avenir de l'homme: Conscience politique de notre temps* (Paris: Buchet-Castel, 1963), 23, 84, 135, 478.

the bomb and consent to a "total sacrifice." Anders confided this remark to his diary: "In the worst case, according to Jaspers, it might become morally inevitable . . . to risk the sacrifice of the victim, and therefore of humanity. I want to know *who,* therefore, according to Jaspers, would sacrifice *whom?* And *to whom* would the sacrifice be made?" He went on to say this:

If only [Jaspers] had contented himself with the sober phrase "suicide of humanity"; that is to say: in the worst case, it might become morally inevitable . . . that humanity kill itself—which would be quite mad enough. For it could not be said that the millions of those who would be annihilated with their children and grandchildren during an atomic war, that these millions meant to collectively commit suicide. They would not sacrifice themselves, they *would be* "sacrificed." The only undeceitful term that would be left [in that case] is "murder." As a consequence: if need be, it might become inevitable to assassinate humanity. Grotesque! I could not believe, until I saw it clearly and with my own eyes, that Jaspers would replace the term "murder" . . . by "sacrificing oneself."[32]

What appalled Anders was the recourse to a religious vocabulary in order to hide an unspeakable abomination. And yet this radical atheist—a German Jew, a former student of Heidegger, and Hannah Arendt's first husband—recognized the existence of a form of transcendence: "What I recognize as being 'religious' in nature is nothing at all positive, but only the horror of human action transcending any human scale, which no God can prevent."[33] What Anders did not grasp was that it is precisely this negative transcendence that legitimizes the terminology of victim and sacrifice. The fundamental disagreement between Anders and Jaspers can be summarized in the following way: whereas Jaspers regarded the bomb as an instrument in the service of an end, and the victims as the necessary price of preserving liberty, Anders argued, in effect, that the use of the bomb could not be considered a sacrificial act, since the only divinity or transcendence that remains in that case is the bomb itself.

32. Günther Anders, "L'Homme sur le pont: Journal d'Hiroshima et de Nagasaki," in *Hiroshima est partout,* trans. Denis Trierweiler et al. (Paris: Seuil, 2008), 123.

33. Anders, *Die Antiquiertheit des menschen;* from the French translation by Michèle Colombo of vol. 2, chap. 28, "Désuétude de la méchanceté," published in *Conférence,* no. 9 (1999): 182.

Now, if Anders had read Hubert's and Mauss's essay on sacrifice, he would have understood that this confusion between the sacrificer, the victim, and the divinity constitutes the very essence of sacrifice. In Mexico, the two anthropologists observed, "at the festival of the god Totec, prisoners were killed and flayed, and a priest donned the skin of one of them and became the image of the god. He wore the god's ornaments and garb, sat on a throne, and received in his place the images of the first fruits." The sacrifice *to* the god was only a form derived from the sacrifice *of* the god: in the beginning, "it is . . . the god who undergoes the sacrifice." In other words, Hubert and Mauss conclude, *"the god was offered to himself."*[34]

In matters of religion, the confusion of categories may be a sign of lucidity, whereas clear and distinct ideas are apt to be misleading. We are accustomed to assume that sacrifice involves the offering of a victim to a divinity through the intercession of an agent, the priest or sacrificer. To the extent that we no longer believe in the existence of a divinity, however, it seems natural to conclude that the sacrifice corresponds to nothing real. But the account given by Hubert and Mauss enjoins us to conflate what rational analysis distinguishes: not only does the god emanate from the victim, "[h]e must still possess his divine nature in its entirety at the moment when he enters . . . into the sacrifice to become a victim himself."[35] To be sure, the circular form of the logic of sacrifice has the appearance of paradox. But this paradox is found at the heart of many philosophical or theoretical systems that like to think of themselves as being perfectly secular. In Rousseau, for example, the form of the social contract is expressed by the formula "Each one, in giving himself to all, gives himself to no one,"[36] where "all"—which is to say the body politic—is constituted only during, and by means of, this act of offering. To paraphrase Hubert and Mauss, one might say that men in a state of nature must already form a body so that they can give themselves to it. If the analogy seems unconvincing, let us turn Rousseau's formula inside out, as Benjamin Constant did so ruthlessly in drawing out the terroristic implication of the principle

34. Hubert and Mauss, *Sacrifice,* 80, 88, 90; emphasis added.
35. Ibid., 81.
36. Rousseau, *The Social Contract,* 1.6; see *The Collected Writings of Rousseau,* 4: 139. [I have preferred a more literal rendering here.—Trans.]

of popular sovereignty, which consisted in "offering to the people as a whole the holocaust of the people taken one by one."[37]

The paradox disappears if one follows Girard in regarding the sacred as the externalization of human violence in relation to itself.[38] One has only to substitute "violence" for "divinity" in the formulas of Hubert and Mauss in order to demystify a conception that stands beneath a halo, as it were. Hypostatized and transfigured, a sacred violence can now be nourished by the "offerings" made to it by ordinary acts of violence. Violence is therefore capable of *externalizing itself,* of *transcending itself* in symbolic and institutional forms—the rites, myths, and systems of prohibitions and obligations that both control and incubate violence, *containing* it in the two senses that I mentioned earlier. Anders's negative transcendence corresponds to this schema.

Religion and Morality

The third fundamental error committed by cognitivists follows from the second. Since they do not notice the preponderant place of ritual in religion, they remain unaware of the essential tension between ritual and the system of prohibitions and obligations that regulate everyday life. This conflict—whose existence forcibly struck Hegel, among others—arises from the fact that ritual frequently works to portray the violation of these prohibitions and obligations, within the clearly delimited space and time of a sacred festival. Dawkins and Boyer almost never use the words "prohibition" or "taboo." And why should they—since for them religion is merely a collection of ideas, beliefs, and concepts? It is only when they examine the relationship between religion and morality that they begin to deal with the questions that must primarily concern any serious student of this subject.

I shall restrict my attention to Boyer's analysis, which at least has the merit of originality. Boyer takes issue with the customary view that morality depends on religion. "Religion," he says, "does not really ground morality,

37. Benjamin Constant, "De l'esprit de conquête et de l'usurpation dans leur rapports avec la civilisation européenne," in *Écrits politiques,* ed. Marcel Gauchet (Paris: Gallimard, 1997), 169.

38. See Girard, *Violence and the Sacred,* esp. 256–73.

it is people's moral intuitions that make religion plausible."[39] Relying as he does on a large body of research conducted throughout the world that explores the neurophysiological substrate of morality and the emergence of cooperative behaviors in evolutionary models, Boyer has scarcely any need of religion in order to naturalize morality. Instead he chooses to take the opposite approach: since creating a physiological basis for religion presents a more formidable obstacle, he looks to naturalize morality first and then to apply this result in naturalizing religion. Let us accept, then, for the sake of argument, that the formation of a moral sense was selected by evolution and incorporated in human minds in the form of a specific capacity for moral reasoning. The question is therefore how religious concepts come to be, in Boyer's phrase, "parasitic upon" moral intuitions.[40]

Before answering this question, it will be instructive to examine the general strategy that evolutionary anthropologists and psychologists typically adopt to account for the genesis of features or characteristics whose putative "adaptive advantage" is by no means clear to the uninformed observer. For these authors, as I say, the quasi-universality of religion in human societies constitutes the supreme challenge, above all in its ritual aspects. If evolution favors "relevance" as much as they maintain, to the point of ruthlessly eliminating everything that confers no advantage, how is it that people who otherwise behave reasonably in everyday life should believe in superstitious nonsense? Why should they waste their time and energy, to say nothing of risking their property and, occasionally, their lives, frantically rushing about and making gifts to nonexistent beings?

In the form given it by Dawkins, this general strategy depends on the notion of a "by-product."[41] Though religion itself does not seem to possess any discernible selective advantage, it may yet have arisen from the dysfunction of one or more cognitive mechanisms that were selected for their usefulness in the reproduction and perpetuation of the human species. Cognitivists therefore apply themselves to the dual task of identifying such "cognitive and inferential modules," whose own usefulness is fairly obvious, and then of analyzing the circumstances under which they depart

39. Boyer, *Religion Explained*, 170. [English text slightly modified, again following the French version.—Trans.]

40. Ibid., 191.

41. See Dawkins, *The God Delusion*, 172–79.

from their intended function and produce something as weird and as harmful, but also as widespread, as religion. The ingenuity shown by these researchers is equaled only by the perfectly arbitrary, and sometimes quite ridiculous, character of their inventions. I shall give only a small number of examples since readers are free to consult the books I cite. Dawkins asks us to consider the situation of a child, for whom believing in authority may often be an absolute condition of survival. If the child happens to cross paths with a tiger, for example, his inability to rapidly analyze the situation obliges him to obey his father's orders, without asking any questions: he must believe what his father says, period. But an undesirable by-product of this faculty of belief is credulity. If his father tells him to throw himself onto the pyre to appease the god, the child willingly goes to his death.[42] Or consider the deeply irrational propensity of human beings to fall in love. It is irrational, yes—but useful. For is not love at first sight, and the neurotic attachment that results from it, in fact an inducement to remain at home once children are born—an indispensable element in the rearing of offspring and therefore in the reproduction of the species? But this same intense fixation on the loved one can misfire, as it were, with the result that it comes to be transferred to this or that divinity.[43]

One cannot help but wonder, and not at all out of spite or mean-spiritedness, whether in order to be an evolutionary anthropologist or psychologist one must have had no personal experience of love, or indeed of many other things in life, such as reading novels or watching films. Myself, I think of one book in particular, Denis de Rougemont's *Love in the Western World*,[44] which served as a sentimental education for many young Europeans of my generation. Romantic love, Rougemont showed, so far from being rooted in biology, is a cultural creation intimately linked to the religious history of the medieval West; what is more, there is an utter incompatibility between romantic love and the institution of marriage, as the *myth* of Tristan and Iseult marvelously illustrates. One

42. See ibid., 174–77.

43. Dawkins considers "especially intriguing" the suggestion made by the philosopher Daniel Dennett that "the irrationality of religion is a by-product of a particular built-in irrationality mechanism in the brain: our tendency, which presumably has genetic advantages, to fall in love"; see ibid., 184–87.

44. Denis de Rougemont, *L'Amour et l'Occident* (Paris: Plon, 1939).

quotation will suffice: "[I]t is unbelievable that Tristan [could] ever marry Iseult. She typifies the woman a man does not marry; for once she became his wife she would no longer be what she is, and he would no longer love her. Just think of a Mme Tristan! It would be the negation of passion."[45]

Boyer's line of argument is superficially less implausible, and in any case it brings us back to the subject at hand, morality. Let us grant that morality has in fact been selected by evolution in the form of cognitive modules that lead us to develop special relationships with our relatives, to exchange gifts, to feel empathy for others, and so on. Unrelated modules have passed through the filter of selection as well, for example, our very great capacity for detecting intentional agents in certain threatening environments—a vestige of our ancestral past as hunters, when it was essential to be able to spot prey and predators in the tangled growth of a forest. The key to the explanation Boyer advances is found in the following claim: "Moral intuitions suggest that if you could see the whole of a situation without any distortion you would immediately grasp whether it was wrong or right. Religious concepts are just concepts of persons with an immediate perspective on the whole of a situation."[46]

In other words, our system for detecting intentional agents is so hypersensitive that it is apt to malfunction and invent such agents for us, even when there are none—and particularly when we violate a taboo. As supernatural agents, they have the singular property of possessing every piece of *strategic* information about our doings. Not that they know everything about us, for this would include a great many things that are not relevant; they are interested only in our moral choices and, most especially, our transgressions. "If you have a concept of [an] agent [as someone having] all the [relevant] strategic information," Boyer says, "then it is quite logical to think of your own moral intuitions as identical to that particular agent's view of the situation."[47] Logical? Myself, I prefer the sentimental and deeply moving force of poetry:

45. Denis de Rougemont, *Love in the Western World,* trans. Montgomery Belgion, rev. and aug. ed. (Garden City, N.Y.: Doubleday, 1957), 35. [Belgion's translation slightly modified.—Trans.]

46. Boyer, *Religion Explained,* 190.

47. Ibid. [English text slightly modified, once more following the French edition.—Trans.]

"Has the eye disappeared?" asked Zillah, trembling.
Cain answered back to her, "No. It's still there."
And then he said to them, "I want to live underground
Like a hermit in his tomb—in some place without sound
Where no one will see me, and I won't see them as well."
And so they dug a ditch, and Cain replied, "You've done well."
Then he went down into the black crypt alone.
And when he was sitting in the darkness on his throne,
And they had sealed the vault in which he would remain,
The eye was in the tomb there and looked straight at Cain.[48]

But Boyer denies that the religious person begins by positing the existence of supernatural beings with absurd and inconceivable properties, and then proceeds to act morally, feeling himself to be watched. The truth of the matter, Boyer says, is opposite: the moral intuitions of ordinary—not necessarily religious—people lead them astray, so that they come to feel that they are interacting with supernatural agents, or else being spied upon by beings with special powers, which in turn gives rise to the belief that these agents exist. One is put in mind of the old joke: "The proof that God exists is that atheists do not believe in Him." This is precisely what a whole tradition of commentary has said about Molière's Don Juan, who claimed not to believe in anything other than "2 + 2 = 4"; yet until his descent into hell, he spent his life defying a god in whom he claimed not to believe.

I shall limit myself to two final remarks in the face of such a baroque construction—far more baroque, in fact, than the system of beliefs entertained by a religious mind. First, it seems extremely odd that cognitivists should insist on transgression as the embodiment of moral evil. For there to be transgression, must there not be taboos? If so, are they part of our moral intuitions, hardwired into our brain? A moment's reflection will show not only that our moral intuitions do not necessarily include the notion of transgression, but that just behavior may actually consist in ignoring prohibitions. There is a Christian illustration that is particularly telling in this regard. It may be objected that I am being inconsistent in choosing it, since at the outset I placed Christianity apart from other religions. Quite so—but here I take

48. Victor Hugo, "La Conscience," in *La Légende des siècles* (1859); from *Victor Hugo: Selected Poetry in French and English,* ed. and trans. Steven Monte (New York: Routledge, 2002), 217.

the point of view adopted by Boyer, who makes no such distinction. I ask you to consider the parable of the Good Samaritan (Luke 10: 25–37), which in my view is the principal source of the Gospels' influence on the modern world.

A lawyer asks Jesus, "And who is my neighbor?"—this neighbor whom the law bids everyone to love as himself. Jesus responds with a story that subsequently spread throughout the nations of the West and beyond, although no supernatural being figures in it; no protective river that, on discovering that an act of incest has been committed, begins to flow backward toward its source; no forest that supplies game only on the condition that one sings to it. Indeed one wonders, following Boyer and Dawkins, how this story could possibly have had the success that it did. For it is a purely human story.

A man who was traveling from Jerusalem to Jericho was attacked by robbers, who left him for dead. A priest passed by, and then a Levite; neither one did anything to help him. But an inhabitant of Samaria—which is to say a foreigner—took pity and did his utmost to give the injured man aid and comfort, and paid for his care. Jesus asked the lawyer, "Which of these three, do you think, proved neighbor to the man who fell among the robbers?" The lawyer replied, "The one who showed mercy on him." At this Jesus said, "Go and do likewise."

This magnificent passage contains nothing that conflicts with our ordinary notions of physics and psychology. Yet it is hard for us today to appreciate how forcefully it must have contradicted the moral intuitions of Jesus's listeners. The dying man might after all have been ritually unclean, and in any case the two clerics could not disregard the duties that awaited them at the Temple in Jerusalem. As for the Samaritan, his obligations of mutual aid extended only to the people of his own community, not to a foreigner. What Jesus meant to tell us is that our neighbor, our true neighbor, can be literally anyone. Jesus's message, then, was that we should ignore the prohibitions and obligations that are conventionally supposed to form the basis of ethics, for they are cultural barriers that turn each people in upon itself. Paul expressed this message in the Letter to the Galatians (3: 28): "There is neither Jew nor Greek, there is neither slave nor free, there is neither male nor female; for you are all one in Christ Jesus."[49]

---

49. Ivan Illich saw in the parable of the Good Samaritan the key to Christianity's extraordinary capacity for destroying traditional social orders; see Cayley, ed., *The Rivers North of the Future*, 29–32.

The second remark that I wish to make about Boyer's account bears upon traditional (or primitive) religions, which are characterized by three elements: myth, rites, and prohibitions and obligations. Consider a rite of enthronement, marriage, passage, or the like, where a sacred boundary is transgressed in the presence of the celebrants (incest, for example, or murder, or the eating of impure foods). One would like to know what the supernatural beings themselves think about this transgression—which, according to Boyer, causes them to intercede. Are they capable of seeing that it is also, within the time and space proper to the rite, an obligation? What sense do they make of the violence inherent in the ritualistic violation of moral injunctions? One thinks in this connection of Durkheim, who took issue with the tendency among anthropologists of his day, as he put it, "to characterize the mentality of lower societies by a kind of unilateral and exclusive penchant for refusing to make distinctions. If the primitive mingles things we keep distinct, conversely, he keeps apart things we yoke together, and he even conceives of these distinctions as violent and clear-cut oppositions." These include a stark contrast between sacred and profane things, which "repel and contradict each other with such force that the mind refuses to think of them at the same time. They exclude one another from consciousness."[50] For cognitivists, who ignore both the central role of ritual and the clear-cut opposition between ritual and prohibitions, such questions have no meaning. One of chief virtues of the anthropology of violence and the sacred elaborated by René Girard, by contrast, is that it illuminates in a very simple and elegant way the radical separation between the prohibitions of ordinary life and the acting out of their violation within the framework of ritual.

At the heart of Girard's analysis, as I say, is the idea that the sacred is a form of human violence, a violence that has been expelled, externalized, hypostatized. The mechanism for making gods operates by means of mimeticism. At the height of a sacrificial crisis, when murderous fury has shattered the hierarchy of distinctions on which social order rests, when everyone is at war with everyone else, the contagious character of the violence triggers a catastrophic swing, causing all the hatreds of the moment to converge arbitrarily on a single member of the group. The killing of this person abruptly reestablishes peace, and gives rise to religion in its three

50. Durkheim, *The Elementary Forms of Religious Life*, 182.

aspects. First, myth: the victim of the foundational event is now regarded as a supernatural being, capable both of introducing disorder and of rec-reating order. Next, rites: always sacrificial in nature to begin with, they mimic the violent decomposition of the group in order the more power-fully to dramatize the restoration of order through the putting to death of a surrogate victim. Finally, prohibitions and obligations: by preventing the recurrence of conflicts that already have embroiled the community, they perform an opposite function to that of ritual, which represents the transgression and the ensuing disorder for the purpose of reproducing the sacrificial mechanism.

The sacred is fundamentally ambivalent, then, because it restrains violence by means of violence. This is clear in the case of the sacrificial gesture that restores order—it is a murder like any other, even if it is meant to put an end to murder once and for all. The same is true of the system of prohibitions and obligations, for the social structures that bind the mem-bers of the community to one another in normal times are the very same ones that polarize it in times of crisis. When a prohibition is transgressed, the obligations of mutual loyalty, by breaking through local boundaries in both time and space (one thinks of the mechanism of the vendetta), draw into an ever-widening conflict people who were in no way parties to the original confrontation.

Scapegoats and Sacrificial Victims

We know these things hidden since the founding of the world, as Girard calls them, for they have now become an open secret. One has only to look at the newspaper, or listen to the radio, to find that the term "scapegoat" is readily adapted to any purpose. Although the word in its current usage points directly to the innocence of the victim, its mean-ing is often misinterpreted—a consequence of the fact that it reveals the mechanism for externalizing violence. A politician, for example, will say, "They want to make me look like a scapegoat, but I won't let them." What he means, of course, is that others want to make him appear to be guilty, when in fact he is innocent. And yet, properly understood, he is really saying the opposite—they want to make him look like an inno-cent victim.

The scapegoat mechanism, by which society causes its wrongs to fall upon an innocent individual or group, or at least an individual or group that is not more culpable than any other, does not function as an intentional act. Persons who persecute others do so without knowing what they do. This, perhaps, is why they must be forgiven: the very act of persecution produces in them, through an unconscious process, the conviction that their victim is guilty. "Innocent persecutors," as one is almost tempted to call them, are persuaded of the well-foundedness of their violence; indeed, in a world of pure persecution, neither the word nor the notion of a scapegoat exists.

The fact that the political use of the term does not create any confusion demonstrates that the scapegoat mechanism has become a matter of common knowledge. It is cynically manipulated, for persecutors no longer themselves believe in the guilt of their victim, or, at the very most, they make believe that they believe in it. Modern-day persecutors have a bad conscience: in order to achieve their aims, they have to portray their victim as a persecutor. In this upside-down world, in which roles are reversed and accusations fly in every direction, one can say the opposite of what one means without anyone noticing it. Everyone understands what is going on, no matter which words are actually used.

A glance at the dictionary reminds us, however, that the political use of the scapegoat is lacking an essential element: the sacred. The scapegoat (in French, *bouc émissaire,* literally "messenger goat"; in English, "the goat that departs") first appeared as part of a particular type of sacrificial ritual, the best known example of which is described in the Book of Leviticus (16: 8–22). On Yom Kippur, the Day of Atonement, the priest symbolically laid all the sins of the people of Israel on the head of a goat, which was then sent away into the wilderness, to the demon Azazel. In *The Golden Bough,* the anthropologist and historian of religion Sir James Frazer claimed that the like of this ritual could be found in the four corners of the earth, beginning with the rite of expulsion associated with the *pharmakós* in ancient Greece, and grouped them under the general rubric of scapegoat rituals. From this point of view, it is at first sight paradoxical, but ultimately no less revelatory, that the entry for "scapegoat" in most Western dictionaries should associate its primary or literal sense with the ritual, and the figurative, derivative, or metaphorical sense with the psychosociological mechanism underlying the ritual. This is a rare instance of the copy coming before the original; of the ritual or theatrical representation of a thing preceding the thing itself. Thus, too, for example, when Girard's book *Le Bouc émissaire* appeared in Japanese, the title chosen was a word that refers to one of the rituals falling under the category defined by Frazer. This was obviously a misinterpretation, for Girard meant to designate the spontaneous mechanism and not its ritual expression. But it may well have been impossible to do any better: the mechanism could not be named because it has no name in Japanese. It is as though the ritual, in blurring the operation of the mechanism beneath a ceremonial veil, was more universal, more transcultural than the understanding of the mechanism itself, which everywhere and always, through the effects of persecution, has transformed the victim into the guilty party.

All of this, Girard says, is proof that the message of the Gospels has penetrated the world through and through, although not everywhere to the same extent. Just so, and notwithstanding statistics that indicate a decline in religious observance, one may rightly speak of the triumph of Christianity in the modern world. The account of Jesus's death on the cross, as nineteenth-century religious anthropology well recognized, is similar to the accounts that one finds at the heart of a great many religions. As far as the *factual* basis of these accounts is concerned, there is no major difference between Christianity and primitive religions—and it is this kinship that makes cognitive anthropologists wrongly believe that there is no difference at all. Yet the *interpretation* that Christianity gave to the story of Jesus's crucifixion, under the influence of its Jewish heritage, was utterly new. Here, paradoxically, Girard renders homage to Nietzsche. The gospel narrative innovates in that it is not told from the point of view of the persecutors; it takes the side of the victim whose perfect innocence it proclaims. This is why Nietzsche accused Christianity of being a slave morality.

The mechanism for manufacturing sacredness in the world has been irreparably disabled by the body of knowledge constituted by Christianity. Instead, as violence loses the ability to externalize and contain itself, more and more violence is produced, and Jesus's enigmatic words suddenly take on unsuspected meaning: "Do not think that I have come to bring peace on earth; I have not come to bring peace, but a sword" (Matthew 10: 34). No progress can be made in comprehending the place of religion in the world today if an attempt has not first been made to elucidate this terrible passage. Anyone who sees religion as a realm filled with omniscient dragons and carnivorous mountains is not in a position even to begin to try.

The triumph of Christianity is everywhere to be seen, but its effects are dreadful. Quite often Christianity is incarnated in the modern world in the form of its monstrous double. I have already mentioned this reversal, by which the concern for victims becomes a ground for persecution, and I shall come back to it at length in the chapter after next. The lesson of Christianity can be applied only if it has first been completely and thoroughly understood: human beings must renounce violence once and for all. For the Kingdom is like the eye of a cyclone: if one tries to reach it by a continuous and incremental path, trying at every step of the way to improve the effectiveness of habitual, which is to say violent, methods for containing violence, one will be cast into the vortex like a wisp of straw, spinning all the more rapidly as one believes that the calm center is drawing nearer. Either one jumps into the Kingdom with both feet—or one dies from getting too close to it.

The False Promise of Salvation by Morality

A recent poll testifying to the rapid decline of Catholicism in France appeared under the headline "The Church Will Be Conquered by Free-Market Liberalism."[51] "This does not mean that there is no longer religious feeling, no longer faith, no longer religious observance," the political scientist Jean-Marie Donegani remarked. "But there is a deinstitutionalization in the sense that, instead of thinking in terms of attachment to a church, people think in terms of attachment to values and of identification, wholly or in part, with a source of meaning." Donegani went on to say: "Subjectivity is overtaking dogma; religion is what I define it to be. In a poll of young people between the ages of twelve and fifteen taken a few years ago, words such as 'justice,' 'truth,' 'liberty,' and 'friendship' were

51. See the special interview with Jean-Marie Donegani, *Le Monde*, 21–22 January 2007, concerning a poll commissioned by the religion section of this newspaper and conducted the same month that showed that only half of the French people identified themselves as Catholics, as against 80 percent thirty years earlier.

considered by a majority of those questioned as religious in nature: that which one most values is religious. Instead of an external, objective, and institutional definition of religion, one finds a personal and fluid definition." Donegani associates this *subjectivism* with the rise of free-market liberalism; the Church, for its part, condemns what it calls the "privatization of religion." Surely many readers in France and elsewhere find little reason to doubt that the end of Catholicism—and, beyond that, of Christianity—is near. But is their expectation justified?

At this point it will be useful to go back in time and listen once more to Émile Durkheim, whose insights have guided us so far. In July 1898, at the height of the controversy surrounding the Dreyfus affair, Durkheim published an article that is no less fresh and pertinent today than it was then. Entitled "Individualism and the Intellectuals,"[52] it was a rejoinder to charges made by the anti-Dreyfusard Ferdinand Brunetière in an article that had appeared several months earlier under the title "After the Trial: Replies to a Few Intellectuals."[53] Brunetière had castigated *individualism*—a "disease" peculiar to a class of scholars who were not yet called social scientists, which led them, in the name of science and a love of truth, to challenge the verdict brought by the authorities competent to rule in the matter, thus imperiling the survival of the nation. Maurice Barrès revived this argument four years later, in 1902, when he defined the intellectual as an "individual who is persuaded that society must be founded on logic and who fails to understand that in fact it rests on necessities that are prior, and perhaps foreign, to individual reason."[54]

I do not doubt that cognitivists, if they were to read these articles, would feel both proud and reassured of the justice of their mission to defend logic and rationality against the attacks of obscurantist and reactionary authors. The interesting question remains, however, how Durkheim—one of the first Dreyfusards, and an active member of the League for the

52. Émile Durkheim, "L'individualisme et les intellectuels," *Revue Bleue,* 4th ser., 10 (2 July 1898): 7–13; reprinted in Durkheim, *L'individualisme et les intellectuels* (Paris: Éditions Mille et Une Nuits, 2002), with an afterword by Sophie Jankélévitch.

53. Ferdinand Brunetière, "Après le procès: Réponses à quelques intellectuels," *Revue des Deux Mondes* 146 (15 March 1898); cited by Jankélévitch in ibid., 46.

54. Quoted by Jankélévitch in ibid., 47.

Defense of the Rights of Man and of the Citizen—managed to defend the intellectuals against the charge of individualism. He did this by showing that individualism was a *religion,* the sole guarantor of social order and, what is more, a religion issued from Christianity.[55]

Durkheim contrasted two types of individualism. The one that served as a target for the attacks of the anti-Dreyfusards, as though it were the only imaginable kind of individualism, is "the narrow utilitarianism and utilitarian egoism of Spencer and the economists."[56] This individualism, which depends on giving free rein to selfish interests, is in fact incompatible with the common good. "However, there exists another individualism over which it is less easy to triumph. It has been upheld for a century by the great majority of thinkers: it is the individualism of Kant and Rousseau and the spiritualists, that which the Declaration of the Rights of Man sought, more or less successfully, to translate into formulae, which is now taught in our schools and which has become the basis of our moral catechism."[57] The ideal sought by this individualism, which Durkheim connects with the great tradition of eighteenth-century liberalism,

goes so far beyond the limit of utilitarian ends that it appears to those who aspire to it as having a religious character. The human person, by reference to the definition of which good must be distinguished from evil, is considered as *sacred, in what can be called the ritual sense of the word.* It has something of that transcendental majesty which the churches of all times have accorded to their gods. It is conceived as being invested with that mysterious property which creates a vacuum about holy objects, which keeps them away from profane contacts and which separates them from ordinary life. And it is exactly this characteristic which confers the respect of which it is the object. Whoever makes an attempt on a man's life, on a man's liberty, on a man's honour, inspires us with a feeling of revulsion, in every way comparable to that which the believer experiences when he sees his idol profaned. Such a morality is not simply a hygienic discipline or a

55. See also the articles published during this time by Charles Péguy in the *Revue Blanche,* where the Dreyfusard "religion" is described as a defense of the innocent.

56. Émile Durkheim, "Individualism and the Intellectuals," in *Durkheim on Politics and the State,* ed. Anthony Giddens, trans. W. D. Halls (Cambridge: Polity, 1986), 79.

57. Ibid., 80.

wise principle of economy. *It is a religion of which man is, at the same time, both believer and god.*[58]

The anti-Dreyfusards criticized the individualism of the intellectuals in the name of a conservative Christian morality. "But are those who take this position unaware," Durkheim objects, "that the originality of Christianity has consisted precisely in a remarkable development of the individual spirit?"[59] And if, he goes on to say, "that restricted individualism which constitutes Christianity was necessary eighteen centuries ago, it seems probable that a more developed individualism should be indispensable today; for things have changed in the interval. It is thus a singular error to present individualist morality as antagonistic to Christian morality; quite the contrary, it is derived from it. By adhering to the former, we do not disown our past; we merely continue it."[60]

Let us compare Durkheim's position with the findings of the poll I mentioned a moment ago on the decline of Catholicism. Yes, Durkheim would say, moral liberalism does threaten Christianity in the strict sense, but only in order to more fully realize its promise. Furthermore, he would take issue with the claim that these findings furnished evidence of "subjectivism." The supreme values shared by the young people Donegani mentions, out of which they have made a religion that permits them to go beyond themselves, to transcend themselves, are anything but catalytic agents of anarchy and anomie. "Once a goal is pursued by a whole people," Durkheim notes, "it acquires, as a result of this unanimous adherence, a sort of moral supremacy which raises it above private goals and thereby gives it a religious character."[61]

In his reply to Brunetière, Durkheim relies heavily on the idea that this religion of humanity, by which "man has become a god for man,"[62] is absolutely indispensable to social cohesion. Speaking of the Dreyfusards, he writes:

If every attack on the rights of an individual revolts them, this is not solely because of sympathy for the victim. Nor is it because they fear that they themselves will suffer

58. Ibid., 81; the emphasis is mine.
59. Steven Lukes, "Durkheim's 'Individualism and the Intellectuals,'" *Political Studies* 17 (1969): 26.
60. Ibid., 27.
61. Ibid., 25.
62. Ibid., 26.

similar acts of injustice. Rather it is that such outrages cannot rest unpunished without putting national existence in jeopardy. . . . A religion which tolerates acts of sacrilege abdicates any sway over men's minds. The religion of the individual can therefore allow itself to be flouted without resistance, only on penalty of ruining its credit; since it is the sole link that binds us to one another, such a weakening cannot take place without the onset of social dissolution. Thus the individualist, who defends the rights of the individual, defends at the same time the vital interests of society.[63]

Here we reach the limits of Durkheim's theory of religion, for which "the idea of society is the soul of religion."[64] At the same time we find ourselves in a position to appreciate the magnitude of the error that Durkheim commits with regard to Christianity.

Durkheim's moral individualism defends humanity in general, humanity *in abstracto*.[65] Like young people today, he is less troubled by the torments of actual individuals than by attacks on what he takes to be the universal and transcendent values of liberty, truth, justice, and reason. Durkheim himself had made this unmistakably clear when, at the beginning of his essay on individualism and intellectuals, published only a few months after Major Esterhazy's acquittal and Zola's trial, while Dreyfus was rotting away on Devil's Island, he wrote, "Let us forget the Affair itself and the melancholy scenes we have witnessed."[66] No doubt a great many Dreyfusards judged that the surrogate victim, Captain Alfred Dreyfus, was unworthy of the noble cause they upheld.

Christianity, as I understand it, stands in complete opposition to this. Neither humanity in general nor some set of supreme values can be divinized without committing idolatry. The person who suffers, the person with a given name, the lost sheep of the flock in the parable, must be saved, even if it means endangering the ninety-nine others.[67] This is the only thing that counts. Far from being the ultimate guarantor of the social order, Christianity acts as a lethal agent of disruption, a source of turmoil that is bound to destroy all humanly constituted authority, all

63. Ibid., 27.

64. Durkheim, *The Elementary Forms of Religious Life*, 314.

65. See Durkheim, "Individualism and the Intellectuals," 80.

66. Lukes, "Durkheim's 'Individualism and the Intellectuals,'" 20.

67. On the fundamentally anti-utilitarian—because anti-sacrificial—character of Christianity, see my earlier book *Le Sacrifice et l'envie*, as well as chapter 5 of the present work.

powers-that-be. If it is destined to triumph, this will be at the expense of everything that makes up our world.

There is a great irony in this, for Boyer and his fellow cognitivists have arrived today, though by a quite different route, at the very same error committed by Durkheim. All of them devalue religion, to the advantage of morality, by denying the religious foundation of human societies. Religion for Durkheim has no morphogenetic power: it is an interpretation—a "collective representation"—of a unique and preexisting reality, namely, society. While such an interpretation may serve to strengthen the social order (Durkheim holds this to be especially true of Christianity and of the morality that flows from it), it does not create society itself. As for the cognitivists, in making morality the offspring of biology they are condemned to see religion as a purely illusory expression of moral intuitions. Ultimately the same impulse of denial is at work, the same blindness in the face of two disconcerting truths. The first truth is that it is the sacred that gives birth to human societies. The second is that Christianity is not a morality, but rather an epistemology: it reveals the truth of the sacred and, by virtue of just this, deprives it of creative power—for better or for worse. Human beings, and human beings alone, will decide which.

4

Rationality and Ritual

THE BABYLON LOTTERY

From Durkheimian sociology to cognitivist psychology and anthropology, the social sciences are united in denying the religious foundation of human societies. The same impulse may be detected in the moral sciences. Modern political philosophy, in particular, has sought to deal with the theological-political problem by imagining a just system of government that makes no reference to religious principles. In attempting to assert its claim to sovereignty in the realm of politics, rationality nonetheless runs up against crippling paradoxes that reveal its hidden debt to religion. Even a procedure as commonplace as voting exhibits a very curious, indeed suspect, relationship to chance that cannot fail to bring to mind the crucial role chance plays in religious practices and beliefs. Here we encounter yet another mark of the sacred.

Chance as a Solution to the Theological-Political Problem

The political problem in its most general form is how something resembling harmonious agreement can be brought forth from a mass of differing opinions and potentially violent conflicts of interest. Religion proposes a solution that depends on assuming the existence of a fundamental source of authority lying outside humanity itself. The modern world, by contrast, has sought to repudiate this logic of exteriority, replacing it with a system of thought in which the principles, laws, and norms that regulate civic life are derived from human resources alone. This amounts to substituting reason for faith, immanence for transcendence, autonomy for heteronomy. Has this secular ambition ever been achieved? Is such a thing possible even in principle? One may be forgiven perhaps for sharing Tocqueville's skepticism: "I doubt whether man can ever support at the same time complete religious independence and [complete] political freedom, and am drawn to the thought that if a man is without faith, he must serve someone and if he is free, he must believe."[1]

If the logic of exteriority is in fact an inescapable feature of human existence, as I maintain, it is not in the least accidental that chance should play a crucial role. In non-modern societies—which is to say, in groups where social bonds are sacred or religious in nature—what we call chance is built into the basic institutions of the community. For anyone who has grown up in a world dominated by the will to self-mastery, this is bound to seem astonishing. Societies dominated by religion have resolved, in effect, to entrust their highest responsibilities to precisely that which, by definition, cannot be mastered. I shall limit myself to a few examples, each of them quite well known.

In the ritual of the scapegoat, as it is described in Leviticus, there were in fact *two* goats: one, associated with good, was sacrificed to Yahweh; the other, the scapegoat proper, was made to bear the full weight of the sins of the community, then driven into the desert and there into the clutches of Azazel, one of the forms assumed by the Devil. This second goat was a direct victim of the community's violence, forced to leap to its death from the top of a cliff—thus restoring the symmetry between good and evil. The choice between these two goats, this fundamental choice between good and evil, was made by drawing lots.

In many traditional societies, the dividing up of land was decided by drawing lots as well. From the Book of Joshua we know that this was done in the Promised Land of the children of Israel. In the case of festivals, especially carnival in its various forms, a "king" is generally chosen by lottery. This personage seems himself to be a substitute for the sacrificial victim who figured prominently in the original rituals from which carnival arose. In many of these rituals the designation of the victim was

1. Tocqueville, *Democracy in America*, 2.1.5, 512.

also left to chance. One finds an analogous structure in crisis situations. Shipwreck presents the outstanding example, in which the person who draws the short straw is the one who will be eaten in order that the others may survive.

It will be recalled, finally, that among the ancient Greeks the democratic method *(isonomy)* of choosing a councilor *(bouleutes)* relied on the use of a mechanical device known as a *klerotérion* that may be considered the ancestor of modern slot machines. Montesquieu and Rousseau both regarded this procedure favorably, contrasting it with the method of electing one among several candidates. "Voting by *lot* is in the nature of democracy; voting by *choice* is in the nature of aristocracy," Montesquieu says.[2]

It needs to be kept in mind that the operation of chance in these various rituals used to be interpreted in a very different way than the one that is common today. We are accustomed to identify chance with randomness, which is to say with a type of uncertainty that is orderly, repeatable, and expressible by the calculus of probabilities associated with the drawing of lots. The classic example is the game of dice—known in Arabic as *az-Zahr* (the source of our word "hazard") and in Latin as *alea* (from which we have "aleatory"). The primitive notion of chance, on the other hand, resisted calculation, because it was believed to have a meaning. Its significance was the consequence of assigning responsibility for choices made by lot to a transcendent being. Chance in this conception has a *subject,* one that is *external* to the human sphere.

What accounts for this need to shift responsibility for decisions on which the life of a community depends away from the members of this community? As a great admirer of the writings of Jorge Luis Borges, I think of the masterly fashion in which he pushed the idea to its logical extreme in his story "The Babylon Lottery."[3] Without some sort of external

2. Charles de Montesquieu, *The Spirit of the Laws,* ed. and trans. Anne M. Cohler, Basia Carolyn Miller, and Harold Samuel Stone (New York: Cambridge University Press, 1989), 2.2, 13.

3. See Jorge Luis Borges, "The Babylon Lottery" (1941), in *Ficciones,* 65–72. "I come from a vertiginous country," says the narrator of this fantastic tale, "where the lottery forms a principal part of reality." In Borges's Babel, a secret Company (the existence of which is denied by certain "masked heresiarchs") determines everything that happens there by means of a lottery, whose drawings

mediation of subjective experience, without appeal to a third party that looks upon them from outside, human beings cannot help but be in thrall to their own violence. The *self-transcendence* made possible by the recourse to chance arises in part from an urge to place this violence outside ourselves by converting it into something sacred; indeed, chance is an essential element in the emergence of the paradoxical loops that I described in the prologue to this book as being so many variations on the form of the sacred. The purpose of dividing up land by drawing lots is clear enough from this point of view: the least favored cannot blame their misfortune on any of their neighbors. With regard to suffrage, Montesquieu observes that the "casting of lots is a way of electing that distresses no one: it leaves to each citizen a reasonable expectation of serving his country."[4]

Evidently it is not incidental that a desacralized society such as our own should have conceived of chance as hazard, or risk, for in this way it was believed the sacred could be made to give way to calculation, and the irrational to yield to rationality. Hazard, by definition, has no subject. In the throw of a die one sees a manifestation, not of fate, but of a deterministic system characterized by weak stability, which is to say a sequence of events that is extremely sensitive to initial conditions, and therefore unpredictable—"deterministic chaos," as it is now usually described.

---

bring ruinous losses and unbearable sufferings as well as fabulous gains and sudden social advancement. Chance is experienced in this land as fate—a merging of contraries that is yet another one of the marks of the sacred. I come back to this point in chapter 6 in connection with the prospect of nuclear apocalypse.

4. Montesquieu, *The Spirit of the Laws*, 2.2, 13. Rousseau takes issue with Montesquieu on this point, objecting that "[t]hose are not reasons." Nevertheless, after elaborating on what he believes Montesquieu fails to grasp, namely, that "the election of leaders is a function of Government, and not of Sovereignty," and so comes under the head of law rather than of contract, Rousseau goes on to say: "In every genuine Democracy, the magistracy is not an advantage but a burdensome responsibility, which cannot fairly be placed on one private individual rather than another. The law alone can impose this responsibility on the one to whom it falls by lot. For then, as the condition is equal for all, and the choice is not dependent on any human will, there is no particular application that alters the universality of the law." See *The Social Contract*, 4.3, in *The Collected Writings of Rousseau*, 4: 202.

In fact, things are not so simple. An essential distinction is introduced if we consider one of the hardest problems contemplated by moral philosophy, on which the major doctrines (and in particular consequentialism and deontology)[5] disagree: the sacrifice of an innocent person. Let us examine the dilemma that has come to be known as "Sophie's choice." In William Styron's novel of the same name, the Nazi officer who greets Sophie on the train platform at Auschwitz forces her to choose which of her two children will be sent to the gas chamber, the other one being spared. If she refuses to choose—itself a choice, or rather a meta-choice—both children will perish. Now, reason—a horribly inappropriate word to use when speaking of such a nightmare, one might feel—forces Sophie *to choose to choose.* Reason is what one hears in Caiaphas's admonition of the high priests and the Pharisees (John 11: 49–50): "You know nothing at all, nor do you consider that it is expedient for us that one man should die for the people, and not that the whole nation should perish." But if Sophie chooses, she bears responsibility for the death of her child. This is the diabolical trap set by the Nazi officer. The question arises whether Sophie could rid herself of this terrible responsibility by drawing lots, even though there would still be a victim. Intuitively, we feel that the answer must be no. We cannot countenance the idea of Sophie's tossing a coin to determine which of her two children will die. That would not change the monstrosity of the situation in the least. It is clear that in this kind of case the resort to chance is powerless to bring about self-exteriorization.

Or consider a symmetrical example—symmetrical because it has to do with the welcoming of life into the world, rather than with the administration of death (or what might be called the rational management of sacrifice). A couple wishes to adopt a child. Again there is a temptation to choose it rationally, by taking various factors into account (sex, skin color, behavior, medical history of the parents, and so on). Suppose this is profoundly repugnant to the couple in question. They wish to reproduce as closely as possible

5. Consequentialism holds that what counts in evaluating an action is the consequences it has for all persons affected by it. Deontology, on the other hand, considers the rightness of an action to consist in its conformity to a norm or a rule, such as Kant's categorical imperative, without regard for its consequences. These two doctrines come into conflict over the question, for example, whether it is morally permissible to put an innocent person to death if, by doing that, the lives of many other persons could be saved.

the conditions of non-mastery that attend the birth of a biological child. That means they must try to recreate by other means the lottery represented by the encounter of a spermatozoon and an ovum. Given a limited supply of adoptable children, should they choose theirs by drawing lots? Imagine that they recoil from this prospect in the same way that they resist the idea of making a deliberate calculation. They need chance to intervene, only a chance that does not assume the form of probabilizable risk, one that arises instead from the contingency of human affairs—contingency experienced as fate. One evening they receive a telephone call from a distant land: a child has been born and abandoned; it is available for adoption, but they must decide that same evening, without seeing it, on the basis of a bare minimum of information. Here the problem of decision under a veil of ignorance assumes a very real and human form.

There is chance, and then there is chance. It would appear that certain methods of generating chance are held to be legitimate and meaningful *exactly to the extent that they create exteriority and transcendence.* Let us test this intuition by examining the practice of voting, which is generally thought to be the very essence of modern democracy. Political life today may be characterized as a search for immanence, in the sense that human beings are assumed to be solely responsible for creating the society they inhabit. In other words, they claim to be exempt from all manner of transcendence. One might expect that they also aspire to emancipate themselves from chance, in view of the intimate relationship between chance and the sacred that I have sketched in the preceding pages. The modern ritual of voting will show how difficult it is, in fact, to detach oneself from old habits of thought.[6]

Reason and the Rite of Election

If democratic institutions owe nothing to an external source of authority, where are their legitimacy and purpose to be looked for if not in the

6. Certain works in the classical liberal tradition can be interpreted as suggesting that the institutionalization of chance serves to guarantee liberty, and free institutions in their turn to generate chance. Yet nowhere is chance construed as risk, in the modern sense of the term, or as a sign of fate, in the ancient sense. Instead it is called contingency or complexity, and it is in this novel guise that it plays its traditional role as a source of exteriority. See Dupuy, *Le sacrifice et l'envie*, 241–91, and chapter 5 below.

unaided faculties of human reason? It is all the more puzzling, then, that every attempt to provide a rational basis for what we are accustomed to regard as the quintessentially democratic procedure—voting, based on the counting of ballots—should lead to paradox. "Except for this primitive contract," Rousseau observed, "the voice of the majority always obliges all the others. This is a consequence of the contract itself."[7] In order for a will to be general, he added, "it is not always necessary for it to be unanimous, but it is necessary that all votes be counted. Any formal exclusion destroys the generality."[8] In saying this much, Rousseau formulated what Schumpeter was later to call the "classical doctrine of democracy,"[9] which seems so obvious to us as to require no comment. And yet rational analysis, when it tries to make sense of these maxims, fails pitiably. In order to understand why this should be so, we must consider at least briefly some of the paradoxes associated with social choice. I shall limit myself here to the three most important ones:

- The concept of the general will in Rousseau remains one of the unresolved enigmas of political philosophy. It is easier to say what the general will is not than what it is. We know that it is altogether distinct from individual wills, and that in no way is it a summing up of them—what Rousseau calls "the will of all."[10] One might even argue that the general will stands in opposition to all individual wills.[11] To the modern mind, by contrast, it is essential to

7. Rousseau, *The Social Contract*, 4.2, in *The Collected Writings of Rousseau*, 4: 200.

8. Ibid., 2.2, 4: 145n.

9. Joseph Schumpeter, *Capitalism, Socialism, and Democracy*, 3rd edition (New York: Harper & Brothers, 1950), 250–52.

10. "There is often a great difference," Rousseau writes, "between the will of all and the general will. The latter considers only the common interest; the former considers private interest, and is only a sum of private wills"; *The Social Contract*, 2.3, in *The Collected Writings of Rousseau*, 4: 147.

11. Quoting the Marquis d'Argenson ("'Each interest . . . has different principles. The agreement of two private interests is formed in opposition to the interest of a third'"), Rousseau observes: "He could have added that the agreement of all interests is formed in opposition to the interest of each. If there were no different interests, the common interest, which would never encounter any obstacle, would scarcely be felt. Everything would run smoothly by itself, and politics would cease to be an art." See *The Social Contract*, 2.3, in *The Collected Writings of Rousseau*, 4: 147n.

the conception of democracy that the common interest be manifested at least as a synthesis, if not a simple summation, of private
interests. When the economist Kenneth Arrow, a future Nobel
laureate, demonstrated in 1951 that no such synthesis satisfying a
set of self-evident axioms can be constructed,[12] his "impossibility"
theorem appeared to deliver a severe blow not only to the theory of
democracy, but to democracy itself. The proof of Arrow's theorem
is a subtle variation on Condorcet's paradox, which turns on the
fact that collective preferences, obtained by the aggregation of individual preferences according to a certain rule, need not always be
transitive[13]—that is, the will of all may rank a candidate or option
A before B, B before C, and yet C before A. The non-transitivity
of a preference ordering is a sign of inconsistency, for depending
on whether A and B are initially placed in competition with each
other, or B and C, or else C and A, the winner will be different.[14]
The final result depends on the wholly contingent way in which
successive rounds of voting are structured. In other words, some
irreducible degree of arbitrariness infects the procedure.

The general will therefore cannot be thought of as a straightfor-
ward aggregation of individual wills, whether by means of majority
voting or some other procedure. Should we really find this disturbing? Could it be that the impossibility identified by Arrow is actually

12. See Kenneth J. Arrow, *Social Choice and Individual Values,* 2nd ed.
(New York: Wiley, 1963), 51–60.

13. In set theory a preference relation is said to be transitive if, *A* being preferred to *B,* and *B* being preferred to *C,* one may deduce that *A* is preferred to *C.*

14. Assume the following non-transitive preference relation: candidate *A*
is ranked ahead of *B, B* ahead of *C,* and *C* ahead of *A.* In that case, if *A* initially faces *B, A* wins and then goes up against *C,* who beats *A.* In other words,
if the balloting starts out with a contest between *A* and *B, C* will emerge vic-
torious in the end. It likewise follows that if one begins with *A* and *C, B* will
win, whereas *A* will prevail if one begins with *B* and *C.* The first round of the
presidential election in France, on 21 April 2002, furnished a perfect illustration of Condorcet's paradox. Many observers thought that Lionel Jospin would
defeat Jacques Chirac, but he was eliminated in the first round by Jean-Marie
Le Pen. As Jean-Marc Daniel put it, "M. Chirac was preferred to M. Le Pen,
who was preferred to M. Jospin, who would have been preferred to M. Chirac"
(*Le Monde,* 12 June 2002).

the saving grace of democracy? Suppose it had been proved that there exists a rational and universal procedure that permits us to say under any set of circumstances, and with regard to any choice, what the will of the people is, so long as the will of each person is known. By programming these individual wills into a central computer we could determine the optimal collective choice, consistent with the will of all. In that case calculation would once and for all have replaced the ritual of voting, and practical reason would dissolve into pure reason. Surely this would be a far more dire predicament, would it not?

One of the criteria that any aggregation rule must satisfy in order for a voting system to be considered rational is what Arrow calls the "non-dictatorship" condition: the rule cannot have the effect always of identifying the preference of a single voter with the collective preference of the electorate as a whole. This condition is already found in Rousseau.[15] Of all the conditions, or axioms, that Arrow lays down, it is the least self-evident. This is why some commentators have considered it also to be the least securely established: if any one of the axioms must be sacrificed, this is it. In that case, however, collective choice becomes a matter of ratifying the decisions of one member of the group, the prince or governor or some other dictator. If it were to be objected that this is a fundamentally undemocratic solution, Schumpeter has already supplied us with an answer. At bottom, he points out, a democracy is simply a society that chooses its own rulers and has the power to change them.

No one seriously believes that the will of a nation's rulers corresponds to the general will; it is a particular will, one will among others—albeit one that, as long as the rulers hold office, enjoys supreme power. Under the dictatorship in ancient Rome, which Rousseau considers to have been a legitimate expedient in view of

---

15. "The Sovereign may well say," Rousseau remarks, "'I currently want what a particular man wants, or at least what he says he wants.' But it cannot say, 'What that man will want tomorrow, I shall still want,' since it is absurd for the will to tie itself down for the future and since no will can consent to anything that is contrary to the good of the being that wills." He then adds, "This is not to say that the commands of leaders cannot pass for expressions of the general will, as long as the Sovereign, being free to oppose them, does not do so." See *The Social Contract*, 2.1, in *The Collected Writings of Rousseau*, 4: 145.

the grave danger facing the republic, the authority of the Senate was temporarily suspended. In such cases, however, the "suspension of legislative authority does not abolish it," Rousseau points out. "The magistrate who silences [the legislature] cannot make it speak; he dominates it without being able to represent it. He can do everything, except make laws."[16] Similarly, one might say, it is precisely because everyone knows that the will of the rulers is nothing more than a particular will that the myth of the general will, or the common interest, can be preserved. In a sense, then, democracy can be seen as a permanent dictatorship.[17] So long as it is interpreted in this fashion, the apparent failure of rational analysis to account for the activity of voting comes close to furnishing a lesson in wisdom.

• Because it depends on the counting of ballots, voting introduces a quantitative element into political science that may be compared to the treatment of value in economics. Voting data permit researchers to explore problems of measurement, correlation, and causation. Having established the existence of regularities, if not laws, they are therefore able to make predictions. It is hard to imagine an election today without polls that forecast the results—sometimes with such precision that voters wonder, not without some annoyance, what use it is to go to the trouble of voting. Indeed, there are some who dream of a computerized democracy operating in real time, in which the perpetual canvassing of opinion makes the state of the general will known at every instant. The question that arises here for our purposes is what distinguishes a poll from an election. Herbert Simon, another future Nobel laureate in economics and one of the founders of artificial intelligence, argued more than fifty years ago that there is no difference in principle between the social and the natural sciences as far as the possibility of making exact predictions is concerned. Simon was not objecting to the claim that

16. Ibid., 4.6, 4: 213.

17. Here I am indebted to Lucien Scubla's profound commentary, "Est-il possible de mettre la loi au-dessus de l'homme? Sur la philosophie politique de Jean-Jacques Rousseau," included in my book *Introduction aux sciences sociales*, 105–43.

observation and forecasting are more difficult in the social sciences, but to the claim that observation and forecasting unavoidably disturb the system that is being observed. On this view, the prediction of a social phenomenon, once known and publicly advertised, is bound to modify the event in question. A poll, for example, by making the state of public opinion known to the public, alters this very state. When a new poll is taken, some respondents, taking note of the prior results, may be inclined to prefer the winner of the earlier poll; others, as Montesquieu long ago suggested, may try to redress the balance by throwing their support behind the runner-up. It is in order to avoid such effects that in some countries, such as France, polling is prohibited in the days just before an election. Simon claimed to refute this argument by showing that public opinion includes a "fixed point," that is, an opinion that always remains stable when informed of its own state.[18] The problem is that Simon did more than this: he showed that there are generally several fixed points. This means that if a polling organization wishes to give the impression that it is able to predict the future, without thereby affecting the actual course of events, it must compute and announce one of the fixed points so that public knowledge of the predicted state will not have an impact on it. The existence of several such fixed points gives pollsters a power to manipulate public opinion that many people are apt to consider improper. Notice, however, that this power would be no less great if pollsters were simply to inform the public of its opinion in its "raw" state, which is to say before it had been so informed—something few people would find improper. Assuming that they know how public opinion will react to information regarding its own state, pollsters, by choosing not to take this knowledge into account, under the pretense of objectivity, are able to shape the development of opinion in a desired direction. The possibility arises, then, that the publication of polls, by condemning them either to inaccuracy or to partisanship, makes it impossible to determine the will of the people. This helps to explain a puzzling remark made by Rousseau in connection with political decision

18. Herbert A. Simon, "Bandwagon and Underdog Effects and the Possibility of Election Predictions," *Public Opinion Quarterly* 18 (1954): 245–53.

making: "If, when an adequately informed people deliberates, the Citizens were to have no communication among themselves, the general will would always result from the large number of small differences, and the deliberation would always be good."[19] How very contradictory it seems to us today to conceive of information without communication!

The scholarly literature on public opinion polls would have us believe that voting is a rational and scientific procedure. But the recursive effects of polling on itself and, ultimately, on elections themselves make it clear that this is an illusion. Reason in this case produces only undecidability. The point of voting is to settle matters, which is to say: to decide the undecidable.

- The third paradox is unarguably the most disconcerting of all. Known to political scientists as the voting paradox, it may be formulated as a variant of an ancient conundrum, the sorites paradox: a few loose stones do not amount to a heap, and adding one more to their number does not make them a heap; yet at some point this collection undergoes a change of state. How many stones have to be added for a non-heap to become a heap? The case of voting is more complicated, however, for it is as though the stones are endowed with free will.

Consider either a national election in which a decision is to be made between two candidates, or a referendum in which citizens must answer "yes" or "no" to a certain question. Except in the extremely improbable case (perhaps one chance in a billion) that the ballots turn out to be equally divided between the two options, no individual ballot can have any effect on the outcome whatever. To the counterfactual question "Would the final result have been different if I had voted otherwise than I did, or if I had not voted at all?" it must be acknowledged that the answer is no. This conclusion is difficult to accept, even if it seems obvious—to take a hypothetical American example—that a voter on the West Coast who knows that the outcome will already have been decided before he casts his vote (owing to the time difference with other parts of the country),

19. Rousseau, *The Social Contract*, 2.3, in *The Collected Writings of Rousseau*, 4: 147.

and who in fact already knows the outcome himself, can do nothing to alter this result. How much more dismaying must it be, then, to realize that the same thing is true even if no one else has yet voted, or if others have voted but the result is unknown. Although it has no effect, each person's vote nevertheless has a cost, measured by the time it takes to go to the polls and the effort required to make up one's mind how to vote—small, no doubt, but nonetheless not insignificant. A rational self-interested voter would never bother to vote.

Cognitive psychologists were naturally curious to know why people went to the trouble of casting a ballot. The answer seemed to have something to do with a mode of reasoning that they called, somewhat contemptuously, "quasi-magical." The average citizen says to himself: If I decide to vote, it is probable that those who tend to vote as I do will decide to vote as well; therefore, by casting my ballot, I will persuade thousands of my fellow citizens to do the same. Morning voters were found to attribute a greater influence to their initiative than evening voters—which, in the context of this sophism (if indeed it is a sophism), nonetheless possesses a certain logic.[20]

All of this strikes French political commentators as utter nonsense. Yet they do not always manage to avoid committing gross absurdities themselves. During the disputed American presidential election of 2000, to which I shall turn in a moment, it was sometimes said with disgust that the final result would depend on the votes cast by a few retired New York Jews sunbathing on the beaches of Florida and a small number of illiterate inner-city blacks.[21] If there is anything magical about the method of

20. See George A. Quattrone and Amos Tversky, "Self-Deception and the Voter's Illusion," in Jon Elster, ed., *The Multiple Self* (New York: Cambridge University Press, 1986), 35–58; also Eldar Shafir and Amos Tversky, "Thinking Through Uncertainty: Nonconsequential Reasoning and Choice," *Cognitive Psychology* 24, no. 4 (1992): 449–74. By "quasi-magical thinking" these authors mean that voters, although they do not *really* believe they have such a counterfactual power, act as though they believe they do.

21. One thinks of Robert Melcher's 9 November 2000 column in *France Soir* ("This geographic appendix of Cuban refugees, Jewish retirees, and descendants of Latin American immigration is somehow going to decide the future of the planet"—the "somehow" is an especially nice touch) and Mathieu Lindon's

reasoning at work here, this is it—the belief that the discovery of a fact has the same causal effect as the fact itself. The fact that the votes in Florida were counted last, after all the other states, did not make their weight any greater or more decisive. Note, too, that the same commentators are in the habit of interpreting the result of extremely close elections as evidence of the very carefully considered choice of a collective subject. In the French referendum concerning the Maastricht Treaty held in September 1992, for example, those who voted in favor of European union came out ahead, but only by the smallest of margins. In their great wisdom, it was said, the French people said "yes" to Europe, but they also wished to issue a warning against moving forward too quickly, and so on. No individual voter wished, thought, or brought any of this about, of course. The collective subject that is appealed to here—the people, the electorate—is a pure fiction. To the vulgar rationalist mind, no greater irrationality can be imagined.

The Lottery in America

The voting paradox therefore constitutes a very serious philosophical enigma.[22] Nothing better illustrates the nature of the difficulty than the American presidential election of November–December 2000. The reaction

---

11–12 November 2000 column in *Libération* ("The president of the United States used to be someone of importance. It used to be kiddingly said that he should be elected by the whole world in view of the fact that his power extended to every part of the planet. This was before the American democratic ideal came to be confided to a few people in Florida"). The mindless anti-Americanism that flourishes in France can take comfort in the fact that it draws its strength as much from the vulgar Right as from the self-righteous Left.

22. The voting paradox has given rise to an abundant literature. Among the most interesting contributions are William H. Riker and Peter C. Ordeshook, "A Theory of the Calculus of Voting," *American Political Science Review* 62 (1968): 25–42, and Paul E. Meehl, "The Selfish Voter Paradox and the Thrown-Away Vote Argument," ibid. 71 (1977): 11–30. See also the discussions in Derek Parfit, *Reasons and Persons* (Oxford: Oxford University Press, 1984) and J. L. Mackie, *Persons and Values: Selected Papers*, vol. 2 (Oxford: Oxford University Press, 1985).

abroad was rather different than in the United States. In France, for example, commentators sought to outdo one another in sarcasm and undisguised mockery: the Americans voted, but they are incapable of determining whom they voted for. The Americans themselves seemed on the whole proud of their system, however. The protracted recounting of ballots gave proof, they said, of the patience and sense of civic duty that are indispensable to a healthy democracy, in which each vote counts, and counts with equal weight. Between this incapacity and this pride, I maintain, there is an essential link.

The illusory and quite misleading precision with which political scientists analyze voting data is beautifully captured in an apocryphal story told by the mathematician John Allen Paulos. A guide at the Museum of Natural History in New York is explaining to his listeners that the majestic tyrannosaur enthroned in the middle of the hall is seventy million and six years old. "What?" a little girl asks. "Seventy million and *six* years? Are you sure?" "Oh, I am quite sure," replies the guide. "When I started work here I was told that it was seventy million years old. And that was six years ago."[23] It seems to me that if Al Gore lost in the end, it is because during the long weeks that followed election day he did not think carefully enough about the point of this story. Right up until the end, he believed that the number of votes that were cast for him and the number that were cast for George Bush were of a definite magnitude, which could be approximated with a margin of error as small as one liked, so long as enough time and money were put into it.[24]

Scientists are trained always to give the result of their experiments with a margin of error. If they failed to do so they would fall short of the ethical standard they demand of themselves. Empirical observations, by their nature, can only be approximate. It is true, of course, that the more time and money one spends, the smaller the margin of error becomes.

23. Quoted in Ellen Goodman, "Numbers Won't Decide Election," *Boston Globe*, 30 November 2000.

24. Of all the commentaries in the press that I checked, two—by American pundits from opposite ends of the political spectrum, as it happens—stand out from the rest for their lucidity on this point. In each case the title alone gives a clear idea of the argument made by the author: Charles Krauthammer, "The 'Will of the People' Can't Be Known—So Just Obey the Rules," *Washington Post*, 28 November 2000, and Goodman, "Numbers Won't Decide Election."

Even so, it can never be reduced to zero. The counting of ballots is not exempt from this rule. What made the situation after 7 November 2000 so remarkable is that the irreducible margin of error exceeded a critical threshold, beyond which it became impossible to say which party had won—*as though the result depended on something that could not be observed.* For reasons independent of the reflexive dynamic introduced by opinion polls, the election was, in the strict sense of the term, undecidable. Notice that a cause so small as to be unknowable, yet large enough to determine a matter of surpassing importance to the future of the world, is the very definition of chance. The American election amounted to flipping a coin on a vast scale—the coin spinning about in the air for a very long time, until finally it fell to the ground, deciding the undecidable.

New Mexico, it turns out, briefly flirted with the idea of resorting to an actual lottery to determine the outcome of the voting there. If that had happened, whether in the form of a game of poker or some other invocation of chance, New Mexico would have quite literally drawn the moral of this story. The news that such a scheme was under consideration caused great mirth among French pundits, who had forgotten, if in fact they ever knew, that the drawing of lots is an ancient method of choosing rulers in many societies, as we just saw. What is more, the system of indirect suffrage used to elect a president in the United States maximizes the role of chance. The Constitution provides that a state must be uniquely represented in the Electoral College by members of the same party, all of them elected by a majority of their constituents. It is the vote of this body, the Electoral College, that determines who will be president, not the national popular vote. A swing in the number of votes cast in favor of one candidate rather than the other within a given state, while it may not be large enough to change the result of the national popular vote, may nonetheless have the effect of transferring the state's representation in the Electoral College from one party to the other, and so possibly of changing the outcome of the election. Permitting the popular vote and the vote of the Electoral College to diverge appears to be a scandalous defect of this system if one believes that voting is a rational procedure meant to reveal the general will. It takes on a quite different aspect, however, if one conceives of it as a way of referring the decision to an authority that transcends the preferences expressed by individual voters—a substitute for fate, as it were.

Benjamin Constant described the political malaise that afflicts moderns more penetratingly than any one before or since: "Lost in the multitude, the individual can almost never perceive the influence he exercises. Never does his will impress itself on the whole; nothing confirms in his eyes his own cooperation."[25] In the 2000 American presidential election, however, something infinitely improbable came to pass, or very nearly so: for once, each person had the sense that his or her vote actually counted. But the point at which the democratic promise comes closest to being fulfilled is also, by logical necessity, the one at which the arbitrariness of the voting process must seem to a neutral observer to reach its height, since the movement of an almost unimaginably small number of votes from one column to the other is liable to have a major impact, amplified by the presence of unavoidable errors in counting—the "noise" in the system—that, in retrospect, appear to have decided the matter. The lesson to be drawn from the American election is therefore the following: *modern democracy never so much resembles what it aspires to be as when it is indistinguishable from a gigantic lottery.*

The link with the voting paradox is readily seen. As a theoretical (if not also a psychological) matter, a person trying to decide whether or not to vote is concerned exclusively with the chance, which must be reckoned to be exceedingly small, that his ballot might tip the overall balance from one party to the other. However small it may be, there is nevertheless a chance that he might wield extraordinary power. But this is an illusion. For in that case, as we have just established, the voting procedure would be so sensitive to the noise in the system as to be indistinguishable from the flipping of a coin.

It may nevertheless be thought that the argument I am making here is vulnerable to another objection. Although many commentators did in fact notice that chance had played a role in the American election, they concluded that it had operated, not on the level of the election as a whole, but on that of individual voters. The same commentators thought that an election ending in a dead heat, whose probability I maintain to be infinitesimal, was in fact bound to occur, as a consequence of the "law

<hr />

25. Benjamin Constant, "The Liberty of the Ancients as Compared with That of the Moderns" (1819), in *Political Writings,* ed. and trans. Biancamaria Fontana (Cambridge: Cambridge University Press, 1988), 316.

of large numbers."[26] Neither the virtual tie between Bush and Gore, they urged, nor the equal distribution of seats in the Senate and their almost equal distribution in the House of Representatives, meant that America was as divided as everyone supposed. Instead the individual voter, a new version of Buridan's ass, was paralyzed in the face of what he regarded as equivalent options and, in effect, flipped a coin before casting his vote.[27] Hence the virtual certainty, given a sufficiently large number of voters, that the final result would be a statistical tie.[28]

But this objection is fallacious as well. Assuming that each person votes at random, and independently of every other voter, the a priori probability of a tie, far from increasing with the number of drawings (in this case, voters), actually *decreases* as this number rises. The probability is one-half for two voters, three-eighths for four voters, and so on, and rapidly tends toward zero as the number of voters approaches infinity. Obviously this does not contradict the law of large numbers. Moreover, if votes are supposed not to be independent of one another, being codetermined by common factors, the a priori probability of a tie diminishes still more rapidly with the number of voters. Calculation shows that in the case of a state the size of New Mexico, it falls to less than one in a hundred million. This mistake here is twofold: first, to conclude from the fact that an event has occurred—namely, a tie vote—that its probability beforehand must have been high; second, to appeal to the law of large numbers in seeking to justify the inference that Americans voted at random. Even infinitely improbable events occur once in a very great while! And even if Americans *had* voted at random, the event would nonetheless have been very improbable.

26. See, e.g., the piece by the political scientist Nicole Bacharan that appeared in *Le Monde,* 30 November 2000, under the headline "États-Unis: La démocratie des petits riens" (United States: A Democracy of Tiny Increments). The law of large numbers, a theorem of probability theory, states that if an experiment (say, the throw of a die) is repeated a large number of times, the frequency of a given outcome approaches its a priori probability ever more closely as the number of trials increases.

27. See ibid. Bacharan asserts that undecided voters, asked to choose between tax cuts and social programs, had a hard time deciding where their present interests lay. "They chose almost at random. A red ball, a blue ball . . ."

28. "A statistician would say: past a few million, the outcome is going to be 50–50." Ibid.

It is hardly plausible to suppose that individual voters flipped a coin. A far likelier possibility, it seems to me, is that each of them very firmly made up his mind according to the usual criteria. If chance did in fact play a role, it was an emergent property of the system located at the level of the overall vote. The sense in which one may legitimately speak here of chance is manifest in the dual meaning of the English noun *draw,* which may refer either to a lottery (that is, something chosen or drawn at random) or to a tie. In French, the words that designate chance—*hasard, chance, aléa*—refer to the throw of a die, which is to say a deterministic system in which a minute variation in the initial conditions has an observable effect on the outcome. When a national election, involving tens of millions of voters, yields a result as close as that of the American election in 2000—the margin of victory being smaller than the irreducible margin of error—one may therefore speak of chance in the sense that unnoticeably small causes producing a miniscule change in the final vote count would have been sufficient to snatch victory away from one candidate and award it to the other.[29]

29. The same analysis applies to the first round of the French presidential election on 21 April 2002, even if the political configuration was more complex. As the *Times* of London observed in an editorial published on 6 May that year, that Le Pen should have knocked out Jospin constituted a *statistical fluke*—a very unlikely event, to be sure, but not a political upheaval. Rejecting the notion that it was an "earthquake" wreaking havoc on the political landscape as an abuse of the language of natural catastrophes, the paper suggested that the support shown for Le Pen more closely resembled the sight of a tornado descending the Thames on a summer's evening: "A quite abnormal conjunction of meteorological conditions can be imagined that would produce such a phenomenon, but do not expect to see it happen twice in your lifetime." In fact, Jospin fell short of reaching the second round by 300,000 votes, out of 40 million ballots cast, or 0.75 percent of the electorate. A very slight realignment due to a largely contingent event (for example, a sudden change in the weather that particular Sunday in April affecting voter turnout), would have produced the anticipated result, and the significance of the election would have been altogether different. In that case, as the *New York Times* noted in an editorial a week later, the event would have gone unnoticed in the international press. It is plain, too, that the result of the election obviously did not constitute a *fixed point* of the electoral process. Had it been anticipated, a good number of voters would have voted differently than they actually did, and Jospin would have come out ahead of Le Pen. Confident

We find ourselves here faced with the situation I called attention to at the outset, in which chance has a subject—"the people"—and, by virtue of this, a meaning. This subject is external to the voters themselves, since the people, whose will is supposed to be expressed by an election, transcends each of the individual persons who, taken together, make up the people. The form assumed by the system that generates chance in the case of voting is therefore decisive. Surely no one in France, for example, imagines that the referendum on the Maastricht Treaty, or the choice between François Mitterand and Valéry Giscard d'Estaing in the 1981 presidential election, could have assumed the form of a coin flip. And yet in the deliberations of the innumerable committees and commissions to which modern societies entrust responsibility for administering public affairs, reliance on anonymous voting is often only a disguised way of delegating to chance a decision that presumptively rational debate proves to be incapable of reaching.

If we are to find a way out from the voting paradox, as we must try to do, it will be necessary to give up treating elections as a rational procedure for choosing leaders and *go back to the ritual origins of democracy.* Some may complain that it has taken me a rather long time to arrive at a conclusion that, had I begun with it instead, would have saved the reader a pointlessly involved detour. I believe the extra effort was not wasted, however, for it is only by looking closely at what separates ritual from rationality that the true nature of ritual can be detected. Ritual is not irrational. It is rational, only in a most peculiar way.

More than any other system in the world for selecting a political leader, the American presidential election normally consists of two sharply contrasting phases. In the first phase, throughout the course of a year or so, a duel takes place between the two major party candidates that is all the more intense as there is nothing that seems really to distinguish one from the other. The more they resemble each other, the more they wear themselves out trying to persuade voters of the reality of invisible differences. This initial period appears to exist only to prepare the way for the second, much briefer period, in which the entire nation rallies around the

---

in their expectation of a Jospin victory, however, they seem to have carelessly supposed that they could "send a message" to the establishment by voting for a candidate from the extremes without this having the least effect on the final result.

victor in a moment of cathartic release. Only a moment earlier it was still divided against itself; yet something unobservably small, or whatever it was that settled the contest, has now suddenly become large enough to make the victor the unifier of the whole polity. In much the same way, the rituals that accompany the signing of a peace treaty or the formation of an alliance *mimic* or *simulate* war in order to throw into relief the state of non-war that has been entered into once a halt is put to the escalation of violence of the first period. This way of symbolizing the negation of violence is customarily marked in traditional societies by sacrifice. The winner produced by the glorious uncertainties of the ritual ball game of the Aztecs, for example, had the honor of being ceremonially slaughtered and offered up to the gods before an altar. However great the difference between sovereign and martyr may appear at first sight, the formal similarity of the procedures followed in choosing either a prince or a victim suggests they are related to each other.

The political crisis that gripped America in late 2000 arose from the fact that, in the absence of a cathartic resolution, the bitter campaign waged until election day was prolonged for weeks afterward. One could not help but be struck by the constant recourse to religious language among even the most unsentimental commentators, who spoke of the need to reaffirm faith—faith in the abiding power of the Constitution, faith in the rule of law and the greatness of a system that puts the law above men. At the same time, one could not fail to detect an undercurrent of fear—fear that these ideals were more fragile than anyone was prepared to imagine, fear that they were not strong enough to resist a protracted struggle, that the system was at risk of losing its legitimacy. In seeking to go beyond violence by mimicking it, the extended rite of campaigning amounts to playing with fire. There is a very real danger that an improbable and unforeseen event will cause the fire to burn out of control, consuming everything in its path. It is revelatory that the two candidates were called upon to sacrifice themselves, so that the nation's ideals might be protected and preserved. The one who consented to offer himself up as a victim would be the symbolic winner and, at some later time perhaps, the actual winner as well.

What Political Philosophy Can Learn
from Anthropology

The foregoing demonstrates that democracy is, at bottom, a ritual whose efficacy depends first and foremost on the participation of all citizens and a scrupulous respect for procedural formalities. The philosopher Claude Lefort has memorably described this priority of form over content: "Nothing . . . makes the paradox of democracy more palpable than the institution of universal suffrage. It is at the very moment when popular sovereignty is assumed to manifest itself, when the people is assumed to actualize itself by expressing its will, that social interdependence breaks down and the citizen is abtracted from all the networks in which his social life develops and becomes a mere *unit of account*. Number replaces substance."[30]

This passage hints at a profound connection between politics and economics, which I have alluded to several times already in this chapter and shall examine more closely in the next. Just as the market and the price mechanism reduce social life to a branch of accounting, by emptying it of all human content, so the essential political act of a democracy—the election of rulers, now identified with the tedious business of counting votes—presupposes the disappearance of the bonds that hold together the various elements of society. Lefort's formulation suggests an analogy that he himself does not explore, between democracy and a type of ritual that brings about cooperation in a society by mimicking its disintegration under the pressure of conflict. The traditional winter festivals of Western Europe (from the Roman Lupercalia to the Iberian carnival) are good examples of this paradoxical union of opposites, where the individual's sense of belonging to a community is raised to its highest point by a stylized enactment of the violent collapse of the community itself. In the ordered disorder of these festivals, the height of holism and the height of individualism seem to coincide.[31] The same

30. Claude Lefort, "The Question of Democracy," in *Democracy and Political Theory*, trans. David Macey (Minneapolis: University of Minnesota Press, 1988), 18–19. My emphasis. [English version slightly modified.—Trans.]
    31. See Dupuy, "Randonnées carnavalesques," in *Ordres et désordres*, 187–210.

paradox, as Louis Dumont has shown, lies at the heart of Rousseau's political philosophy.[32]

The troubling proximity between democratic ideals and their despotic offspring cannot be avoided. Rereading Tocqueville, with a view to isolating the necessary conditions for a just democratic society, the historian and philosopher Marcel Gauchet was led to reformulate the theological-political problem in the following terms. Primitive and traditional societies, dominated by religion, imagine that both social order and the meaning of this order are due to a higher will that is separate from human volition. By contrast, what we call modernity is suffused with the conviction that human beings owe the laws of political life to themselves alone. The emergence of state-based societies marks the beginning of a long historical process in which what had been external to them becomes internalized, so that the alienation of society from itself that characterized the logic of the sacred assumes the form of the alienation of the governed from their governors.

It was long hoped that this process of internalization would logically, and necessarily, put an end to social division. The history of democratic societies, however, together with a growing awareness of their inherent instability and an appreciation of the lessons of totalitarianism, suggests that this ideal is not only unachievable, but profoundly dangerous as well. The absolute sovereignty of a people over itself paradoxically tends to produce its opposite—the most complete alienation from this sovereignty imaginable, through the concentration of unlimited and arbitrary power in institutions that are completely cut off from the rest of society. A political body can therefore be its own subject only so long as it accepts that the instruments it provides itself with for the purpose of exercising its sovereignty serve to one extent or another to dispossess it of this very sovereignty.

In a democratic society, Gauchet holds, this rule is confirmed by the behavior of the bureaucratic and administrative state as well as by the institutionalization of political conflict. Both make it plain that, although social bonds and the experience of living in society are a fundamental part of what it means to be human, no human institution

32. See Louis Dumont, *From Mandeville to Marx: The Genesis and Triumph of Economic Ideology* (Chicago: University of Chicago Press, 1977), 21.

can make them its own property. This is the logic of what might be called betweenness. Nowhere is it clearer than in the case of the state: "Everything takes place *between* humans—and the state's all-pervasiveness is there to substantiate the complete repossession of collective-being. But everything also occurs through it in such a way that the social actors cannot possibly appropriate the ultimate meaning of collective-being—whether in individual, dictatorial, collective, or self-managed form—because meaning would then no longer be *between* them, but *in* them."[33]

Lefort characterizes what he takes to be a radical transformation of the symbolic representation of power brought about by democracy in very similar terms:

Power was embodied in the prince, and it therefore gave society a body . . . . This model reveals [what is] revolutionary and unprecedented [about] democracy. The locus of power becomes *an empty place.* There is no need to dwell on the details of the institutional apparatus. The important point is that this apparatus prevents governments from appropriating power for their own ends, from incorporating it into themselves. The exercise of power is subject to procedures that periodically cause it to be redistributed. It represents the outcome of a controlled contest with permanent rules, which in turn implies an institutionalization of conflict. The locus of power is an empty place, it cannot be occupied—it is such that no individual and no group can be consubstantial with it—and it cannot be represented.[34]

It would be wrong, Lefort adds, "to conclude that power now resides *in* society on the grounds that it emanates from popular suffrage."[35]

This view stands in striking contrast with Schumpeter's conception of democracy, which we considered earlier. As the philosopher and anthropologist Lucien Scubla has pointed out (elaborating on an example given by A. M. Hocart, one of the greatest anthropologists of the last century), it holds that

33. Marcel Gauchet, *The Disenchantment of the World: A Political History of Religion,* trans. Oscar Burge (Princeton, N.J.: Princeton University Press, 1997), 198–99. The emphasis in the first instance, echoed by the final line, is mine. [English version slightly, but crucially, modified at the end.—Trans.]

34. Lefort, "The Question of Democracy," in *Democracy and Political Theory,* 17. Emphasis in the original.

35. Ibid. Emphasis in the original.

if the general will is inalienable, no one can be the possessor of it; if the general will cannot be represented, no thing or person, not even the people speaking with one voice, can be its representative. And yet for a limited time the chief of state will occupy an inviolable place. Like the king of the Ashanti, who sits under [his throne] because no one can sit on it,[36] he will be, so to speak, placed under the protection of the general will, without at all being able to identify himself with it. [He is] neither supreme leader, nor representative of the sovereign, but *guardian of an empty place* from which no one can talk because no one can occupy it.[37]

This empty place is the absent content, the invisible substance around which social and political order is organized. Political ritual requires some such substance (be it the common interest, general will, justice, or something else), but only so long as no one can say what it is or speak in its name. The intangible and unspeakable character of this substance is perhaps what makes a democratic regime fundamentally different than any other. Even if so, however, we are not prevented from asking which *mechanisms* made it possible to pass from non-democratic rituals (which, strictly speaking, are religious rather than political) to the rituals of democracy—a transition that casts light, in its turn, on what is irreducibly religious about politics.

On this difficult question Scubla makes an interesting suggestion with reference to an Ivory Coast ritual, described by the structuralist anthropologist Ariane Deluz:

The Guro presently resolve certain disputes by organizing a decisive competition between the two parties. In 1928, for example, there were many arguments in the villages of the *gura* and the *bwavere* tribes. Since a female hyena had never been captured during a hunt, some maintained that there were no female hyenas, the others that there were. This controversy was a source of chronic dissension among the villagers, who were divided into two camps. Finally it was decided to settle the issue. A great net-hunting expedition was organized. Those who upheld the existence of female hyenas were sent out on their own, and those who contradicted them on theirs. The hunting party that brought back the most game would be said to have reason on its side. Those who claimed that female hyenas exist caught six does in their net, the others none. The two parties ate the meat

36. See A. M. Hocart, *Kings and Councillors: An Essay in the Comparative Anatomy of Human Society,* ed. Rodney Needham (Chicago: University of Chicago, 1970), 94.

37. Scubla, "Est-il possible de mettre la loi au-dessus de l'homme?" in Dupuy, *Introduction aux sciences sociales,* 141.

together and the *zavogi* [dispute] came to an end. Henceforth it was understood that female hyenas do exist, and it was forbidden to claim otherwise.[38]

Scubla remarks:

One can imagine how such a rite might be transformed. First, the communal meal is abandoned and only the ritual hunt, which has the function of differentiating or deciding between the groups, is retained. Then it is decided to give up the ritual hunt and count votes instead of game. In other words, the ritual hunt is transformed into a political version of Aunt Sally, in which human "victims" are substituted for animal victims. . . . Counting votes is obviously no more rational than [counting] game in order to determine the sex of hyenas. But the essential thing, in both cases, is universal participation in the rite. For the general will truly to be expressed, it is important that each person's voice be heard. Universal participation guarantees the efficacy of democratic election, just as it guarantees the efficacy of the sacrificial rite.[39]

If this is really the true nature of democracy, if the essence of democracy is its *formal* or *procedural* aspect, then societies that claim to be democratic are faced with a question of staggering consequence. What institutions, what procedures can they devise that will be capable of giving genuine substance to political debate? Who, in other words, will say what the sex of a hyena is? When the modern equivalent of this question involves a dire threat to the future of humanity—the dangers posed by new technologies, for example, or the attempt to avoid mass destruction by producing weapons of mass destruction, or the alarming growth of environmental degradation—reliance on procedural formality too often serves as an excuse for avoiding meaningful discussion of the issues themselves. Is wisdom always on the side of the majority? Here it was the great Rousseau who stated the problem more succinctly than any ancient or modern: "[W]here do one hundred who want a master get the right to vote for ten who do not?"[40]

38. Ariane Deluz, "Un dualisme africain," in Jean Pouillon and Pierre Maranda, eds., *Échanges et communications: Mélanges offerts à Claude Lévi-Strauss à l'occasion de son 60ème anniversaire*, 2 vols. (The Hague: Mouton, 1970), 2: 783.

39. Scubla, "Est-il possible de mettre la loi au-dessus de l'homme?" in Dupuy, *Introduction aux sciences sociales*, 142. ["Aunt Sally" is the British name for an old fairgrounds (now pub) game in which contestants throw sticks at a target; the French equivalent is a bowling game, known as *jeu de massacre*, in which the pins represent well-known politicians.—Trans.]

40. Rousseau, *The Social Contract*, 1.5, in *The Collected Writings of Rousseau*, 4: 138.

5

Justice and Resentment

CORRUPTION OF THE BEST

The secularization—I prefer to follow Max Weber in saying the disenchantment *(Entzauberung)*, or, better still, the desacralization—of the world was the result of a long process by which the gospel message eroded primitive and traditional religious structures that until the advent of the modern age, as René Girard emphasizes, had constituted so many barriers and obstacles to the spread of mimetic desire. Human beings ceased to believe in the sorcerer's evil eye. This is why scientific reason was able to flourish—notwithstanding the modern myth that substitutes cause for effect by attributing to the triumph of reason the virtue of having demystified religious beliefs.

Rituals lost their efficacy, and the distinction between the profane and the sacred—a distinction that is governed by the rules of the sacred—was replaced by the banal (which is to say essentially functional) alternation of the weekdays and Sundays of life, to borrow a phrase from Hegel. Work now supplanted piety. The old systems of prohibitions and obligations, weakened by the loss of their sacred character, gave way to economic activity of unprecedented scope and dynamism. As Adam Smith's brilliant forerunner Bernard de Mandeville rightly perceived, it was the unbridling of private vices and invidious passions that constituted both the engine and the source of energy for what formerly had been the least important branch of human activity. There resulted from this, if not the happiness, then at least the wealth of nations.

No one can deny that the unleashing of mimetic desire in communities that now found themselves detached from the sacred, and the unrestrained competition between human beings to which this novel state of affairs gave rise, had extremely positive consequences. Still less can it be doubted that these things also had extremely negative consequences, particularly for the mental health of modern society. With the rapid growth of disruptive passions, the cardinal evil of resentment came to rule the world.

If what I call economy constitutes the essence of modernity, it is not only because of the importance that production, consumption, and commerce have acquired over the past several centuries, but also, and above all, because an economistic mode of thinking has become the dominant way of understanding social, moral, and political phenomena.[1] Not only do economic theorists today not hesitate to pronounce on matters having to do with social justice, property rights, and the punishment of criminal behavior; they take pride in the fact that a good part of contemporary moral and political philosophy has been decisively shaped by economic theory and, in particular, by normative economics. The most influential doctrine in this domain of philosophy in recent times, of course, is found in John Rawls's famous work, *A Theory of Justice.*

When it considers problems of social justice, economic theory claims to limit itself to the resources of rational analysis and, still more restrictively, to instrumental rationality, which is interested solely in the adequacy of means to ends, without troubling to inquire into the value of these ends. Weber showed that the rise to power of instrumental reason in human affairs, which accompanied the growth of Christianity under the influence of the Protestant ethic, was itself a religious phenomenon. But his argument was fiercely contested. Setting to one side the attempts of German idealism to provide a ground for reason in reason itself, it is fair to say that modern scientism has relied mainly on theories of evolution to explain the emergence of instrumental rationality and its selection as the mode of reasoning best suited to the development of the human race. It

---

1. I develop the concept of economy in both its normal and pathological forms in *L'avenir de l'économie: Sortir de l'économystification* (Paris: Flammarion, 2012). An English translation is forthcoming from Michigan State University Press.

should be noted that Darwinism started out, like Freudianism, as a species of economism, and to a large extent remained one in its later versions. So long as the main dynamic of biological evolution was seen to depend on maximization principles, the mental outlook remained unchanged.

A through examination of theories of justice that purport to ground themselves in reason, and reason alone, reveals that they are deeply influenced in spite of themselves by Christianity, or at least by the Christian injunction to show meekness and humility and to take the side of the victim. In seeking to ground this injunction on what amount to tautologies, such theories produce impossibly baroque, Escher-like constructions that unwittingly depend on the very thing they intend to demonstrate by deductive argument. This peculiar blindness renders them defenseless against the onslaught of disruptive passions—a threat that itself feeds and sustains another phenomenon, which rationalist theories of justice are unable to account for: the characteristically modern retreat from the sacred. Nowhere has the denial of the religious foundation of human societies had more deleterious effects than in economic life.

Justice is Not Reducible to Logic

Why is inequality an evil? And is it necessarily an evil? Even in the domain of economy, fundamental questions of this sort have to do primarily with human relationships, not with relationships between people and things. Our dealings with one another bring us joy or suffering, make us rich or poor, give us hope or plunge us into despair. They can also be the source of immense danger. All human societies have sought to reduce the chance of violence by creating institutions that block opportunities for direct confrontation between their members. In contemporary societies dominated by economic competition, the chief institution serving this purpose is called wealth. A person who is mainly interested in maximizing his own wealth is naturally less interested than he would otherwise be in the moral vices and virtues of his neighbors.

Adam Smith, who was first and foremost a moral philosopher, saw that wealth is desired, not for the material satisfactions that it brings, but because it is desired by others. Whoever possesses it concentrates on himself the "sympathy" of those who regard him—an ambiguous feeling compounded of admiration and envy that corrupts social morality.[2] It is altogether deplorable that economists, who see Smith as the founding father of their discipline, should have completely forgotten his teaching.[3]

Any analysis of the evil and injustice of inequality must begin with the triangular relationship uniting a subject, an object, and a third party. Economic theory, in reifying wealth, sees only the subject in his relation to the object. From the very outset, then, it condemns itself to what Rawls approvingly calls a kind of moral geometry, in which the joy and suffering of human beings are measured by simplistic logic and trivial mathematics. And yet, at the same time, economic theory dares to compete with moral and political philosophy by making what it supposes to be a fresh—and, moreover, a scientific—start in undertaking to reconsider its oldest questions, not least the question of distributive justice. It looks with special favor on the notion of "equity," defined as the absence of "envy." These words must be placed within quotation marks, for in the sterile world of microeconomics they do not have the meaning they have in ordinary language. One individual is said to envy another if he prefers that person's situation to his own, measured according to his own system of preferences. Equity is achieved when no one envies anyone else, which is to say when each person considers himself better off than anyone else.

This notion gained currency because it allows individual situations to be compared without obliging economists to renounce what remains their chief article of faith, namely, the incommensurability of individual preferences. That Jones's satisfaction might have diminished because Smith's has increased (or decreased) is beyond the power of economists to imagine, for it would require them to admit the feasibility of interpersonal comparisons. By conceiving of envy in the peculiar way I have just mentioned, however, it becomes possible to square the circle: Jones evaluates Smith's situation by putting himself in Smith's place, but the criterion of evaluation—the only one available to him—continues to be his own system of preferences.

It seems very odd indeed that persons having no feelings toward one another should be capable of envy. Where is the suffering the envious

2. See Smith, *The Theory of Moral Sentiments*, 1.3.3.1, 72.
3. See Jean-Pierre Dupuy, "Invidious Sympathy in *The Theory of Moral Sentiments,*" *Adam Smith Review* 2 (2006): 96–123.

person feels in contemplating the happiness of another? Where are the destructive urges that this suffering inspires in him? They are nowhere to be found, for they are inexpressible under the assumptions of neoclassical economics. Whether or not someone envies another (in the economist's impoverished sense of this term) changes nothing, neither his satisfaction nor his behavior. This is because the envy of which economic theory speaks is not the relation of one subject to another, but the relation of an individual to an object. If Jones prefers to have what Smith possesses, and we replace Smith with Taylor, who has the same thing, Jones's "envy" will remain the same. The actual person who is envied is of no importance whatever.

Economists are adept at justifying what must seem to anyone else to be an obvious defect in their theory. If equity, defined as the absence of envy, is desirable, this is because it does not involve human passions, but consists instead in the design of ethical norms. Whenever equity obtains, they say, members of society are treated "symmetrically"; that is, there is no favoritism or inequality of opportunity. Let us suppose that all members of society have open to them an identical set of possibilities. It is plain, then, that there will be no envy. For Jones to envy Smith would mean that he did not choose wisely, since he prefers to his own situation one that is identical to Smith's, which by hypothesis could be his as well. The economist is prepared to concede that what he calls envy has nothing in common with the disruptive passion bearing this name. Exploiting a distinction made by Rawls (who speaks here in a way that must be regarded as unusual, to say the least), the economist construes it as resentment, in the sense of "excusable" or "legitimate" envy: whoever considers himself treated unfairly by comparison with another is justified in complaining of it; but since he is within his rights to do so, he is immune to the torments of envy. Why would he envy someone who owes his good fortune only to injustice?

Reason (or logic, or else geometry) dictates the principle that, if all persons are considered to be equal, they ought to be treated equally. It is therefore reason (or logic, or geometry) that is harmed by an "unfair" state of affairs, and not the self-esteem of human subjects. If they are troubled by injustice, it is insofar as they are moral logicians or geometers, not creatures having desires and passions. The naïveté of this position is staggering. Even Rawls, who has the audacity to cite to Freud in this connection, does not allow himself to be taken in by it. Envy is a sickness that one attempts to conceal or suppress, since otherwise self-respect and the sense of one's own worth would be in jeopardy. All societies have invented symbolic devices for the purpose of facilitating this dissimulation. Ethical rules are an outstanding example. In Protestant societies, for example, envy assumes the form of moral indignation. But the basic facts of experience are too psychological—too anthropological—to be taken seriously by a discipline that seeks to ground the universality of moral judgment on logical truths.

The principles of justice to which Rawls attempts to give a foundation in social contract theory underlie an ordering rule known as "leximin." In each of the domains to which justice applies (basic civil liberties, personal security, economic opportunity), this rule prescribes that absolute priority be given to the person who is worst off, then to the one who is next worse off, and so on. Leximin does indeed have interesting logical properties.[4] But it has no interest in the individual person, only in the rank individual persons occupy in a hierarchy of ill-being. When it comes to comparing two states of society, the one in which the most disadvantaged group enjoys greater favor is declared more just than the other, but this judgment does not require that the members of the most disadvantaged group in each of these two states be the same. Justice is concerned simply with discovering whether a certain overall pattern of wealth distribution is respected or not. If there is any concern for a poor person, it is not because he is *a person,* but because he is *poor.*

A student revolt some ten years ago against the teaching of economics in France, provoked by dissatisfaction with the growing mathematization of the discipline, misdiagnosed the true source of the problem—as though the patient were to blame the thermometer for his illness. This

---

4. Leximin is compatible with the basic meta-ethical criterion that normative economics seeks to satisfy, namely, Pareto preordering (also known as Pareto efficiency), which obtains when no individual can be made better off without making another worse off. From a normative point of view, this criterion scarcely advances beyond the obvious: in any ranking that involves several dimensions, a candidate who ranks higher than another on *each* of these dimensions ranks higher overall, in accordance with the Pareto preordering. It is better, in other words, to be rich and handsome than poor and ugly!

may be why the revolt has had no impact whatsoever on how economics is taught in France today. What must be challenged instead is an entire way of thinking about economic life that encourages the almost exclusive reliance on mathematical models and methods. For it is only by neglecting the whole gamut of moral passions and sentiments[5] that animate human relationships (whether people are assumed to be equal or unequal) that it becomes possible to abandon oneself to the solitary pleasures of geometry and algebra, under the pretense of constructing a human science.

Social Inequality and Humiliation

Novelists and philosophers have exhaustively described and analyzed the passions of inequality—those "modern" passions of which Stendhal and Dostoyevsky spoke: jealousy, envy, impotent hatred, the feeling of humiliation, and so on—as well as the passions of equality—those "democratic" passions of which Tocqueville spoke, which "burn the brighter in those very times when they have the least fuel."[6] All these authors know how intensely such passions may be felt and what dangers they hold for both personal and social equilibrium. This classic theme can be seen in a new light if we consider the extent to which not only social ideologies (understood as systems of ideas and values)[7] but also theories of society have had to be forced to undergo strange contortions, remarkable for their diversity and their ingenuity, in order to contain the passionate energies of modernity within manageable limits. I shall now proceed to examine four symbolic systems—hierarchy, demystification, contingency, and complexity—that appear to be united by a common interest in doing everything possible to ensure that inferior social status is not experienced as something humiliating. Let me make it clear at the outset that I make no claims for the effectiveness of these systems. I simply suggest that they may usefully be thought of as attempts to combat a formidable threat.

5. Or by placing people behind a "veil of ignorance," to use the phrase favored by Rawls, for whom persons deliberating about questions of justice are supposed to be indifferent to the interests of others.

6. Tocqueville, *Democracy in America*, 2.4.3, 782.

7. I therefore use the word "ideology" in the neutral sense given it by Louis Dumont, detached from any value judgment.

Hierarchy

Here it will be instructive once again to borrow Louis Dumont's characterization.[8] Dumont, it will be recalled, considers hierarchy to be the social form peculiar to all traditional or archaic societies in which social ties are guaranteed by the sacred. In these societies, what we call social inequality is the very form of justice itself. What is utterly novel about modernity, by contrast, is its egalitarian conception of social relationships—not that equality is fully realized, of course, but it nonetheless furnishes the collective imagination with an ideal.

Hierarchy is a way of totalizing society, by making it part of a cosmos that is itself conceived as a hierarchy of values. Hierarchy refers neither to an inequality of economic wealth nor to an inequality of political power. It is the form, not of political or economic categories (classes), but of categories such as honor and prestige that derive from a system of social relations protected by religion (status groups, orders, estates, castes, and so on). In this system, values are ranked in such a way that the "higher" element is nowhere dominant, for it is neither superior nor preferable to "lower" elements in the ordinary sense of these terms. It differs from them as a whole differs from the parts it encompasses, or as one part that is preeminent with respect to the internal arrangement of a whole differs from other parts. The relation of hierarchy is intelligible only in the context of a holistic ideology, which is to say within a system of ideas and values that subordinate individual persons to the society of which they are all members.

The essential point, for our purposes, is that hierarchical superiority does not signify a higher personal value. Hereditary monarchy, among other hierarchical social forms, makes this manifest by leaving the essential institutional mechanism for transmitting authority from one generation to the next to the chance of genetic endowment. "The value of heredity," one defender of royalist prerogatives has urged, "does not reside in any chromosome map or bloodline, for this would raise the question of qualities and set in motion exactly the competition it is meant to dispense with."[9] What ultimately is of greatest importance for the hierarchical

8. See especially the postface ("Toward a Theory of Hierarchy") to Dumont, *Homo hierarchicus*, 239–45.

9. Dominique Decherf, "La succession: Un débat pour des nouveaux arguments monarchistes," *Royaliste* 388 (September–October 1983).

model of society, in other words, is avoiding a situation in which individual values are placed in rivalry with one another.

Anthropological research has shown that, in many traditional cultures, social advancement is legitimate only to the extent that it can be explained by reference to chance, luck, or else the protection of some figure who, by bringing another person within his circle or orbit of influence, transforms that person's status. It is amusing to note that the very same things that are thought to legitimize inequalities in traditional societies are considered bad things in egalitarian, competitive, and meritocratic societies today, and serve to morally disqualify whoever benefits from them (thus a person is disapprovingly said to have achieved success owing to connections, or simply to sheer luck). The reason these things are good or bad, depending on the case, is always the same: they exclude any appeal to individual value or personal merit.

Demystification

In egalitarian, competitive, and meritocratic societies, demystification serves much the same purpose as hierarchy in traditional societies, by opposing the tendency to regard the favorable situation enjoyed by another person as the rightful consequence of his own virtue. The work of the sociologist Pierre Bourdieu is exemplary in this regard. Bourdieu's lasting influence is due in large measure to his analysis of the role of power relations in the struggle for domination that is constantly being waged beneath a hypocritical veneer of social legitimacy. Using new critical methods (hence the name "critical sociology"), he sought to rob meritocratic values of their mystique by revealing the transmutation of "social heritage into individual grace or personal merit."[10]

Thus, for example, the modern educational system claims to select the best and the brightest—which is to say those whom nature has most generously provided with abilities and talents, and who are the most diligent in trying to develop them—and to assure their success in life. But in fact it only reproduces the social ranking that previously existed, while entrenching it further by means of the fiction of individual merit. It is a

10. Pierre Bourdieu and Jean-Claude Passeron, *Inheritors: French Students and Their Relation to Culture,* trans. Richard Nice (Chicago: University of Chicago Press, 1979), 70; see also my discussion in *Le sacrifice et l'envie,* 203–13.

golden rule of critical sociology that social phenomena are determined by social factors alone. Accordingly, social and cultural "heritage" are held to be infinitely more powerful than supposedly natural endowments in producing social differences.

A practiced demystifier ought to feel no admiration or envy whatever for those who dominate the economic and political landscape, and least of all for those who are uncouth enough to boast of the effort by which they have managed to pull themselves all the way up to the top of the ladder. For the meritocratic ideal of hard work and steadfast determination unwittingly betrays the shameful, and quite opposite, reality of the social order as the arbitrary outcome of hidden power struggles. Yet critical sociology, still more than meritocracy itself, is a child of the competitive spirit. If critical sociology rejects competition, it is not owing to a lack, but rather to an excess, of this very spirit. Certainly the torments of envy are by no means foreign to it.

Contingency

By "contingency" I refer to the lottery appointed by the natural and social circumstances of a person's birth. That the principal theories of social justice should all be non-meritocratic, and indeed in some cases anti-meritocratic, can hardly be a coincidence. Rawls's theory, with respect to problems of economic and social justice, asserts that inequalities are legitimate only to the extent that they help to improve as far as possible the lot of the worst-off. This so-called difference principle can be used to justify inequalities insofar as they have the effect of creating what economists call an "incentive": if people redouble their efforts and work harder, it is not because they seek to ameliorate the general welfare or the quality of social justice, but because they *are motivated* to do so, typically by the prospect of being rewarded for their perseverance with higher pay, higher either than what they used to receive or than what others earn. In the just society imagined by Rawls, it follows that talent and effort are remunerated, not for moral reasons (as would be the case in a meritocratic society), but in order to attain a moral end by making the most unfortunate better off. The state of social differentiation licensed by a difference principle of this sort therefore has a purely functional value. By means of this principle, Rawls hopes to neutralize the inequalities due to the lottery of nature and society—not by eliminating them, but by placing them in the service of those who are most disadvantaged.

The logical structure of Rawls's argument concerning merit therefore reduces to the following syllogism:

(a) Justice implies a positive correlation between talent and effort, on the one hand, and shares of social wealth, on the other, calibrated in such a way that the smallest share will be as large as possible (difference principle);

(b) No personal merit is associated with such talent and effort;

(c) The correlation between talent and effort, on the one hand, and shares of social wealth, on the other, therefore does not express a meritocratic principle.

This syllogism is perfectly coherent, but it is also profoundly odd. It exposes Rawls to criticism as much from the Right (which protests that the individual is wrongfully dispossessed of what makes him who he is— his gifts, his willingness to devote time and effort to develop them, his readiness to make sacrifices and to take risks, and so on) as from the Left (which rebels against the idea that inequalities might be legitimized by natural facts and circumstances). One cannot help but wonder why Rawls placed himself in such an awkward position.

The reason, I believe, is that he had no choice, in view of the threat posed to any such theory of justice by envy and resentment.[11] Rawls's just and well-ordered society is one that everyone publicly agrees to be just, and one that seeks as far as possible to bring about genuine equity by promoting equality of opportunity. It is nevertheless an inegalitarian society, in which inequalities are correlated with—and therefore reveal—differences in talent and effort. How can those who are at the bottom of the ladder blame anyone but themselves for their own inferiority? Indeed, they ought to be grateful that they are not worse off than they are—and, what is more, ought to give thanks for this "privilege" to their more favored fellow citizens.

Envy has a free hand in such a society. To prevent it from wreaking havoc, merit—which is to say differences in individual worth—must be eliminated. For it is in imagining that another person deserves his good fortune that the torments of envy are unleashed, and not in imagining the opposite, which is the only possibility to be openly contemplated. Hence

---

11. See Dupuy, *Le sacrifice et l'envie,* 161–89.

Rawls's insistence, so paradoxical in the context of his own ideology, on the "arbitrariness" not only of natural endowments and social circumstance, but also of individual effort, and on the absence of any personal credit or discredit associated with such effort—an anti-meritocratic position for which his fellow liberals never forgave him.

Oversimplifying somewhat, one is tempted to say that the poor man in Rawls's just society does not suffer from any sense of inferiority, since he knows that if he is poor, it is because his genes did not permit him to aspire to a higher station in life; as for the rich man, he has no reason to feel superior to others, because he knows that his talents and his capacity for hard work are nothing more than means—which he has inherited from nature, and which have a merely functional value—for making society more just. Rawls's solution to the problem of justice and disruptive passions could be considered plausible only if the members of society were themselves persuaded that merit plays no role here. But the modern individual, having been born into a world of competition, will not allow a whole part of himself to be taken away from him, all those things that make him deserving of reward or punishment—in a word, his *desert.* Winners do not wish to be robbed of their prestige, nor losers of their anguish.

Complexity

At the other extreme of the ideological spectrum from Rawls, similar contortions and distortions may be detected at the heart of the social and political philosophy of Friedrich Hayek, and, as I have tried to show elsewhere, for the same reasons.[12] In Hayek's writings the "invisible hand" of the market has a very different sense from the one it has in the neoclassical model, first devised by Léon Walras, which provides the framework for economic theory as it is taught today in every university in the world. Hayek does not have in mind the spontaneous harmonization of behaviors that, although they aim at no common interest, nonetheless remain, at least on the individual level, guided by a spirit of calculation and a concern for rationality. The market in his view displays something more like the self-organization observed in a termite colony—albeit a colony

12. See ibid., 241–91.

in which imitation has taken over from instinct. Individual behaviors, though they are blind, constitute an efficient system thanks to a process of cultural "selection" that eliminates all that is superfluous, unnecessary, or counterproductive.

There is a great deal of suffering in Hayek's version of economic life, at least as much as in the markets of the real world: people lack work or lose their jobs, businesses fail, suppliers are abandoned by long-standing customers, speculators gamble and lose everything, new products find no buyers, fresh discoveries elude the best efforts of researchers, and so on. These disappointments are experienced as strokes of fate, unjustified, unpredictable, incomprehensible. Hayek's objection to policies aimed at achieving social justice is not that they disrupt the system of economic incentives, since quite obviously there are no effective incentives in this case. It is that such policies can themselves only be blind, for no one can tell a spontaneous social order what it must do. As I indicated earlier, in the prologue, government regulation that ignores the spontaneous self-regulation of the market is bound to fail.

This argument follows from the existence of what Hayek calls social complexity. No one can fix the value of a unit of labor in advance, or of the effort it involves, or of the product that comes of it, for these are things only the market can decide, and its determinations cannot be anticipated. Economic agents have no access to the collective knowledge represented by prices *before* they are established by the market. Suppose a worker in France loses his job—the result of some multinational corporation having decided to close the factory where he worked because global economic conditions had made it more profitable to move operations overseas to Singapore or Brazil. He now discovers that the value attached to his qualifications and abilities by the community to which he belongs has suddenly become equal to zero. In a world of perfect information, of course, such as the one economists are pleased to imagine exists, the same worker would have been able to anticipate his impending unemployment and would either have moved to another country or acquired a new set of job skills. But in the real world, Hayek observes, the complexity of social processes prohibits this. It is revealing that he often characterizes this state of affairs in terms of chance, luck, or misfortune, rather than of complexity. And yet, as we saw in the preceding chapter, there is a profound connection between chance and complexity. Individual merit and moral worth are therefore not the only things that can be blindly disregarded by the market; hard work, talent, skill, and considered strategic choices are liable to meet the same fate. There is no guaranteed reward in the face of the hazards and contingencies of social life.

Hayek is by no means unaware of the risk that the market may exacerbate disruptive passions. Envy is bound to be a familiar presence in a competitive society where success and failure are the only things that count. Since failure signifies an inability to satisfy the needs of others, it inevitably leads to a loss of their esteem—and so to a loss of self-esteem. Hayek's remedy, insofar as it consists in an appeal to a form of exteriority, is altogether traditional. Its novelty resides in the nature of the exteriority appealed to—the complexity of social dynamics. Hayek describes the operation of chance in this domain with considerable eloquence:

> Inequality is undoubtedly more readily borne, and *affects the dignity of the person much less,* if it is determined by impersonal forces than when it is due to design. In a competitive society it is no slight to a person, *no offense to his dignity,* to be told by any particular firm that it has no need for his services or that it cannot offer him a better job. . . . But the unemployment or the loss of income which will always affect some in any society is certainly less degrading if it is the result of *misfortune* and not deliberately imposed by authority.[13]

As in Rawls, the problem is that this can be an adequate solution only on the condition that economic agents share the philosopher's conviction, namely, that they are dealing here with a true exteriority. No one will surrender to the impersonal forces that Hayek considers to be providential if he has good reason to doubt that they are leading the world in the right (or at least a promising) direction. After all, an extended market order in Hayek's sense can easily close in upon itself and become "locked-in"—a prelude to catastrophe, as historical experience has regularly demonstrated.

13. Friedrich A. Hayek, *The Road to Serfdom* (Chicago: University of Chicago Press, 1944), 106. The emphasis is mine.

What Economics Can Learn from Anthropology and Political Philosophy

If I have dwelt at such length on the violence of the passions to which inequalities among human beings give rise and on the ways in which various ideologies try to disarm these passions, and if I criticize the economistic vision of the world so harshly, it is because I cannot help but think the tragedy of our present condition. The world having become a universal theater, it is now on a worldwide scale that the attempt must be made to ensure that humiliating inequalities, and the widespread sense of resentment they feed, do not culminate in the worst abominations. Those who prefer to make the study of society a branch of applied mathematics, in the expectation of arriving at a unique and definitive solution to the problem of social justice, are free to go on playing in their corner of the sandbox. For the rest of us, it is urgent that we make an effort to raise ourselves up to the height of the dangers our new world demands that we confront.

The Violence of Resentment

To gauge the strength of man's hateful passions, I have so far proceeded indirectly by pointing out the deformations they have produced in the logic of various theories of justice. But the direct method works just as well. There are any number of reputable authorities one may cite, especially among the greatest classical authors. The most profound of these still seems to me to be Rousseau, whose concept of *amour-propre* remains unsurpassed.

Rousseau regarded *amour-propre* as the essence of human desire, the force that moves men and engenders all the vices. He contrasted it with *amour de soi,* which reigned in the state of nature.[14] The extraordinary account that Rousseau left us of *amour-propre* in the *Dialogues* (also known as *Rousseau, Judge of Jean-Jacques,* a sort of sequel to the *Confessions*) contains this remarkable passage:

14. Rousseau describes *amour de soi* as a "natural feeling," common to both man and animals, that causes them to take an interest in their own well-being. In human beings, guided by reason and shaped by pity, it gives rise to humanity and virtue.

The primitive passions, which all tend directly toward our happiness, focus us only on objects that relate to it, and having only *amour de soi* as a principle, are all loving and gentle in their essence. But when, being *deflected from their object by obstacles, they focus on removing the obstacle rather than on reaching the object,* then their nature changes and they become irascible and hateful. And that is how *amour de soi,* which is a good and absolute feeling, becomes *amour-propre,* which is to say a relative feeling by which one makes comparisons; the latter feeling demands preferences, and *its enjoyment is purely negative, as it no longer seeks satisfaction in our own benefit but solely in the harm of another.*[15]

Amour-propre is a destructive force, one that has broken loose from the logic of self-interest that restrains *amour de soi.* And yet *amour-propre* has its origin in *amour de soi.* It is when people's interests intersect ("cross each other," Rousseau says), that this transformation occurs.[16] It arises from the *crossing* of one person's gaze with another's, which brings about in turn the sidelong glance—the invidious look (Latin *invidia,* from the verbal form meaning "to cast an evil eye upon")—and so, though envy, leads to jealousy, hatred, and all the other disruptive passions. These passions are not only evil. They are also irrational, for, in prompting us to focus on a rival (the "obstacle" that stands in our way), they cause us to lose sight of what we actually desire. The task Rousseau sets for a good society in the *Social Contract* is to reestablish the transcendent supremacy of *amour de soi* (whose collective expression is the general will) over *amour-propre* (expressed by particular wills); in other words, to bring about the triumph of reason over emotion, of interests over passions.

The *obstacle* that we seek to remove, even more ardently than we seek to attain what we desire, is plainly *another person,* whose desire—as if by chance, identical to our own—stands in our way on the road that leads us to the object of our desire. The triangular relationship I spoke of at the outset is now in place: rivalry emerges from the eclipse

---

15. Jean-Jacques Rousseau, *Rousseau, Judge of Jean-Jacques: Dialogues* (1776), in *Collected Writings of Rousseau,* 1: 9. The emphasis is mine. Here and elsewhere I have modified the English translations found in this edition, which not infrequently suffer from grave errors of interpretation.

16. "When . . . men begin to cast their eyes upon their fellows. . .[,] their interests cross each other ... [and] *amour de soi*[,] put into fermentation[,] changes into *amour-propre*"; see *Letter to Beaumont* (1763), in *Collected Writings of Rousseau,* 9: 28–29.

of the individual subject's relationship to his object by his relationship to another subject. The economistic way of looking at the world, which sees only relations between subjects and objects, between people and things, is condemned to remain blind to the force of passions—a fateful handicap that, as Rousseau's dazzling analysis makes clear, is inherent in this perspective.

The terrorist attacks of 11 September 2001 have typically been interpreted with reference to the beliefs and the *interests* of their authors. Much effort has been devoted to inquiring into their objectives, which is to say the *objects* they aimed at. One would have done better to reread Rousseau and his disciple Dostoyevsky. Elsewhere I have tried to show that the error lies in trying to make sense of the senseless by asserting the radical foreignness of those who commit senseless acts.[17] In the case of 11 September, the criminals desired the same things we did; they were no less motivated by the passions of competition than we were. The simple fact of the matter is that when the fever of rivalry spreads throughout the world, with the result that some nations (or ethnic groups within nations) repeatedly come out on the losing end, it is inevitable that the evil of resentment—no matter which name we give to it: pride, wounded pride, envy, jealousy, hateful passion, or any other—should have devastating consequences. Anyone who is fascinated by those whom he judges, in spite of himself, to be superior is pitiably and tragically crushed by all the obstacles that he finds in his way, like the moth that is consumed in the candle flame or the jihadists aboard the two planes that crashed into the towers of power—and this *because he is more concerned with the obstacle than his object.*

Common sense has been so thoroughly corrupted by the spirit of demystification that the word "interest" has now come exclusively to designate self-interest. But interest, as Hannah Arendt reminds us, is that which, in coming *between* people, "gathers us together and yet prevents our falling over each other, so to speak." It is for this reason, she says, that "[t]o live together in the world means essentially that a world of things is between those who have it in common, as a table is located between those who sit around it; the world, like every *in-between,* relates and separates

17. See Dupuy, *Avons-nous oublié le mal?* 11–67; also the first chapter of the present work.

men at the same time."[18] Resentment, the ultimate evil, occurs when nothing any longer comes between human beings, when no concern for the world, no *interest* in the world, prevents them from falling over each other. In the absence of an intermediary, rivals are bound to clash with one another in a free-for-all of pure violence, having lost all idea of their own individual interests, to say nothing of a common interest.

There is something fundamentally sane about this way of looking at the matter, despised by both economists and critical sociologists. Indeed, if the logic of interest in Arendt's sense governed human affairs, the world would be a much happier place. By a remarkable paradox, both the economist and the critical sociologist fail to see that, in making self-interest an ineliminable fact of human nature, they overlook the possibility that a situation might arise in which there no longer is any interest, any object of desire, any common world—a situation in which there is only pure violence. No one wishes to be accused of naïveté and innocence, however, for these things are today considered to be grave sins.

The Sacralization of the Victim

The problem of inequality in the world is not primarily a theoretical problem—as though we have only to work out a theory of justice in order to be done with it. It is an eminently practical problem. Indeed, to the extent that it is encrusted by layers of historical, political, and even anthropological context, a kind of moral geometry is exactly what is *not* wanted. The chief obstacle to thinking clearly about the problem of inequality arises from the fact that someone who considers himself to be in a position of inferiority is apt today to pose as a victim of injustice. And yet, in the Judeo-Christian world, the victim is sacred. The sacralization of victims is therefore the real problem.

Nothing more strikingly reveals the degree to which civilization has assumed a global character than the almost universal concern for victims. Everywhere it is in the name of the victims that others are alleged to have persecuted, killed, massacred, or mutilated that they themselves are persecuted, killed, massacred, or mutilated in their turn. It was in the name of the victims of Hiroshima that the Islamic kamikazes struck America. For

18. Arendt, *The Human Condition*, 52. My emphasis. Recall that the word "interest" itself comes from the Latin *inter* (between) and *esse* (to be).

decades now in the Middle East, the Israelis and Palestinians have been "fighting to be the victim."[19] Here we find an abominable perversion of the compassionate regard for human suffering that Nietzsche, that most anti-Christian of philosophers, saw as the mark of Christianity and of the slave morality he considered it to have brought forth. The source of this perversion, as both Illich and Girard have emphasized, is Christianity itself—a corrupt Christianity.[20]

The influence of this depraved doctrine is measured by the fact that the word "sacrifice" has come to mean self-sacrifice—so thoroughly, and to such an extent, that scarcely a week after 11 September, some of the current representatives of a long tradition of anti-Americanism in France refused to condemn the criminals, on the ground that they had given their own lives. Astonishingly, from this moment on, the word "victim" was used, not to designate the doomed occupants of the towers, but the terrorists themselves, declared to have been doubly victimized by the injustice of the world and by the necessity of martyring themselves. It may nevertheless be the case, as the anthropologist Eric Gans has argued, that the attacks of 11 September, by their very enormity, signaled the demise of the ideology of the victim. "Just as the Holocaust inaugurated the postmodern era by making victimary resentment the preeminent criterion of political change," Gans wrote a month after the attacks, "September 11 ended it by demonstrating the horrors such resentment can produce." He goes on to ask: "Does the end of victimary thinking mean that we should no longer seek justice? Of course not. But it does mean that justice cannot be sought simply by 'taking the side of the victim.'"[21]

19. Thus the title of an article in the 4 April 1994 issue of *Newsweek* by its Jerusalem correspondent, Jeffrey Bartholet.

20. Hence my allusion in the subtitle of the present chapter to the Latin maxim *corruptio optimi quae est pessima* (corruption of the best is the worst), often quoted by Ivan Illich in his indictment of the modern world, which he saw as having been shaped by a fatal misinterpretation of the Gospel. See 34–39 above.

21. Eric Gans, "Window of Opportunity," *Chronicles of Love and Resentment* 248 (20 October 2001), www.anthropoetics.ucla.edu/views/vw248.htm. Note that "victimary resentment" is not (or not necessarily) the same thing as victims' resentment, that is, the resentment felt by the victims of injustice themselves; it refers instead to the resentment of those who use the victimization of others, whether real or imagined, as a pretext for persecuting their persecutors.

This optimistic analysis throws light upon a sharp controversy that broke out in the spring of 2002 in the pages of the *Jerusalem Post* and *The Economist*. Many Americans, who after 11 September regarded their country as a classic victim, watched with disbelief and amazement as the rise (in some cases the resurgence) of anti-Americanism in Europe gathered momentum in the months that followed, all the more since it was accompanied by gains for the extreme Right at the polls and by the growth of a resolutely anti-Israeli attitude in connection with the Middle East conflict. This conjunction of events seemed to them to be irrefutable proof of a corresponding outburst of anti-Semitism. The American columnist Charles Krauthammer, writing in the *Jerusalem Post* in April 2002, charged that

[w]hat we are seeing [in Europe at this moment] is pent-up anti-Semitism, the release—with Israel as the trigger—of a millennium-old urge that powerfully infected and shaped European history.

What is odd is not the anti-Semitism of today, but its relative absence during the last half-century. That was the historical anomaly. Holocaust shame kept the demon corked for that half-century. But now the atonement is passed. The genie is out again.

This time, however, it is more sophisticated. It is not a blanket hatred of Jews. Jews can be tolerated, even accepted, but they must know their place. Jews are fine so long as they are powerless, passive, and picturesque. What is intolerable is Jewish assertiveness, *the Jewish refusal to accept victimhood*. And nothing so embodies that as the Jewish state.[22]

While conceding that events might appear to justify such an interpretation, the editors of *The Economist* vigorously dissented, calling it grossly mistaken and an unforgivable slander. No, they insisted, anti-Semitism is not rearing its ugly head in Europe; it is simply that Europeans, above all since 11 September, are no longer afraid to criticize the government of Israel. This is not a sign of deepening anti-Semitism, it is a sign of weakening anti-anti-Semitism. Why? Because the attacks of 11 September deprived the victim of its sacred status.[23]

22. Charles Krauthammer, "Please Excuse the Jews for Living," *Jerusalem Post*, 29 April 2002. The italics are mine.

23. See "Europe and the Jews: Is Anti-Semitism Surging Back?" *The Economist*, 4 May 2002.

To address the question of inequality by constructing a theory that gives the interests of the most disadvantaged a preponderant and unchallengeable weight in deliberations about social justice amounts in turn, then, to proceeding in exactly the opposite direction to the one that needs to be followed, for it serves only to perpetuate the sacralization of the victim. What, then, *as a practical matter,* can be done?

Escaping the Victim Syndrome

The French columnist Roland Hureaux, writing in February 2003, very aptly described the predicament that faces us today:

There has been a great deal of foolish talk about bin Laden and the al-Qaida network. Some . . . say that terrorism is a result of poverty: it is a matter of the poor taking revenge against the rich. To this others rightly reply that the leaders of al-Qaida, most of whom come from the Arab upper-middle class, . . . are not exactly the "wretched of the earth." Who does not see that the true wellspring of terrorism is humiliation? National and, more generally, cultural humiliation. *It may be, contrary to a widely held opinion, that the poor readily forgive the rich for being rich.* The rhetoric of a North-South war based on the discrepancy in wealth can hardly be taken seriously: no terrorist has ever come from sub-Saharan Africa. *What the "poor"—or the members of a dominated civilization--do not forgive is that the rich humiliate them.* The rich who are also the powerful. That they should find no other argument than force: "I am stronger than you are, therefore I shall swat you like a fly and there is nothing you can do about it"— this is what is unbearable. The absolute denial of the other's dignity. Not only the physical annihilation of the other person, but the moral annihilation. . . . If the United States, with all the means at its disposal, crushes Iraq, it will not only be the Iraqis . . . who will resent it, but all those who, finding themselves in a position of inferiority, tell themselves that the same thing could happen to them, or who simply "sympathize" with the victims.[24]

Here Eric Gans has some very suggestive things to say, particularly in relation to the Middle East conflict. When one party is more powerful than another party, or is seen to be more powerful, and when that party humiliates the other, it encourages the weaker party to cloak itself in the convenient status of victim, with the consequence that negotiation becomes

24. Roland Hureaux, "L'humiliation, terreau terroriste," *Libération*, 18 February 2003. Again, the emphasis is mine.

impossible. Negotiation between parties that are unequal in power requires that they see themselves as equals in the eyes of the law and morality. But morally, within the framework of victimary justice, it is the inferior who absolutely dominates the superior, as a vengeful god does his sinful creatures. In the guise of compensation, the persecutor is made to remunerate his victim for the resentment this person feels, and only an infinite price will allow the persecutor to repay his debt. A way out from this impasse can be found on one condition, that the two parties agree to talk to each other, since it is only in entering into a dialogue that moral equality can at least to some extent be reestablished. Plainly the responsibility for initiating this dialogue falls upon the more favored of the two parties, or at least the one that appears to a disinterested observer to have the greater advantage. A foolish dream? Not at all. Consider the transformation of conflict between the rich and the poor, between capital and labor in industrialized countries during the twentieth century. There the class struggle gradually gave way to dialogue; victimary rhetoric yielded to wage negotiations. Over time, business owners and union leaders came to see themselves as partners having both divergent and convergent interests.

Things are not everywhere the same, of course, or at least not similar to the same degree. The victimary model of labor relations remains in force to some extent in France, more so at any rate than in the United States. Brazil, one of the most inegalitarian nations in the world, in which the transition from a holistic and hierarchical society to a modern, individualist, and egalitarian society has not yet been fully achieved, presents an interesting case. The left-wing governing Workers Party argues that the country's enormous disparities are true inequalities, the result of the exploitation of labor by capital, and not the mark of social hierarchy. And yet at the same time, in its single-minded pursuit of civil and criminal justice, the party repudiates the popular view of Brazil as one big, happy democratic family, a tropical mixed-race society blessedly free of racism.

Portuguese America, on emancipating its slaves in the 1870s, proudly proclaimed the advent of a society whose members would be "different but united"—in pointed contrast to the spirit of the segregationist slogan "separate but equal" that epitomized the Jim Crow laws of the same period in the United States. Today the Workers Party denounces this expression of holism, which it regards merely as a means of masking official approval of social exclusion. Observing that social inequalities are perfectly correlated with skin color, it concludes that Brazil is a fundamentally racist society. The rhetorical benefit of combining two apparently incompatible narratives—on the one hand, the Marxist discourse of capitalist exploitation, on the other, the victimary discourse of racial persecution—is clear: the outcast and poor of the present day can be represented as the remote victims of inexpiable crimes committed in the past by a slaveholding society. Whether this strategy is well calculated to promote the cause of racial democracy is rather less obvious, however.

The fundamental philosophical error of theories of justice (and particularly of Rawls's theory) is *to believe that there exists a solution to the problem of justice, and that this solution also disposes of the challenge posed by disruptive passions.* The mistake, in other words—the sin, in fact—is to believe that a society that is just, and that knows itself to be just, is a society that has succeeded in abolishing resentment. For it is in precisely such a society, one that makes a point of advertising its own fairness, that those who find themselves in an inferior position cannot help but feel resentful. The fatal conceit, as Hayek might well have said, is to suppose that the Saint George of moral geometry has slain the dragon of envy. It is fatal because it distracts our attention from what can and must be done here and now. Resentment will never be wholly eliminated. The only relevant question is how it can be minimized and its effects postponed, having been redirected to serve benign, perhaps even productive purposes. It is on the international level—about which Rawls's philosophy has exactly nothing to say—that a plan for doing this must be devised and successfully carried out.

The hold of what I call economy over modern societies is identical with the retreat from the sacred on which they are founded.[25] This retreat is itself intimately associated with the explosive growth of competition among human beings, and of the destructive energies that accompany it, on a scale never before seen. The massive paradox that I have tried to illuminate in this chapter arises from the fact that economic theory, no less than the political vision it inspires, nonetheless denies that there is any threat either to the stability of contemporary society or to the welfare of

25. I have developed this argument in a series of works over the past thirty years; see in particular my book with Paul Dumouchel, *L'enfer des choses* (1979), *Le sacrifice et l'envie* (1992), and *L'avenir de l'économie* (2012).

its members. Until quite recently economists sought to justify this denial by means of the oxymoronic expression "perfect competition"—a formula meaning that people do not actually need to meet one another or to exchange anything other than commodities, still less to love one another, in order to form an efficient and peaceable society. This utopia, which has now assumed the form of a nightmare, is perhaps the price that must be paid for a society deprived of the protections that the sacred once afforded it. Economy, at once idea and reality, now occupies the place that used to be filled by the sacred. It is the supreme mark of the sacred.

6

The Nuclear Menace

A NEW SACRAMENT FOR HUMANITY

The desacralization of the world is not something that gradually, as though by necessity, will lead to the complete and definitive elimination of religion. Secondary episodes of resacralization have regularly punctuated this long retreat from the sacred in its primitive form and perpetuated its outstanding characteristic: by *containing* violence, in the two senses of the word, the sacred acts as a barrier to violence through its own violent methods. It used to be said of the atomic bomb, especially during the years of the Cold War, that it was our new sacrament. Very few among those who were given to saying this sort of thing saw it as anything more than a vague metaphor. But in fact there is a very precise sense in which nuclear apocalypse can be said to bear the same relation to strategic thought that the sacrificial crisis, in René Girard's mimetic theory, bears to the human sciences: it is the absent—yet radiant—center from which all things emerge; or perhaps, to change the image, a black—and therefore invisible—hole whose existence may nonetheless be detected by the immense attraction that it exerts on all the objects around it.

From bin Laden to Hiroshima

One of the most remarkable theoreticians of the human sciences in our time was a man named Osama bin Laden. His ideas, which have only recently been made known, deserve to be carefully considered.

Everyone knows that the site on which the twin towers stood in New York is now called "Ground Zero." Already by the evening of 11 September 2001, this name had entered into everyday language, having been spontaneously adopted by print and television journalists, by ordinary New Yorkers, and then by all Americans, before it came into common use by people the world over. But the origin of the term may be less familiar. In the mind of every educated American, Ground Zero inevitably recalls the precise spot (named Trinity) where the first atomic bomb explosion in human history occurred, on 16 July 1945 at Alamogordo, New Mexico. It was Robert Oppenheimer himself who chose this name, in the feverish state of excitement surrounding the development of the bombs that were to demolish Hiroshima and Nagasaki. From the first, then, Americans compared the terrible attack of 11 September with the nuclear strikes that brought imperial Japan to its knees. Now, this is exactly what Osama bin Laden intended to happen.

In May 1998, bin Laden was asked by John Miller, an ABC News reporter who visited him at his mountaintop camp in southern Afghanistan, about the fatwa that called upon all Muslims to kill Americans whenever and wherever the opportunity presented itself. Miller inquired whether the target was limited to military personnel or whether it included every American. Bin Laden replied: "The Americans started it and retaliation and punishment should be carried out following *the principle of reciprocity,* especially when women and children are involved. Through[out] history, America has not been known to differentiate between the military and the civilians or between men and women or adults and children. Those who [dropped] atomic bombs and used the weapons of mass destruction against Nagasaki and Hiroshima were the Americans. Can the bombs differentiate between military and women and infants and children?"[1]

We know today that, in the months leading up to 11 September, the United States had many warnings of a spectacular attack. One of them, a message from al-Qaida intercepted by the CIA in August 2000, was particularly frightening. It boasted that bin Laden's organization was

---

1. From the transcript provided by the PBS news program "Frontline," on which Miller's interview aired later that year, posted at www.pbs.org/wgbh/pages/frontline/shows/binladen/who/interview.html. The emphasis is mine.

planning "a Hiroshima-type event" against America.[2] The generalized use of the expression "Ground Zero" is unmistakable evidence that Americans got the message bin Laden meant for them.

It will have been noted that bin Laden refers to the "principle of reciprocity," as if he were citing the famous chapter that Claude Lévi-Strauss devoted to this idea in *The Elementary Structures of Kinship* (1949). As absurd as the suggestion of a link between bin Laden and Lévi-Strauss may seem at first sight, its pertinence is unexpectedly confirmed if one considers the remarks made by the architect of 11 September in the only televised interview he gave thereafter, in October of the same year. Asked about his role in the attacks, bin Laden replied: "[I]f killing those who kill our sons is terrorism, then let history be witness that we are terrorists." And further on: "We kill the kings of the infidels, kings of the crusaders and civilian infidels in exchange for those of our children they killed. *This is permissible in Islamic law, and logically.*" The interviewer sought to make sure that he had correctly understood: "So what you are saying is this is a type of *reciprocal treatment*—they kill our innocents, so we kill their innocents?" Bin Laden: "So we kill their innocents. And I say it's permissible *in Islamic law and logic.*"[3]

This is astonishing. In the ongoing debate over the form and function of symbolic exchange inaugurated by the publication of Marcel Mauss's landmark essay *The Gift* (1924), in which some of the greatest French intellectuals have taken an active part (not only Lévi-Strauss, but also Pierre Bourdieu, Jacques Derrida, and Michel Serres), bin Laden explicitly and resolutely sides with Lévi-Strauss. The human law that imposes reciprocity of exchange is the expression, he says, of a logical—and therefore a mechanical—necessity. One cannot help but acknowledge bin Laden's decisive contribution to this debate, for he has succeeded dramatically in demonstrating what Bourdieu and others were incapable of grasping, namely, that this "logic" is the logic of evil, of violence and resentment.

2. See the transcript of the 3 October 2002 PBS "Frontline" program, posted at www.pbs.org/wgbh/pages/frontline/shows/knew/etc/script.html.

3. From the English-language transcript of the interview conducted by Al-Jazeera correspondent Tayseer Alouni in October 2001, aired on CNN on 1 February 2002; see www.transcripts.cnn.com/TRANSCRIPTS/0202/01/ltm.04.html. Again, the emphasis is mine.

As scandalous and as paradoxical as it may seem, Islamic terrorism thereby stands revealed as the monstrous reflection of the Christian
West that it abhors. This is made manifest by its victimary rhetoric, which
speaks of a duty falling upon the Muslim kamikazes of 11 September to
avenge the victims of Hiroshima. The very fact that our vocabulary is limited to the Japanese word for persons who commit suicide attacks shows,
by the way, that this terrorist practice is hardly rooted in Islam. Its source
is to be found in the West and in Japan, even if today Islamist groups seem
to have claimed a virtual monopoly on it for themselves, in the Middle
East and elsewhere.

Osama bin Laden usefully reminds us of something that many
people in the West would rather ignore, namely, that it was the West that
did away with the principles of just war. These include the principle of
discrimination, which requires that fighting be limited to enemy com-
batants, sparing people who are considered to be innocent, in particular
women, children, and the elderly; and the principle of proportionality,
which requires that the degree of violence be calibrated to suit the political and strategic objectives in view. These principles—meant to convert
war into a ritual that is both violent and measured in its effects, a ritual
that *contains* violence by means of violence—died a gruesome death at
Hiroshima, and their remains were vaporized in the radioactive blast that
then leveled Nagasaki. It is true, of course, that these same principles had
already suffered grave harm only a few months earlier, with the fire bomb-
ings of Dresden and Tokyo.

Theoretician of the Atomic Age

On 6 August 1945, an atomic bomb reduced the Japanese city of
Hiroshima to radioactive ashes. Three days later, Nagasaki was struck
in its turn. In the meantime, on 8 August, the International Military
Tribunal at Nuremberg had provided itself with the authority to judge
three types of crime: crimes against peace, war crimes, and crimes against
humanity. In the space of three days, then, the victors of the Second
World War inaugurated an era in which unthinkably powerful arms of
mass destruction made it inevitable that wars would now be judged criminal by the very norms that these victors were laying down at the same

moment. This colossal irony was forever to mark the thought of the most neglected German philosopher of the twentieth century, Günther Anders.

Anders was born Günther Stern, on 12 July 1902, to German Jewish parents in Breslau (now the Polish city of Wrocław). His father was the well-known child psychologist Wilhelm Stern, remembered for his concept of an intelligence quotient (or IQ). When Günther Stern was starting out as a journalist in Berlin, his editor, Bertolt Brecht, suggested that he write under another name, something other than Stern. From then on he wrote under the name Anders ("other" or "different" in German). This was not the only thing that set him apart. There was also his manner of doing philosophy, which he had studied at Marburg with Husserl and Heidegger. Anders once said that to write moral philosophy in a jargon-laden style accessible only to other philosophers is as absurd and as contemptible as a baker's making bread meant only to be eaten by other bakers. He practiced what he called occasional philosophy, a kind of philosophy that "arises from concrete experiences and on concrete occasions."[4] Foremost among these occasions was the conjunction of Auschwitz and Hiroshima, which is to say the moment when the destruction of humanity on an industrial scale entered the realm of possibility for the first time. It is to topics such as this, Anders believed, that the philosopher must devote all of his energies and every minute of his waking life.

Anders seems not to have been very well liked, at least not by his first wife, Hannah Arendt, who had been introduced to him by their classmate at Marburg, Hans Jonas. Both Arendt and Jonas had studied under Heidegger, as he had; each of them was Jewish, as he was; each of them was destined to become a more famous philosopher, and a far more influential one, than he would ever be. The memory of Günther Anders matters because he is one of the very few thinkers who have had the courage and the lucidity to link Hiroshima with Auschwitz, without in any way depriving Auschwitz of the sad privilege it enjoys as the incarnation of bottomless moral horror. He was able to do this because he understood (as Arendt herself did, though probably somewhat later) that even if moral evil, beyond a certain threshold, becomes too much for human beings to bear, they nonetheless remain responsible for it; and that no ethics,

---

4. Quoted in Paul van Dijk, *Anthropology in the Age of Technology: The Philosophical Contribution of Günther Anders* (Atlanta, Ga.: Rodopi, 2000), 1.

no standard of rationality, no norm that human beings can establish for themselves has the least relevance in evaluating its consequences.

It takes courage and lucidity to link Hiroshima and Auschwitz because still today, in the minds of many people—including, it would appear, a very large majority of Americans—Hiroshima is the classic example of a necessary evil.[5] With the recent death of Paul Tibbetts, the pilot of *Enola Gay*, the B-29 that dropped "Little Boy" on Hiroshima, old wounds were reopened and the argument from necessary evil trotted out once again, though this time not without resistance. Having invested itself with the power to determine, if not the best of all possible worlds, then at least the least bad among them, America placed on one of the scales of justice the bombing of civilians and their murder in the hundreds of thousands, and, on the other, an invasion of the Japanese archipelago that, it was said, would have cost the lives of a half-million American soldiers. Moral necessity, it was argued, required that America choose to put an end to the war as quickly as possible, even if this meant shattering once and for all everything that until then had constituted the most elementary rules of just war. Moral philosophers call this a consequentialist argument: when the issue is one of surpassingly great importance, deontological norms—so called because they express a duty to respect absolute imperatives, no matter what the cost or effects of doing this may be—must yield to the calculus of consequences. But what ethical and rational calculation could justify sending millions of Jewish children from every part of Europe to be gassed? There lies the difference, the chasm, the moral abyss that separates Auschwitz from Hiroshima.

In the decades since, however, persons of great integrity and intellect have insisted on the intrinsic immorality of atomic weapons in general, and the ignominy of bombing Hiroshima and Nagasaki in particular. In 1956, the Oxford philosopher and Catholic thinker Elizabeth Anscombe made an enlightening comparison that threw into stark relief the horrors to which consequentialist reasoning leads when it is taken to its logical conclusion. Let us suppose, she said, that the Allies had thought at the beginning of 1945 that, in order to break the Germans' will to resist and to compel them to surrender rapidly and unconditionally, thus sparing

---

5. It is ironic, or perhaps merely a proof of cynicism, that the B-29 bomber that carried the team of scientists responsible for studying the conditions and effects of the atomic explosion on 6 August 1945 was named *Necessary Evil*.

the lives of a great many Allied soldiers, it was necessary to carry out the massacre of hundreds of thousands of civilians, women and children included, in two cities in the Ruhr. Two questions arise. First, what difference would there have been, morally speaking, between this and what the Nazis did in Czechoslovakia and Poland? Second, what difference would there have been, morally speaking, between this and the atomic bombing of Hiroshima and Nagasaki?[6]

In the face of horror, moral philosophy is forced to resort to analogies of this sort, for it has nothing other than logical consistency on which to base the validity of its arguments. In the event, this minimal requirement of consistency did not suffice to rule out the nuclear option, nor to condemn it afterward. Why? One reply is that because the Americans won the war against Japan, their victory seemed in retrospect to justify the course of action they followed. This argument must not be mistaken for cynicism. It involves what philosophers call the problem of moral luck.[7] The moral judgment that is passed on a decision made under conditions of radical uncertainty depends on what occurs *after* the relevant action has been taken—something that was completely unforeseeable beforehand, even as a probabilistic matter.

Robert McNamara memorably describes this predicament in the extraordinary set of interviews conducted by the documentarian Errol Morris and released as a film under a most Clausewitzian title, *The Fog of War* (2003). Before serving as secretary of defense under Presidents Kennedy and Johnson, McNamara had been an advisor during the war in the Pacific to General Curtis LeMay, who was responsible for the firebombing of sixty-seven cities of imperial Japan, a campaign that culminated in the dropping of the two atomic bombs. On the night of 9–10 March 1945 alone, one hundred thousand civilians perished in Tokyo, burned to death. McNamara approvingly reports LeMay's stunningly lucid verdict: "If we'd lost the war, we'd all have been prosecuted as war criminals."

6. See G. E. M. Anscombe, "Mr. Truman's Degree," in *Collected Philosophical Papers*, vol. 3: *Ethics, Religion, and Politics* (Minneapolis: University of Minnesota Press, 1981), 62–71. The title of this essay refers to Oxford's awarding of an honorary degree to President Truman in June 1956.

7. See Bernard Williams, "Moral Luck," in *Moral Luck: Philosophical Papers, 1973–1980* (Cambridge: Cambridge University Press, 1981), 20–39.

Another possible reply is that consequentialist morality served in this instance only as a convenient pretext. A revisionist school of American historians led by Gar Alperovitz has vigorously pleaded this case, arguing that in July 1945 Japan was on the point of capitulation.[8] Two conditions would have had to be satisfied in order to obtain immediate surrender: first, that President Truman agree to an immediate declaration of war on Japan by the Soviet Union; second, that Japanese surrender be accompanied by an American promise that the emperor would be allowed to continue to sit on his throne. Truman refused both conditions at Potsdam. The day before the conference opened, on 16 July 1945, the president had received the "good news" that the bomb was ready—as the successful test at Alamogordo had just demonstrated.

Alperovitz concludes that Truman sought to steal a march on the Soviets, before they were prepared to intervene militarily in the Japanese archipelago. The Americans played the nuclear card, in other words, not to force Japan to surrender, but to impress the Russians. In that case the Cold War had been launched on the strength of an ethical abomination, and the Japanese reduced to the level of guinea pigs, for the bomb was not in fact necessary to obtain the surrender. Other historians reckon that, whether it was necessary or not, it was not a sufficient condition of obtaining a declaration of surrender. Some years ago Barton J. Bernstein proposed a "new synthesis" of the various revisionist accounts.[9] It had long been known that the day after Nagasaki, the Japanese war minister, General Korechika Anami, and the vice chief of the Naval General Staff, Admiral Takijiro Ōnishi, urged the emperor to authorize a "special attack *[kamikaze]* effort,"[10] even though this would mean putting as many as twenty million Japanese lives at risk, by their own estimate, in the cause of ultimate victory. In that case, two bombs would not have

8. See Gar Alperovitz, *The Decision to Use the Atomic Bomb and the Architecture of an American Myth* (New York: Knopf, 1995); also Barton J. Bernstein, "A Postwar Myth: 500,000 U.S. Lives Saved," *Bulletin of the Atomic Scientists* 42 (June–July 1986): 38–40.

9. See Barton J. Bernstein, "Understanding the Atomic Bomb and the Japanese Surrender: Missed Opportunities, Little-Known Near-Disasters, and Modern Memory," *Diplomatic History* 19 (Spring 1995): 227–73.

10. See Robert J. C. Butow, *Japan's Decision to Surrender* (Stanford, Calif.: Stanford University Press, 1954), 183; also 205.

been enough. So convinced were the Americans of the need to detonate a third device, Bernstein says, that the announcement of surrender on 14 August—apparently the result of chance and of reversals of alliance at the highest level of the Japanese government, still poorly understood by historians—came as an utter surprise.[11] But Bernstein takes the argument a step further. Of the six options available to the Americans to force the Japanese to surrender without an invasion of the archipelago, five had been rather cursorily analyzed, singly and in combination, and then rejected by Truman and his advisors: continuation of the conventional bombing campaign, supplemented by a naval blockade; unofficial negotiations with the enemy; modification of the terms of surrender, including a guarantee that the emperor system would be preserved; waiting for Russia to enter the war; and a non-combat demonstration of the atomic bomb. The sixth option, the military use of the bomb, was never discussed—not even for a moment: it was simply taken for granted. The bombing of Hiroshima and Nagasaki followed from the bomb's very existence. From the ethical point of view, Bernstein's findings are still more terrible than those of Alperovitz: dropping the atomic bomb, perhaps the gravest decision ever taken in modern history, was not something that had actually been decided.

Revisionist interpretations do not exhaust the questions that need to be asked. There are at least two more. First, how are we to make sense of the bombing of Hiroshima and—more troubling still, because of the grotesquely absurd determination to persist in infamy—of Nagasaki? Second, how could the consequentialist veneer of the official justification for these acts—that they were extremely regrettable, but a moral necessity just the same—have been accepted as a lawful defense, when it should have been seen instead as the most execrable and appalling excuse imaginable?

---

11. Bernstein, for his part, holds that bombing, if it was to have any immediate effect, would have had to be combined with Soviet entry into the war (on 8 August) and reversals of alliance among high Japanese officials—and so was a necessary, but not a sufficient, condition of obtaining surrender by 14 August. He nevertheless believes, as I do, that surrender very probably could have been obtained later, before the planned 1 November 1945 invasion of Kyushu, without using the bomb at all, under one of two scenarios; see Bernstein, "Understanding the Atomic Bomb and the Japanese Surrender," 254. In that case, the bomb was neither necessary *nor* sufficient—it was irrelevant!

The work of Günther Anders not only furnishes an answer to these questions, it does so by relocating them in another context. A German Jew who had emigrated to France and from there to America, and then come back to Europe five years after the war's end—everywhere an exile, the wandering Jew of legend—Anders recognized that on 6 August 1945, human history had entered into a new phase, its last. Or, rather, that the sixth day of August was only a *rehearsal* for the ninth—what he called the "Nagasaki syndrome." The atomic bombing of a civilian population, once it had occurred for the first time, once it had made the unthinkable real, inevitably invited more atrocities, in the same way that an earthquake is inevitably followed by a series of aftershocks. History, Anders said, became obsolete that day. Now that humanity was capable of destroying itself, nothing could ever cause it to lose this "negative all-powerfulness," not even a general disarmament, not even a total denuclearization of the world's arsenals. *Apocalypse having been inscribed in our future as fate, henceforth the best we can do is to indefinitely postpone the final moment.* We are now living under a suspended sentence, as it were, a stay of execution. In August 1945, humanity entered into an era of reprieve *(die Frist)*, the "second death" of all that had existed: since the meaning of the past depends on future actions, it follows from the obsolescence of the future, from its programmed end, not that the past no longer has any meaning, but that it never had one.[12]

To inquire into the rationality and the morality of the destruction of Hiroshima and Nagasaki amounts to treating nuclear weapons as a means in the service of an end. A means loses itself in its end as a river loses itself in the sea, and ends up being completely absorbed by it. But the bomb exceeds all the ends that can ever be given to it, or ever found for it. The question whether the end justifies the means suddenly became obsolete, like everything else. Why was the bomb used? Because it *existed*. The simple fact of its existence is a threat, or rather a promise that it will be used. Why has the moral horror of its use not been perceived? What

---

12. See Günther Anders, *Die atomare Drohung: Radikale Überlegungen zum atomaren Zeitalter* (Munich: Beck, 1981). Lest anyone suppose that Sartre's work inspired these remarks, Sartre himself frankly acknowledged it was Anders who had influenced his thinking.

accounts for this "blindness in the face of apocalypse"?[13] The answer is that, beyond certain thresholds, our power of making and doing infinitely exceeds our capacity for feeling and imagining. Anders called this irreducible gap the "Promethean discrepancy." Whereas Hannah Arendt diagnosed Eichmann's psychological disability as a "lack of imagination,"[14] Anders showed that this was not the weakness of one person in particular; it is the weakness of every person when mankind's capacity for invention, and for destruction, becomes disproportionately enlarged in relation to the human condition.

"Between our capacity for making and our capacity for imagining," Anders says, "a gap is opened up that grows larger by the day." The "too great" leaves us cold, he adds. "No human being is capable of imagining something of such horrifying magnitude: the elimination of millions of people."[15]

The Impotence of Deterrence

Imagine a man who is in the habit, while driving, of spraying elephant-repellent from the window of his car. The proof that doing this removes the danger of an unexpected collision with an elephant crossing the road, he believes, is that he has never seen one. To say that nuclear deterrence has saved humanity from perishing in an atomic holocaust for more than a half-century now, on the basis of the fact that no such catastrophe has occurred during the interval, is really no different.

A pacifist would urge that the best way for humanity to avoid a nuclear war is not to have any nuclear weapons. This argument, which borders on the tautological, was irrefutable before the scientists of the Manhattan Project developed the atomic bomb. Alas, it is no longer valid

13. See the eight chapters that make up the section titled "On the Bomb and the Causes of Our Blindness in the Face of Apocalypse," in Günther Anders, *Die Antiquiertheit des Menschen*, 2 vols. (Munich: Beck, 1980), 1: 233–324.

14. Hannah Arendt, *Eichmann in Jerusalem: A Report on the Banality of Evil* (New York: Viking, 1963), 287.

15. Günther Anders, *Wir Eichmannsöhne: Offener Brief an Klaus Eichmann* (Munich: Beck, 1964); quoted from the French edition, *Nous, fils d'Eichmann*, trans. Sabine Cornille and Philippe Ivernel (Paris: Payot & Rivages, 1999), 50, 54, 65.

today. Such weapons exist, and even supposing that they were to cease to exist as a result of universal disarmament, they could be recreated in a few months. Errol Morris, in *The Fog of War,* asks McNamara what he thinks protected humanity from extinction during the Cold War, when the United States and the Soviet Union permanently threatened each other with mutual annihilation. Deterrence? Not at all, McNamara replies: "We lucked out." Twenty-five or thirty times during this period, he notes, mankind came within an inch of apocalypse.

I have tried in my own work to enlarge the scope of Günther Anders's analysis by extending it to the question of nuclear deterrence.[16] For more than four decades during Cold War, the debate over mutual vulnerability (or, as it is almost universally known, mutually assured destruction) assigned a major role to the idea of *deterrent intention,* on both a strategic and a moral level. And yet, as we shall now see, it is exactly this idea that constitutes the principal obstacle to understanding the logic of deterrence.

In June 2000, meeting with Vladimir Putin in Moscow, Bill Clinton said something amazing. His words were echoed almost seven years later by George W. Bush's secretary of state, Condoleezza Rice, speaking once again to the Russians. The antiballistic shield that we are going to build in Europe, they said, is only meant to defend the United States against attacks from rogue states and terrorist groups. *Therefore rest assured:* even if we were to take the initiative and attack you first with a nuclear strike, you could easily get through the shield and annihilate us. Plainly the logic of deterrence under the new world order created by the collapse of Soviet power was no less insane than it had been before. This logic requires that each nation expose its own population to certain destruction by the other's reprisals. Security becomes the daughter of terror: for if either nation were to take steps to protect itself, the other might believe that its adversary considered itself to be invulnerable; therefore, in order to prevent a first strike, it would hasten to launch this strike itself. It is not for nothing that the doctrine of mutually assured destruction came to be known by its acronym, MAD. In a nuclear regime, nations are at once vulnerable and invulnerable: vulnerable because they can die from attack by another nation; invulnerable because they will not die before having killed their

16. See Dupuy, *Petite métaphysique des tsunamis,* 93–107.

attacker—something they will always be capable of doing, no matter how powerful the strike that will have brought them to their knees.

There is another doctrine, known as NUTS (Nuclear Utilization Target Selection), that calls for a nation to be prepared to use nuclear weapons in a surgical fashion, for the purpose of eliminating the nuclear capabilities of an adversary, while protecting itself by means of an anti-missile shield. It will be obvious that MAD and NUTS are at odds with each other, for what makes a type of weapon or vector valuable in one case robs it of much of its utility in the other. Consider submarine-launched missiles, which have imprecise trajectories and whose mobile hosts are hard to locate. Whereas nuclear-equipped submarines hold little or no theoretical interest from the perspective of NUTS, they are very useful—indeed, almost ideal—from the perspective of MAD, since they have a good chance of surviving a first strike and the very imprecision of their guidance systems makes them effective instruments of terror. The problem facing the United States was that it had said that it would like to go on playing MAD with Russia (and perhaps China), while practicing NUTS with North Korea, Iran, and, until a few years ago, Iraq. This obliged the Americans to show that the missile defense system they had been hoping to build in Poland and the Czech Republic would be penetrable by a Russian strike while at the same time capable of stopping missiles launched by a rogue state. The reconfigured system proposed by Washington in September 2009 is subject to the same constraint.

That the lunacy of MAD, whether or not it was coupled with the craziness of NUTS, should have been considered the height of wisdom, and that it should have been credited with having kept world peace during a period whose return some strategists still yearn for today, passes all understanding. Thirty years ago, however, few persons were at all troubled by this state of affairs, apart from American bishops—and President Reagan. Once again we cannot avoid asking the obvious question: why? For many years the usual reply was that what is at issue here is an intention, not the carrying out of an intention. What is more, it is an intention of an exceedingly special kind, so that the very fact of its being formed has the consequence that the conditions that would lead to its being acted on are not realized. Since, by hypothesis, each side is dissuaded from launching a first strike, there is no need to preempt such an attack by attacking first, which means that no one makes a move. One forms a deterrent intention, in other words, *in order* not to have to put it into effect. Specialists speak of such intentions as being inherently "self-stultifying."[17] But plainly this does no more than give a name to an enigma. It does nothing to resolve it.

No one who inquires into the strategic and moral status of deterrent intention can fail to be overwhelmed by paradox. What seems to shield deterrent intention from ethical rebuke is the very thing that renders it useless from a strategic point of view, since such an intention cannot be effective in the absence of a meta-intention to act on it if circumstances so require. From the moral point of view, deterrent intention, like primitive divinities, appears to unite absolute goodness (since it is thanks to this intention that nuclear war has not taken place) with absolute evil (since the act of which it is the intention is an unutterable abomination).

Throughout the Cold War, two arguments were made that seemed to show that nuclear deterrence in the form of MAD could not be effective.[18] The first argument has to do with the non-credible character of a deterrent threat under such circumstances: if the side threatening a simultaneously lethal and suicidal response to aggression that endangers its "vital interests" is assumed to be at least minimally rational, calling its bluff—say, by means of a first strike that destroys a part of its territory—ensures that it will not carry out its threat. The very purpose of this regime, after all, is to issue a guarantee of mutual destruction in the event that either side upsets the balance of terror. But what statesman, having in the aftermath of a first strike only remnants of a devastated nation left to defend, would run the risk—by launching a retaliatory strike—out of a desire for vengeance, of putting an end to the human race? In a world of sovereign states exhibiting this minimal degree of rationality, the nuclear threat has no credibility whatever.

Another, quite different argument was put forward that likewise pointed to the incoherence of the prevailing strategic doctrine. To be effective, nuclear deterrence must be absolutely effective. Not even a single failure can be allowed, since the first bomb to be dropped would already be one too

17. See Gregory S. Kavka, *Moral Paradoxes of Nuclear Deterrence* (New York: Cambridge University Press, 1987), 20–21.

18. See the excellent summary of this debate in Steven P. Lee, *Morality, Prudence, and Nuclear Weapons* (New York: Cambridge University Press, 1993).

many. But if nuclear deterrence is absolutely effective, it cannot be effective. As a practical matter, deterrence works only if it is not completely reliable. Think, for example, of the criminal justice system: violations of the law must occur and then be punished if citizens are to be convinced that crime does not pay. But in the case of nuclear deterrence, the first transgression is fatal. Deterrence, though it is therefore incapable of deterring, nonetheless *prefigures* something essential—the prophecy of doom.

The most telling sign that nuclear deterrence does not work is that it did nothing to prevent an unrestrained and potentially catastrophic arms buildup. If nuclear deterrence did work, it ought to have been the great equalizer. As in Hobbes's state of nature, the weakest nation—measured by the number of nuclear warheads it possesses—would be on exactly the same level as the strongest, since it could always inflict "unacceptable" losses, for example, by deliberately targeting the enemy's cities; and indeed France enunciated a doctrine ("deterrence of the strong by the weak") to this effect. Deterrence is therefore a game that can be played—indeed, that must be able to be played—with very few armaments on each side.

Belatedly, it came to be understood that in order for deterrence to have a chance of succeeding, it was absolutely necessary to abandon the notion of deterrent *intention*.[19] The idea that human beings, by their conscience and their will, could control the outcome of a game as terrifying as deterrence was manifestly an idle and abhorrent fantasy. In principle, the mere *existence* of two deadly arsenals pointed at each other, without the least threat of their use being made or even implied, is enough to keep the warheads locked away in their silos. Even so, the specter of nuclear apocalypse did not disappear from the world; nor did a certain form of transcendence. Under the name of "existential" deterrence, the perils of the old game were transformed in such a way that mutual annihilation now loomed as the *fate* of humanity, its destiny. To say that deterrence worked means simply this: so long as one does not recklessly tempt fate, there is a chance that it will forget us for a time—perhaps a long, indeed a very long time, but not forever. From now on, as Günther Anders was the first to understand, and to announce from an utterly opposite philosophical perspective, we are living on borrowed time.

19. See, e.g., Bernard Brodie, *War and Politics* (New York: Macmillan, 1973), 392–432.

If the theory of existential deterrence is to be believed, nuclear weapons have managed to keep the world at peace until now by projecting evil outside the sphere of human experience, by making it an evil *without harmful intent;* an evil capable of annihilating civilization, though with no more malice than an earthquake or a tsunami; an evil whose destructive force makes nature's wrath look timid by comparison. The threat hanging over the heads of the world's leaders has caused them to exercise the caution necessary to avoid the biblical abomination of desolation promised by thermonuclear war, which would decimate entire nations and, in the worst case, extinguish life on earth.

The paradox that lies at the heart of this theory is none other than the mark of the sacred. Consider once more the two reasons given in support of the view that deterrent intention is impotent to achieve its purpose. First, a threat of retaliation is not credible: if deterrence were to fail, such a threat would never be carried out. Second, perfectly effective deterrence would be self-negating: the deterred party could never be sure that the deterring party really means to carry out his threat of retaliation if deterrence were to fail. This paradox can be escaped only if the reality of nuclear apocalypse is made a part of our future, as it were, so that it is apprehended as *fate* or *destiny.* It may seem surprising to find these words in the writings of existential deterrence theorists, who think of themselves as "rational" thinkers and hard-headed strategists. But a moment's reflection will make it clear that their own argument is no sooner stated than it is swallowed up by the abyss of self-refutation: the condition under which deterrence is effective—that we regard nuclear apocalypse as our fate—contradicts the very purpose of deterrence, namely, to ensure that nuclear apocalypse does *not* take place.

To dispel this apparent contradiction, one must take seriously—more seriously than Robert McNamara did himself—what McNamara emphasizes in his memoirs[20] and in *The Fog of War:* not once, but several dozen times during the Cold War, humanity came ever so close to disappearing in a radioactive cloud. Was this a failure of deterrence? Quite the opposite: it was precisely these unscheduled expeditions to the edge of the black hole that gave the threat of nuclear annihilation its dissuasive force.

20. Robert S. McNamara, *In Retrospect: The Tragedy and Lessons of Vietnam* (New York: Times Books, 1995).

"We lucked out," McNamara says. Quite true—but in a very profound sense it was the repeated flirting with apocalypse that saved humanity: whereas accidents are needed to precipitate an apocalyptic destiny, an accident, unlike fate, is not inevitable. An accident *can* not occur.

The distinctive form assumed by self-refutation in this case is typical of a whole series of paradoxes to which I have given the fine name of Jonah—in reference not only to the twentieth-century German philosopher Hans Jonas, but also to his predecessor in the eighth century BCE, the biblical prophet Jonah.[21] Both were faced with the same dilemma, the very one that confronts every prophet of doom: he must foretell an impending catastrophe as though it belonged to an ineluctable future, but with the purpose of ensuring that, as a result of his doing just this, the catastrophe will not occur. The Jonah of the Bible, called upon by God to prophesy the destruction of Nineveh, sought to evade his mission and fled. We know the price he paid for that! The same paradox is at the heart of a classic figure of literature and philosophy, the killer judge, who "neutralizes" all those of whom it is written that they shall commit a crime—with the result that their crimes will not be committed.[22] Intuitively, one feels that the paradox derives from the failure of the past prediction to be joined with the future event in a closed loop.[23] But the very idea of such a loop makes no sense in our ordinary metaphysics, as the modal logic of prevention shows. Prevention consists in taking action to ensure that an unwanted action is relegated to the ontological realm of non-actualized possibilities. The catastrophe, even though it does not occur, retains the status of a possibility, not in the sense that it would still be possible for it to take place, but in the sense that it will forever remain true that it could have taken place. When one announces that a catastrophe is imminent, *in order to avert it,* this announcement does not possess the status of a *prediction,* in the strict sense of the term: one does not claim to say what the future will be, only what it would

21. "Jonas" is the French spelling of the biblical name Jonah.—Trans.

22. One thinks in particular of Voltaire's *Zadig* (1747). Philip K. Dick contrived a subtle variation on this theme in his 1956 short story "The Minority Report"; the 2002 film by Steven Spielberg that Dick's story inspired unfortunately falls short of the standard it set.

23. As Danny Witwer, the government investigator in Spielberg's film, puts it, "It's not the future if you stop it."

have been had preventive measures not been taken. There is no need for any loop to close here. The announced future does not have to coincide with the actual future, the forecast does not have to come true—for the announced "future" is not in fact the future at all, but a possible world that is, and will remain, non-actual.[24]

The prophet of doom cannot be satisfied with a sort of supermarket metaphysics in which possible worlds make up a very long aisle of options from which the futures shopper is free to choose. As a fatalist, the prophet tells of events that will come to pass, come to pass as they are written down on the great scroll of Fate —immutably, ineluctably. How, then, can one prophesy a future one does not wish for, *so that* it will not occur? This is the Jonah paradox, whose logical structure is exactly the same as that of the paradox of perfect (self-refuting) deterrence. The key to the enigma is found in the dialectic of fate and accident that forms the core of existential deterrence, in regarding nuclear apocalypse as something that is *at once necessary and improbable.* But is there anything really new about this idea? Its kinship with tragedy, classical or modern, is readily seen. Consider Oedipus, who kills his father at the fatal crossroads, or Camus's "stranger," Meursault, who kills the Arab under the blazing sun in Algiers—these events appear to the Mediterranean mind both as accidents and as acts of fate, in which *chance and destiny are merged and become one.*

Accident, which points to chance, is the opposite of fate, which points to necessity; but without this opposite, fate cannot be realized. A follower of Derrida would say that accident is the *supplement* of fate, in the sense that it is both its contrary and the condition of its occurring. What complicates the present case is that the fate is one we absolutely do not wish for ourselves, one that we must try as far as possible to distance ourselves from. Accident, as both an instrument of fate and its negation, gives us the means to do this.

24. One thinks, for example, of highway news bulletins whose purpose is to steer motorists away from routes that are expected otherwise to be backed up with traffic. See Jean-Pierre Dupuy, "The Precautionary Principle and Enlightened Doomsaying: Rational Choice Before the Apocalypse," *Occasion: Interdisciplinary Studies in the Humanities* 1 (15 October 2009), at http://arcade.stanford.edu/journals/occasion/articles/precautionary-principle-and-enlightened-doomsaying-rational-choice-apocalypse-by-jean-pierr.

If we reject the Kingdom—that is, if violence is not universally and categorically renounced—all that is left to us is a game of immense hazard and jeopardy that amounts to constantly playing with fire: we cannot risk coming too close, lest we perish in a nuclear holocaust (this is the principle of existential deterrence); nor can we risk standing too far away, lest we forget the danger of nuclear weapons (this is the Jonah paradox). We must neither believe too much in fate nor refuse too much to believe in it. We must, that is, believe in fate exactly as one believes in a work of fiction. In principle, the dialectic of fate and chance permits us to keep just the right distance from the black hole of catastrophe: since apocalypse is our fate, we are bound to remain tied to it; but since an accident has to take place in order for our destiny to be fulfilled, we are kept apart from it.

Notice that the logical structure of this dialectic is exactly the same as that of the sacred in its primitive form, as elucidated by Girard. One must not come too near to the sacred, for fear of causing violence to be unleashed; nor should one stand too far away from it, however, for it protects us from violence. I repeat, once again: the sacred *contains* violence, in the two senses of the word.

The End of Hatred and Resentment

The profound analogy between existential deterrence and the sacred in its primitive form leads us back to the question of evil. It is probably owing to the influence of Christianity that evil has come to be most commonly associated with the intentions of those who commit it. And yet the evil of nuclear deterrence in its existential form is an evil disconnected from any human intention, just as the sacrament of the bomb is a sacrament without a god. It is for this reason that the end of hatred and resentment augured by the advent of nuclear weapons is to be feared above all things.

In 1958, Günther Anders went to Hiroshima and Nagasaki to take part in the Fourth World Conference against Atomic and Hydrogen Bombs. After many conversations with survivors of the catastrophe, he noted in his diary: "Their steadfast resolve not to speak of those who were to blame, not to say that the event had been caused by human beings; *not to harbor the least resentment, even though they were the victims of the greatest of crimes*—this really is too much for me, it passes all understanding." And he adds: "They constantly speak of the catastrophe as if it were an earthquake or a tidal wave. They use the Japanese word, *tsunami*."[25]

The evil that inhabits the so-called nuclear peace, unmoored from any malign intention, inspires these words of terrifying insight in Anders's book *Hiroshima ist überall* (Hiroshima Is Everywhere): "The fantastic character of the situation quite simply takes one's breath away. At the very moment when the world becomes apocalyptic, and this owing to our own fault, it presents the image . . . of a paradise inhabited by murderers without malice and victims without hatred. Nowhere is there any trace of malice, there is only rubble."[26] Anders's prophecy sends a chill down the spine: "No war in history will have been more devoid of hatred than the war by tele-murder that is to come. . . . [T]his absence of hatred will be the most inhuman absence of hatred that has ever existed; absence of hatred and absence of scruples will henceforth be one and the same."[27]

Violence without hatred is so inhuman that it amounts to a kind of transcendence—perhaps the only transcendence yet left to us.

25. Günther Anders, "L'homme sur le pont: Journal d'Hiroshima et de Nagasaki," in *Hiroshima est partout*, trans. Ariel Morabia with the assistance of Françoise Cazenave, Denis Trierweiler, and Gabriel Raphaël Veyret (Paris: Seuil, 2008), 168. I have deliberately modified both the French translation and the German original.

26. Ibid., 171–72.

27. Ibid., 202.

Epilogue

Self-References

Jorge Luis Borges, a virtuoso of self-referential paradoxes, once asked:

Why does it make us uneasy to know that the map is within the map and the thousand and one nights are within the book of *A Thousand and One Nights?* Why does it disquiet us to know that Don Quixote is a reader of the *Quixote* and Hamlet is a spectator of *Hamlet?* I believe I have found the answer: those inversions suggest that if the characters in a story can be readers or spectators, then we, their readers or spectators, can be fictitious. In 1833 Carlyle observed that universal history is an infinite sacred book that all men write and read and try to understand, and in which they too are written.[1]

Looking back on my past, it seems to me not only that I was a faithful spectator of *Vertigo,*[2] but that my life actually became a part of this fiction from

1. Jorge Luis Borges, "Partial Enchantments of the *Quixote,*" in *Other Inquisitions: 1937–1952,* trans. Ruth L. C. Simms (Austin: University of Texas Press, 1965), 46.

2. *Vertigo* was made by Alfred Hitchcock in 1958. As a courtesy to readers who have not seen the film, I have been persuaded to give a brief synopsis of the plot, though I do so with grave misgivings: first, because it will spoil the pleasure—I beg your pardon, the traumatic shock—they would otherwise feel on seeing it for the first time; second, and above all, because, for deep reasons that will become apparent as they read this epilogue, a work of art as complex as *Vertigo* cannot be briefly summarized. Still, I shall try.

the first moment I encountered it. I am not the only one who feels this way. There are many others for whom Hitchcock's masterpiece is much more than a film. In order to protect confidences that should remain private, I shall say no more than this, except to add that this is the first time I have written about *Vertigo*. My reluctance to analyze the film until now was probably the

---

Scottie Ferguson (played by James Stewart) is a detective recently discharged from the police force because of a medical condition, acrophobia, which first manifested itself during a manhunt across the rooftops of San Francisco when Scottie was unable to prevent an officer who had come to his aid from falling to his death. An old friend, Gavin Elster, asks Scottie to follow his wife, Madeleine (played by Kim Novak), whose odd behavior has caused him to fear that she might try to take her life. After much hesitation, Scottie agrees to monitor Madeleine Elster's movements. Her extraordinary beauty has made up his mind for him. He shadows Madeleine, keeping a safe distance as he follows her strange wanderings through San Francisco, which lead her to a flower shop, the cemetery at Mission Dolores, the museum gallery of the Legion of Honor, and finally the foot of the Golden Gate Bridge, where she throws herself into the cold waters of the Bay. Scottie saves her from drowning. On getting to know Madeleine afterward, he soon falls madly in love with her. His feeling appears to be reciprocated. From then on, instead of following Madeleine, Scottie accompanies her to various places in the city and the surrounding area.

Madeleine's suicidal impulses seem more and more evident to him. Earlier Scottie had learned that she was haunted by the specter of her great-grandmother, Carlotta Valdez, who herself had committed suicide after her daughter (Madeleine's grandmother) had been taken away from her by a wealthy lover. At the Franciscan mission of San Juan Bautista, paralyzed by his fear of heights, Scottie is unable to stop Madeleine from climbing to the top of the bell tower and hurling herself into the abyss. He reaches a landing part way up the stairs just in time to look through a window and see her body fall onto the red-tile roof of the cloister below.

In the days that follow Scottie struggles with acute depression. He is found innocent by a jury, which concluded that Madeleine's death was a suicide, though the coroner's cruel insinuations of moral culpability called attention to the fact that that this was the second time that he had been powerless to prevent a fatal plunge. Tormented by terrible nightmares, Scottie is finally committed to a clinic, where the music of Mozart has little therapeutic effect.

Later we see Scottie wandering through the streets of San Francisco, revisiting places where he had gone with Madeleine. One day he sees a woman in the street who reminds him of her. He follows her to her room in the Empire Hotel and learns that her name is Judy Barton, that she comes from Kansas, and that

result of a fear that in doing this I would destroy its enchantment for me. As Denis de Rougemont observed about *The Romance of Tristan and Iseult,* it "is *'sacred'* for us precisely to the extent that it seems *'sacrilegious'*... to attempt to analyze it."[3] This is exactly the feeling I have in offering up these few reflections—of shattering a taboo, of overstepping a boundary.

Looking back on my past, in the light of the effort that writing this epilogue has cost me, I now perceive that I owe my passion for logic and philosophy, and particularly metaphysics, to the emotional shock I felt on seeing this film when it first came out in France. I was seventeen years old. I see now that my most abstract works, my most abstruse researches, have inexorably been woven with the fabric of its plot. Self-reference, self-transcendence, circular time, the peculiar mechanism of self-exteriorization (by which a system is projected outside of itself), the catastrophe that reveals the meaning of the events that preceded it—it was *Vertigo* that

---

she works in a local department store. He insists that she go out to dinner with him. Reluctantly, she agrees.

Then, by an extraordinary feat of cinematic legerdemain, Hitchcock allows the viewer to enter into Judy's mind. From a flashback we learn that she is "Madeleine"—Elster's accomplice in the murder of his wife, the real Madeleine Elster. It was Judy who climbed the stairs to the top of the tower, where Elster waited for her with the dead body of his wife, which he then threw over the edge of the terrace.

In the last part of the film we see Scottie gradually turn Judy into Madeleine, the memory of whom continues to obsess him. He makes Judy wear the same clothes, makes her adopt the same mannerisms, makes her wear her hair in the same style. Horrified at first, Judy finally allows herself to be completely transformed, down to the least detail, for she realizes that this is the only way that Scottie, whom she loves, will love her in return.

No sooner is their love complete than Judy makes a fatal mistake. She puts on a necklace that belonged to Madeleine's great-grandmother, Carlotta Valdez, which Scottie remembers from the portrait of Carlotta he saw in the gallery. Scottie now understands the trap into which he has fallen. He brings Judy back to Mission San Juan Bautista. Conquering his vertigo, he forces her to climb to the top of the tower and there makes her tell him the truth. A dark shadow suddenly rises up. With a cry of horror, Judy recoils and falls over the edge, plunging into the abyss. The nun who has just appeared at the top of the stairs rings the tower bell.

3. De Rougemont, *Love in the Western World,* 24. My emphasis.

planted all these ideas in my mind, along with many others that have long fascinated me and that I have described in the prologue to the present work. It is therefore not so much an interpretation of the film itself that I propose here as an interpretation of my own work, seen through the prism of *Vertigo*. I shall speak in particular about the metaphysics of the age of catastrophe that awaits us, a topic that has occupied my attention for many years now and that forms the central theme of my most recent books, this one included.

On Madeleine's Mode of Existence

Whoever has been can no longer not have been: henceforth this mysterious and profoundly obscure fact of having been is one's viaticum for eternity.
—Vladimir Jankélévitch, *L'irréversible et la nostalgie* (1974)[4]

Like everyone else, I call the person with whom Scottie falls in love "Madeleine." And like everyone else, in doing this, I will be committing an error, for that is what it is. In the tale invented by Hitchcock and titled *Vertigo,* there is only one Madeleine—Madeleine Elster, the wife of Gavin Elster, whom Scottie describes very near the end of the film as "the real wife." The character whom we call "Madeleine," and whom we ought to call "the false Madeleine," "the "pseudo-Madeleine," or "Madeleine in quotation marks," is a fictional character *in* the fiction that we call *Vertigo.*

In an essay of some thirty-five years ago that remains the standard reference on the subject for analytical philosophers, the logician and metaphysician David K. Lewis tried to elucidate the concept of truth in fiction.[5] Lewis assumes an implicit convention, or understanding, between narrator and reader (or film viewer): the narrator pretends to

---

4. "Celui qui a été ne peut plus désormais ne pas avoir été : désormais ce fait mystérieux et profondément obscur d'avoir vécu est son viatique pour l'éternité." These words appear on a plaque installed on the façade of 1, Quai des Fleurs in the fourth arrondissement of Paris, where Jankélévitch lived from 1938 until his death in 1985.

5. See David K. Lewis, "Truth in Fiction," *American Philosophical Quarterly* 15 (1978): 37–46; reprinted with postscripts in *Philosophical Papers* (New York: Oxford University Press, 1983), 261–80.

tell the truth about things he knows and the reader (or viewer) pretends to take him at his word. Lewis recognizes that his theory does not cover all possible cases—for example, when the narrator pretends to lie (where lying is understood, of course, in relation to the convention of truth *in fiction*). In that case, Lewis admits, a fiction is introduced into the fiction. This iteration is not a problem in itself, he says, but it poses the following questions: "Why doesn't the iteration collapse?" And how do we "distinguish pretending to pretend from really pretending"?[6] To these questions, by his own admission, the greatest metaphysician of the twentieth century has no answer.

Madeleine is a fictional character, fictional in fiction. Her death is revelatory, because it enlightens us about her mode of existence. Madeleine's death does not simply put an end to her existence; it has the fantastic consequence that Madeleine never existed—even though before she died it is the case that, like every real person, like every fictional person, she existed. It may be true as a general proposition that (in Malraux's fine phrase) death turns every life into fate. In Madeleine's case, however, death converts the past (and past love), not into something that took place and is now no more, but instead into something that never took place at all.

As she rushes from the lawn in front of the cloister at San Juan Bautista and up the bell tower stairs to Gavin Elster—the one who made her, in the sense of having fabricated her ("He made you over," Scottie says later)—Madeleine knows that. This is the most poignant moment of the film in my view, the moment on which everything else turns. To share this view, one must accept that the main character of the film is Madeleine, the false Madeleine, and not Scottie. Feminists who accuse Hitchcock of making male films could not be more mistaken. Madeleine knows that her imminent "death" is about to lead her into a nothingness more absolute than that of death itself. Her final words—the last ones she will ever utter—must be understood as a naïve and desperate attempt to avert the infinite anxiety that seizes her at the edge of the abyss:

Madeleine: You believe that *I* love you?
Scottie: Yes.

6. Ibid., 280.

Madeleine: And if you lose *me,* you'll know that *I* loved you and wanted to go on loving you.
Scottie: I won't lose you.[7]

The title of the crime novel by Boileau-Narcejac, *D'entre les morts* (From the Dead),[8] which Alec Coppel and Samuel Taylor used as the basis for their screenplay, by itself illustrates the chasm that separates the plot of the original police procedural from the dizzying descent into metaphysical bewilderment that Hitchcock created from it. From the dead? No, Madeleine will never be able to come back from the dead—in the form of Judy Barton or anyone else—since in order to come *back* to life, she must have lived a first time. Nor is it true, as so many critics have insisted (repeating Hitchcock's own claim), that Scottie, when he discovers the nature of the trap into which he has fallen, is in love with a dead woman. Necrophilia is a ridiculously trivial conceit by comparison with what is going on here. In the final sentences that Madeleine utters—the first and last words that she speaks in complete sincerity, the first and the last words that do not figure in the script written for her by Elster—the problematic element is the referent of the first-person pronoun. This "I" cannot refer to Judy, whom Scottie does not know. It can refer only to Madeleine—yet the person who utters these words knows that she is not Madeleine, just as the actress who embodies Juliet in Shakespeare's play knows that she is not Juliet, no matter how much feeling and intensity she is able to summon on stage in delivering her heart-rending declaration of love.

Death is sweet for this reason, that the person who has died continues to live on in the minds of those who remember. Of a love that is no

7. This and all other dialogue excerpts are taken from the screenplay of *Vertigo,* posted at www.dailyscript.com/scripts/vertigo.html. In every case the emphasis is mine. [The script transcript of the dialogue as it actually occurs in the film, which differs slightly in many places from the screenplay by Coppel and Taylor, may be found at www.script-o-rama.com/movie_scripts/v/vertigo-script-transcript-alfred-hitchcock.html. Some of the dialogue in the screenplay was cut by Hitchcock at the editing stage.—Trans.]

8. The novel by Pierre Boileau and Thomas Narcejac, written in 1954 under the pseudonym Boileau-Narcejac, remained unpublished in French for almost two decades. An English version nevertheless promptly appeared as *The Living and the Dead* (London: Hutchinson, 1956), later reissued under the title *Vertigo* (London: Bloomsbury, 1997).—Trans.

more one can at least say, no matter how great may have been the bitterness, the anger, the resentment it left behind, that it *was*. But Madeleine's death *falsifies* the words that Scottie utters when he advances toward Judy at the top of the bell tower: "I loved you so, Madeleine." It *was* true that Scottie loved a person named Madeleine. Now that she is "dead," it is not true that Scottie *will have* loved Madeleine. Judy and Scottie kiss, and the screenplay says: "Scottie's eyes are tight with pain and the emotion of hating *her* and hating himself for loving *her*."

To whom, then, does the feminine personal pronoun, the direct object of Scottie's hate and love, refer? To Judy, one is tempted to say—to her physical body, her luscious lips, her shapely hips. But note that in response to Judy's plea at the top of the tower, "Love me . . . keep me safe . . . ," Scottie murmurs to himself: "Too late . . . too late . . . there's no bringing *her* back." Here the "her" unambiguously refers to Madeleine—that phantom, that ghost.

There's no bringing her back: the meaning of this phrase is not at all that a person cannot be brought back from the dead (as in Henri-Georges Clouzot's film *Les Diaboliques*, likewise based on a novel by Boileau-Narcejac). It means that no one can be brought back from ontological nothingness. Madeleine knew this. Now it is Judy's turn to know it. The person who has just begged Scottie to protect her from danger and death now tears herself from his embrace when the figure in black suddenly appears. This is the *fourth* time that Scottie has found himself powerless to prevent a fatal plunge—first the police officer fell to his death, then the true Madeleine and the false Madeleine, now Judy. For Judy, however, it is the first and last time that she surrenders to despair.

Catastrophe and Time

Madeleine's mode of existence can be described only by a very particular metaphysics, in which the basic elements of standard modal logic—possibility, contingency, and necessity (the three ontological categories contemplated by this logic, represented by modal operators); temporality; and existence predicates—are governed by unfamiliar rules. These rules completely elude the axiomatic system developed by Lewis,[9] whose work

9. See David K. Lewis, *On the Plurality of Worlds* (Oxford: Blackwell, 1986).

on possible worlds has led some to compare him with Leibniz. One can imagine, for example, the following state of affairs: an object *O* possesses the property *P* until time *t;* after *t,* it is not only the case that the object *O* no longer has the property *P,* but also that *O* never had *P.* In that case the truth value of the proposition "The object *O* has the property *P* at instant *t"* would depend on the moment when the proposition is stated. I have myself devised a theory of modal logic that accepts this type of restriction, drawing not only on the thinking of Heidegger, Bergson, and Bergson's pupil Sartre, but also on the philosophy of quantum mechanics.[10]

Bergson spoke of something similar in connection with artistic creation. In an essay entitled "Le possible et le réel" (The Possible and the Real), published in 1930, he wrote: "I believe in the end we shall consider it evident that the artist in executing his work *is creating the possible as well as the real."*[11] In other words, "[a]s reality is created as something unpredictable and new, its image is reflected behind it into the indefinite past; thus it finds that it has from all time been possible, but it is at this precise moment that it *begins to have always been possible,* and that is why I said that its possibility, which does not precede its reality, will have preceded it once the reality has appeared."[12]

It was in reflecting, not upon a work of artistic creation, but upon the prospect of global ruin, that I arrived at much the same conclusion. Following in the footsteps of three of Heidegger's intellectual offspring— Hannah Arendt, Hans Jonas, and above all Günther Anders—I became particularly interested in the harbingers and portents of mankind's self-destruction. Madeleine's death in *Vertigo* is, in a sense, a metonymy of the disappearance of humanity. I now realize, however, that for me it was the opposite: I wound up devoting myself to this topic because the disappearance of humanity seemed to me a metonymy of Madeleine's death. Rather than describe how I came to terms with the problem of doomsaying, I

10. See Jean-Pierre Dupuy, "Philosophical Foundations of a New Concept of Equilibrium in the Social Sciences: Projected Equilibrium," *Philosophical Studies* 100 (2000): 323–45.

11. Henri Bergson, "The Possible and the Real," in *The Creative Mind: An Introduction to Metaphysics,* trans. Mabelle L. Andison (New York: Philosophical Library, 1946), 121. My emphasis.

12. Ibid., 119. Again, the emphasis is mine.

would prefer—and all the more strongly since the present book in its entirety bears witness to my method—to illustrate it by means of a magnificent parable. A few years ago I placed this parable, which is due to Günther Anders, at the head of my brief treatise on the metaphysics of catastrophes.[13]

Noah had grown tired of being a prophet of doom, forever announcing a catastrophe that never came and that no one took seriously. One day,

he clothed himself in sackcloth and covered his head with ashes. Only a man who was mourning [the death of] a beloved child or his wife was allowed to do this. Clothed in the garb of truth, bearer of sorrow, he went back to the city, resolved to turn the curiosity, spitefulness, and superstition of its inhabitants to his advantage. Soon a small crowd of curious people had gathered around him. They asked him questions. They asked if someone had died, and who the dead person was. Noah replied to them that many had died, and then, to the great amusement of his listeners, said that they themselves were the dead of whom he spoke. When he was asked when this catastrophe had taken place, he replied to them: "Tomorrow." Profiting from their attention and confusion, Noah drew himself up to his full height and said these words: "The day after tomorrow, the flood will be something that will have been. And when the flood will have been, *everything that is will never have existed.* When the flood will have carried off everything that is, everything that will have been, it will be too late to remember, for there will no longer be anyone alive. And so there will no longer be any difference between the dead and those who mourn them. *If I have come before you, it is in order to reverse time,* to mourn tomorrow's dead today. The day after tomorrow it will be too late." With this he went back whence he had come, took off the sackcloth [that he wore], cleaned his face of the ashes that covered it, and went to his workshop. That evening a carpenter knocked on his door and said to him: "Let me help you build the ark, *so that it may become false.*" Later a roofer joined them, saying: "It is raining over the mountains, let me help you, so that it may become false."[14]

13. Dupuy, *Petite métaphysique des tsunamis,* 10.

14. Quoted in Thierry Simonelli, *Günther Anders: De la désuétude de l'homme* (Paris: Éditions du Jasmin, 2004), 84–85. The emphasis is mine. Simonelli very closely follows Anders's German text, found in the first chapter of *Endzeit und Zeitenende* (Munich: Beck, 1972), a work that has not yet been translated into either French or English. Anders told the story of the flood elsewhere and in other forms, particularly in *Hiroshima ist überall* (Munich: Beck, 1982).

The temporal metaphysics that structures the parable of Noah according to Anders is the very same one that underlies the Jonah paradox, which I discussed in the preceding chapter in connection with nuclear apocalypse. As we have seen, the Jonah paradox—which is to say the doomsayer's paradox—is subject to the following constraint: the prospect of catastrophe, if it is to be credible, must be made to fully exist in the future, so that the suffering and deaths foretold will be believed to be inevitable, the inexorable result of something like fate. The present conserves the memory of it, so to speak, allowing the mind to project itself into the aftermath of the catastrophe and treat the event in the future perfect tense. There exists a moment in the present, then, when one may say that the catastrophe *will have taken place*; when one may say, "The day after tomorrow, the flood will be something that will have been." What is it, then, that is "perfect" (or completed) in the future perfect that is not so in the grammatical tense that we call simply "future"? The future tense reflects a negative property of the future, namely, that it is fundamentally indeterminate. The future, in other words, lacks a property that the past fully possesses: the fixity of what has already been determined by its occurrence. Now, the future perfect accomplishes the remarkable feat of granting the future tense, and therefore the future itself, exactly this property. For from the point of view of the day after tomorrow, tomorrow belongs to the past.

The paradox is that if one succeeds too well in fixing a catastrophic future, one will have lost sight of the purpose of the metaphysical exercise, which is precisely to stimulate awareness, and thus bring about action, so that the catastrophe does not occur: "Let me help you build the ark, so that it may become false."

The way out from this paradox, I believe, is to regard the catastrophic event simultaneously as something fated to occur and as a contingent accident, one that need not occur—even if, in a completed future, it appears to be necessary. Note, by the way, that this metaphysics is the metaphysics of the ordinary person, of the naïve and untutored mind. It consists in believing that if a memorable event occurs, such as a catastrophe, this is because it could not *not* occur; while at the same time thinking that so long as it has not occurred, it is not inevitable. It is therefore the actualization of the event—the fact that it occurs—that retrospectively creates necessity.

This metaphysics is also the metaphysics of the sacred—and, as we shall see, the metaphysics of *Vertigo*. One must not suppose that I am deliberately trying to model a certain way of looking at the future on Hitchcock's masterpiece. I have only now come to realize that it was the hidden effects of watching *Vertigo*, unconsciously at work deep within my mind, that enabled me many years later to discover this way of looking at the future and the past.

The Object of Desire

In 1941, the year of my birth, the brilliant Adolfo Bioy Casares, friend and collaborator of Jorge Luis Borges, published in Buenos Aires one of the masterpieces of twentieth-century literature, *La invención de Morel* (Morel's Invention).[15] The narrator, a fugitive hounded by the political authorities of his country, finds refuge on an island that he believes to be deserted, having been abandoned by its inhabitants in the aftermath of a terrible epidemic. Very quickly he discovers that quite the opposite is true: the island is populated by human beings, among them a woman, Faustine, with whom he falls madly in love. He nevertheless does not dare to approach her, or her companions, for fear of being recognized and taken into custody. Strange events take place, which the narrator follows from a distance, but with growing amazement, for he notices that they are repeated in identical fashion each week. He realizes that the beings he has taken for humans are in fact animated three-dimensional images, projected by a machine invented by Morel, one of the phantoms who inhabit the island. Morel, it turns out, filmed the last week in the lives of the people the narrator has been watching, his own last days included, in order to be forever united with Faustine in an endlessly repeated sequence of events—an eternal recurrence. The narrator then resolves to enter into the world of the machine, in the hope that one day, having now become an image himself, technology will allow him to penetrate Faustine's soul.

15. Adolfo Bioy Casares, *The Invention of Morel*, trans. Ruth L. C. Simms (New York: New York Review of Books, 2003). Casares's book has inspired a number of films, both in the cinema—most notably Alain Resnais's own masterpiece, *Last Year at Marienbad*—and on television—the American series *Lost*.

Now let us return to *Vertigo* and the Bergsonian metaphysics that underlies Hitchcock's tale. Once she is "dead," it is false to say that Madeleine *will ever have existed*—and yet there was a time when she did exist. Much more than Elster's machinations and the script he has written for Madeleine to follow, it is Scottie's love that brings about this miracle. Can one love a fictional character, and by doing this give it existence? Inside a fiction one can, because one can *in real life*. Anyone who has fallen in love with Madeleine will know what I mean.

I was seventeen years old when I fell head over heels for Madeleine. It was love at first sight. The first time I saw the film, I was glued to my seat for three showings in a row (in those days you did not have to leave the theater at the end of a film and pay to see it again). A dozen times in the next three weeks I went back to satisfy my passion. In the fifty years that came after I was often reunited with Madeleine, perhaps another fifty times. There is only one remedy for an obsession like this: like the narrator of *La invención de Morel*, I would have had to enter into the film and become a character myself, to contrive a reflection of myself and say to Madeleine what Scottie says to Judy when she lets him into her room at the Empire Hotel: "I just want to see you as much as I can." To be with Madeleine, to see her, without touching her—to Judy's great displeasure: "Why? Because I remind you of someone? That's not very complimentary. [Pause] And nothing would . . . happen. . . . " "No," Scottie concedes. "That's not very complimentary, either," Judy replies.

But obviously that was impossible. The next best thing was to learn everything I could about Kim Novak. Feverishly I combed the weekly and monthly magazines that specialized in celebrity news back then. My fatal mistake was to commit the same category error that Scottie commits in searching for Madeleine in Judy.

Madeleine exists only through Scottie's love. It may nonetheless be doubted whether this love is authentic. Why does Scottie love Madeleine and wish to possess her? Because she is possessed by Carlotta Valdez, and therefore he cannot possess her. Why is Scottie fascinated by her, to the point of losing his mind? Because she herself is fascinated by death. Here one cannot help but be reminded of Denis de Rougemont's analysis of the myth of Tristan and Iseult. Recall the passage that I quoted in chapter 3—only now replace the names of the myth with those of Hitchcock's fiction: "[I]t is unbelievable that Scottie [could] ever marry Madeleine. She typifies the woman a man does not marry; for once she became his wife she would no longer be what she is, and he would no longer love her. Just think of a Mrs. Ferguson! It would be the negation of passion."

The voluntary chastity of the married knight, on which de Rougemont lays such emphasis, is disturbingly echoed by Scottie's impotence, on which the film dwells at almost undue length. One of the most unbearable scenes is the inquest conducted on the very site of the alleged suicide—unbearable not least for the withering scorn in the voice of the coroner (played by the wonderful Henry Jones) when he utters the cruel words that Scottie will go on endlessly repeating to himself: "[Mr. Elster] could not have anticipated that Mr. Ferguson's 'weakness,' his 'fear of heights,' would have made him powerless when he was most needed." De Rougemont concludes: "'Passion' triumphs over desire. Death triumphs over life."[16] Here we encounter another troubling resonance. In the Tristan myth there are two Iseults: Iseult the Fair, King Mark's wife and Tristan's passion; and Iseult of the White Hands, whom Tristan marries.

Scottie cannot possess Madeleine because Madeleine is possessed by Carlotta Valdez, but it is because she is possessed by another that Scottie wishes to possess her. The desire for possession and control is necessarily engulfed by its opposite, powerlessness. Hitchcock returns to this fatal reversal again and again, imparting impetus to a pattern of spiraling descent—the plunge into the abyss—that gives the film its very form. The downward spiral begins innocently enough with the story Gavin Elster tells of his wife's strange behavior.[17] He recounts the great excitement she felt on coming to San Francisco and discovering the city for the first time: "[H]er delight was so strong, so fiercely *possessive!* These things were *hers.* And yet she had never been here before. . . . [T]here was something feverish about the way she embraced the city. She *possessed* it." Then he describes the sudden change that comes over Madeleine one day: "I don't know what happened that day: where she went, what she saw, what she did. But on that day, the search was ended. She had found what she was looking for. . . . And something in the city *possessed* her."

16. Rougemont, *Love in the Western World*, 45.
17. Hitchcock included only a part of this account in the final version of the film.

Thus Madeleine's relationship to the city assumes the form of a tangled hierarchy, which we examined in the prologue. Madeleine was possessed by the very thing that she wanted to possess, in the same fashion that, according to Borges (quoting Carlyle), we are written by the very thing that we write. And it is when Scottie, at Mission San Juan Bautista, believes he is free at last to possess Madeleine, which is to say to establish his full control over her ("[N]o one possesses you . . . you're safe with me . . . my love . . . "), that he loses her forever.

Yet Scottie's nightmare has only begun. The horror will reach its height when, having transformed Judy into Madeleine, having finally made Madeleine his creature, which is to say a person whom he has entirely created, wholly fabricated, Scottie realizes that he has only done again, exactly, down to the least detail, down to the shape and style of her chignon, what Elster did to the same Judy. Our shock on discovering this plunges us, as viewers, into the abyss once we realize that the same compulsion (or "repetition automatism," as Lacan translated Freud's notion of *Wiederholungszwang*), which twice sends Madeleine to her death, manifested itself in Hitchcock's cruel, if not actually sadistic, treatment of Kim Novak during pre-production and rehearsals.

The rage and chagrin that Scottie cannot repress at the moment when he suddenly grasps what we, as viewers, have known since we were allowed to enter into Judy's mind are as feeble and pathetic as Madeleine's anguished expression of love when she was about to descend into nothingness was powerful and sincere: "Who was at the top when you got there? Elster? With his wife? . . . And she was the one who died. Not you. The *real* wife. You were the copy, you were the counterfeit." And then, a moment later: "You played his wife so well, Judy! He made you over, didn't he? He made you over, didn't he? Just as I've done. *But better!*"

Envy, that most destructive of all passions—all the world's envy is condensed in those two emphatic words: "But better!" The "Madeleine" whom Scottie has made is only a mediocre copy, a pale imitation of the Madeleine whom Elster had succeeded in making, who herself in turn is only a counterfeit of the *real wife*, Madeleine Elster. Scottie's Madeleine is only a copy of a copy—a simulacrum—of the real object, who herself holds no interest apart from the wealth that her presumptive suicide will bring to Elster. The futility of desire could not be illustrated more force-fully, or with more devastating irony.

What touches Scottie to the quick in this moment of crushing rev-elation is not the fact that Judy was Elster's mistress—Scottie could not care less about Judy!—but that he remade Madeleine less faithfully than Elster did. Scottie was the victim, in other words, of *mimetic desire*. He desired Madeleine only because she was possessed by someone else—not by Elster, but by Carlotta. There is nothing in the least theoretical about this revelation; it is an altogether practical discovery, arrived at through his own actions, his own compulsive behavior. He realizes—viscerally, from the innermost depths of his being—that what he desired was only an *image* that had been fabricated by another. He realizes this because he has in his turn fabricated the same image. That "Madeleine" is nothing more than an image is now clear to him because he sees that he has slav-ishly copied it.

The Sense of the Past

Henry James left two works unfinished at his death in 1916. One was called *The Sense of the Past*. James was a friend of H. G. Wells, whose short novel *The Time Machine* (1895) he had long wished to rewrite in his own fashion. Some years later the formidable complexities of James's novel were admirably clarified by the poet Stephen Spender, in a study of mod-ern writers entitled *The Destructive Element* (1935), which in turn inspired Jorge Luis Borges ten years later to write a metaphysical masterpiece, "The Flower of Coleridge." From this latter work I take the following summary of James's novel:

In *The Sense of the Past* the nexus between the real and the imaginative (between present and past) is not a flower [as in the query by Coleridge from which Borges's essay takes its title],[18] but *a picture* from the eighteenth century that mysteriously represents the protagonist. Fascinated by this canvas, he succeeds in going back to the day when it was painted. He meets a number of persons, including the

18. "If a man could pass through Paradise in a dream, and have a flower presented to him as a pledge that his soul had really been there, and if he had found that flower in his hand when he awoke—Ay!—and what then?"

artist, who paints him with fear and aversion, because he senses that there is something unusual and anomalous in those future features. James thus creates an incomparable *regressus in infinitum*, when his hero Ralph Pendrel returns to the eighteenth century because he is fascinated by an old painting, but Pendrel's return to this century is a condition for the existence of the painting. *The cause follows the effect, the reason for the journey is one of the consequences of the journey.*[19]

I do not know if Coppel and Taylor knew of James's novel, Spender's study, or Borges's essay (all of them published prior to the release of *Vertigo*) when they wrote the screenplay for Hitchcock's film, but it must be said that the echoes of the figure of Madeleine, fascinated by the portrait of Carlotta Valdez, who is reincarnated in her, induce a sense of—vertigo. Nor do I know if the filmmaker Chris Marker had read Borges when he made *La jetée* (1962), one of the most brilliant ruminations on *Vertigo*. Once again, the structural analogy with James's novel sends shivers down the spine.

At the heart of my thinking about catastrophe I have placed this same temporal metaphysics, which takes the form of a circle linking the future to the past and the past to the future. It cannot be by chance that I should have thus rediscovered, forty years later, the central figure of *Vertigo:* it had never ceased to inhabit me. I call this metaphysics "projected time," in homage to Bergson and Sartre. It is, as the reader will have suspected, a metaphysics ideally suited to the purposes of a prophet of doom. What is more, it has the same form as the primitive conception of the sacred:

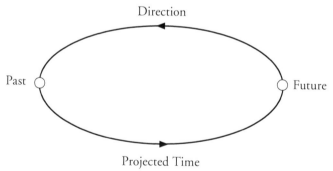

Projected Time

19. Jorge Luis Borges, "The Flower of Coleridge" (1945), in *Other Inquisitions, 1937–1952*, 12. The emphasis is mine. [Simms's translation used here in preference to Suzanne Jill Levine's more recent and very similar version.—Trans.]

In order for projected time to be experienced, the loop must be closed on its origin. Its origin is not the past; it is the future, which has acquired from the past, as a metaphysical effect of the future perfect tense, the property of being determinate and fixed. We have seen that if the closing of the loop is prevented from occurring, the future is stopped by the causal consequences of the actions that its anticipation brings about. It is as though the future were trying to pull itself up by its bootstraps, and falls apart instead. In projected time the future is inevitable; but if the loop is not closed, the future does not happen—an intolerable paradox. Illustrations of this paradox abound, from the prophecy that goes unfulfilled by virtue of the fact that it is publicly announced (the Jonah paradox) to the case of the killer judge, who eliminates all those individuals of whom it is "written" that they will commit a murder (Voltaire's *Zadig*, Dick's "The Minority Report," the official American doctrine of preemptive nuclear strike, and so on).[20]

The fiction (within the fiction) of the temporal circle that unites Madeleine and Carlotta is a perfect example of a loop that is closed at its point of departure. By contrast, when Scottie—with Judy's complicity—attempts to imitate Madeleine in throwing himself back into the past, only to be forever swallowed up by the very attempt, the loop is not closed—and that is the tragedy. It is essential to grasp the reason for this. In Hitchcock's world, such a reason is called a "MacGuffin." As he explained to François Truffaut, a MacGuffin is "actually nothing at all," something "of no importance whatever." Nevertheless, it has very important consequences.[21]

What is it the MacGuffin in *Vertigo?* The very thing that prevents the loop from being closed at its origin, its point of departure. Scottie and Judy have made a pact (probably with the devil) to travel back into the past, in order once again to become Scottie and Madeleine, and to save a love that, as they should realize by now, will have never existed. The voyage into the past reaches its end, not without protests and resistance on the part of Judy, but without there having been any need of a time

20. A general theory of such cases, where the loop is not closed, may be found in Dupuy, *Pour un catastrophisme éclairé*, 175–97.

21. See François Truffaut, *Hitchcock*, rev. ed. (New York: Simon & Schuster, 1985), 138–39.

machine of the sort imagined by Wells—for Scottie, in his powerlessness and absolute desire for control, has been able to provide all the necessary energy. It is at this very moment that an object suddenly appears that prevents the temporal loop from closing upon itself. Since the necklace Carlotta is shown wearing in the portrait would have had to have disappeared with Madeleine, it is causally impossible that Judy—once more made over, transformed into Madeleine—should still be wearing it. This is why the true form of *Vertigo* is not a circle. It is a circle that wants to be closed on itself, but that is powerless to bring about this result. Instead it becomes a downward spiral, the swirling descent into the abyss.

Alcmena's Paradox

A way out from the infinitely morbid universe of *Vertigo* can be found, I believe, in the form of a conception of love suggested by the philosopher Monique Canto-Sperber that escapes the perverse logic of mimetic desire. Before we examine this conception, however, permit me to recall a story told to me by my late friend Heinz von Foerster, one of the founders of cybernetics and, on account of this, an early pioneer of cognitive science.[22]

The story takes place in Vienna toward the end of 1945. The psychiatrist Viktor Frankl had just returned there, having miraculously survived the Auschwitz-Birkenau camp, only to discover that his wife, his parents, his brother, and other members of his family had been exterminated. He decided to resume his practice. Frankl was soon to achieve fame with the publication of *Man's Search for Meaning* (1946), a work that sold tens of millions of copies throughout the postwar world and made the technique of logotherapy a rival to Freudian analysis. Frankl developed logotherapy in order to help survivors talk about their experience in the death camps. Von Foerster, a friend of Frankl, left us the following account:

Concentration camps were the setting for many horrific stories. Imagine then the incredulous delight of a couple who returned to Vienna from two different camps to find each other alive. They were together for about six months, and

22. This story first appeared in English as part of the preface to the MIT Press edition of my book *The Mechanization of the Mind*, retitled *On the Origins of Cognitive Science*, xix–xxi; on von Foerster himself, see pages 10–11.

then the wife died of an illness she had contracted in the camp. At this her husband lost heart completely, and fell into the deepest despair, from which none of his friends could rouse him, not even with the appeal "Imagine if she had died earlier and you had not been reunited!" Finally he was convinced to seek the help of Viktor Frankl, known for his ability to help the victims of the catastrophe.

They met several times, conversed for many hours, and eventually one day Frankl said: "Let us assume God granted me the power to create a woman just like your wife: she would remember all your conversations, she would remember the jokes, she would remember every detail: you could not distinguish this woman from the wife you lost. Would you like me to do it?" The man kept silent for a while, then stood up and said, "No thank you, doctor!" They shook hands; the man left and started a new life.

Von Foerster wished to know how this astonishing change could have come about. Frankl explained it this way: "You see, Heinz, we see ourselves through the eyes of the other. When she died, he became blind. But when he *saw* that he was blind, he could see!"[23]

This, at least, is the lesson that von Foerster drew from this story—in typical cybernetic fashion. But I think that another lesson can be drawn from it, one that extends the first. What was it that this man suddenly saw, which he did not see before? The thought experiment that Frankl invited his patient to perform echoes one of the most famous Greek myths, the story of Amphitryon. In order to seduce Amphitryon's wife, Alcmena, and to pass a night of love with her, Zeus assumes the form of Amphytryon:

All through the night, Alcmena loves a man whose qualities are in every particular identical to those of her husband. The self-same description would apply equally to both. All the reasons that Alcmena has for loving Amphitryon are equally reasons for loving Zeus, who has the appearance of Amphitryon, for Zeus and Amphitryon can only be distinguished numerically: they are two rather than one. Yet it is Amphitryon whom Alcmena loves and not the god who has taken on his form. If one wishes to account for the emotion of love by appeal to arguments meant to justify it or to the qualities that lovers attribute to the objects of their love, what rational explanation can be given for that "something" which

23. Translated from the German ("Wir sehen uns mit den Augen des anderen. . . . Als er aber erkannte, daß er blind war, da konnte er sehen!"); see Heinz von Foerster, "Mit den Augen des anderen," in *Wissen und Gewissen: Versuch einer Brücke*, ed. Siegfried J. Schmidt, 350–63 (Frankfurt: Suhrkamp, 1993).

Amphitryon possesses, but that Zeus does not, and which explains why Alcmena loves only Amphitryon, and not Zeus?[24]

When we love somebody, we do not love a list of characteristics, even one that is sufficiently exhaustive to distinguish the person in question from anyone else. The most perfect simulation still fails to capture something, and it is this something that is the essence of love—that magnificently impoverished word, which says everything and explains nothing.

Viktor Frankl's patient suddenly realized that the love that bound him to his wife was unique and irreplaceable. For that very reason it stood apart from the flood of time, the time we are accustomed to regard as a receptacle for the events that emerge in it. If Scottie had loved Madeleine as she loved him, he would never have conjured her up from the nothingness that in truth she never left.

24. Monique Canto-Sperber, "Amour," in idem, ed., *Dictionnaire d'éthique et de philosophie morale*, 4th ed. (Paris: Presses universitaires de France, 2004), 41.

Cultural Memory in the Present

Henri Atlan, *Fraud: The World of Ona'ah*

Niklas Luhmann, *Theory of Society, Volume 2*

Ilit Ferber, *Philosophy and Melancholy: Benjamin's Early Reflections on Theater and Language*

Alexandre Lefebvre, *Human Rights as a Way of Life: On Bergson's Political Philosophy*

Theodore W. Jennings, Jr., *Outlaw Justice: The Messianic Politics of Paul*

Alexander Etkind, *Warped Mourning: Stories of the Undead in the Land of the Unburied*

Denis Guénoun, *About Europe: Philosophical Hypotheses*

Maria Boletsi, *Barbarism and its Discontents*

Sigrid Weigel, *Walter Benjamin: Images, the Creaturely, and the Holy*

Roberto Esposito, *Living Thought: The Origins and Actuality of Italian Philosophy*

Henri Atlan, *The Sparks of Randomness, Volume 2: The Atheism of Scripture*

Rüdiger Campe, *The Game of Probability: Literature and Calculation from Pascal to Kleist*

Niklas Luhmann, *A Systems Theory of Religion*

Jean-Luc Marion, *In the Self's Place: The Approach of Saint Augustine*

Rodolphe Gasché, *Georges Bataille: Phenomenology and Phantasmatology*

Niklas Luhmann, *Theory of Society, Volume 1*

Alessia Ricciardi, *After* La Dolce Vita: *A Cultural Prehistory of Berlusconi's Italy*

Daniel Innerarity, *The Future and Its Enemies: In Defense of Political Hope*

Patricia Pisters, *The Neuro-Image: A Deleuzian Film-Philosophy of Digital Screen Culture*

François-David Sebbah, *Testing the Limit: Derrida, Henry, Levinas, and the Phenomenological Tradition*

Erik Peterson, *Theological Tractates*, edited by Michael J. Hollerich

Feisal G. Mohamed, *Milton and the Post-Secular Present: Ethics, Politics, Terrorism*

Pierre Hadot, *The Present Alone Is Our Happiness, Second Edition: Conversations with Jeannie Carlier and Arnold I. Davidson*

Yasco Horsman, *Theaters of Justice: Judging, Staging, and Working Through in Arendt, Brecht, and Delbo*

Jacques Derrida, *Parages*, edited by John P. Leavey

Henri Atlan, *The Sparks of Randomness, Volume 1: Spermatic Knowledge*

Rebecca Comay, *Mourning Sickness: Hegel and the French Revolution*

Djelal Kadir, *Memos from the Besieged City: Lifelines for Cultural Sustainability*

Stanley Cavell, *Little Did I Know: Excerpts from Memory*

Jeffrey Mehlman, *Adventures in the French Trade: Fragments Toward a Life*

Jacob Rogozinski, *The Ego and the Flesh: An Introduction to Egoanalysis*

Marcel Hénaff, *The Price of Truth: Gift, Money, and Philosophy*

Paul Patton, *Deleuzian Concepts: Philosophy, Colonialization, Politics*

Michael Fagenblat, *A Covenant of Creatures: Levinas's Philosophy of Judaism*

Stefanos Geroulanos, *An Atheism That Is Not Humanist Emerges in French Thought*

Andrew Herscher, *Violence Taking Place: The Architecture of the Kosovo Conflict*

Hans-Jörg Rheinberger, *On Historicizing Epistemology: An Essay*

Jacob Taubes, *From Cult to Culture*, edited by Charlotte Fonrobert and Amir Engel

Peter Hitchcock, *The Long Space: Transnationalism and Postcolonial Form*

Lambert Wiesing, *Artificial Presence: Philosophical Studies in Image Theory*

Jacob Taubes, *Occidental Eschatology*

Freddie Rokem, *Philosophers and Thespians: Thinking Performance*

Roberto Esposito, *Communitas: The Origin and Destiny of Community*

Vilashini Cooppan, *Worlds Within: National Narratives and Global Connections in Postcolonial Writing*

Josef Früchtl, *The Impertinent Self: A Heroic History of Modernity*

Frank Ankersmit, Ewa Domanska, and Hans Kellner, eds., *Re-Figuring Hayden White*

Michael Rothberg, *Multidirectional Memory: Remembering the Holocaust in the Age of Decolonization*

Jean-François Lyotard, *Enthusiasm: The Kantian Critique of History*

Ernst van Alphen, Mieke Bal, and Carel Smith, eds., *The Rhetoric of Sincerity*

Stéphane Mosès, *The Angel of History: Rosenzweig, Benjamin, Scholem*

Pierre Hadot, *The Present Alone Is Our Happiness: Conversations with Jeannie Carlier and Arnold I. Davidson*

Alexandre Lefebvre, *The Image of the Law: Deleuze, Bergson, Spinoza*

Samira Haj, *Reconfiguring Islamic Tradition: Reform, Rationality, and Modernity*

Diane Perpich, *The Ethics of Emmanuel Levinas*

Marcel Detienne, *Comparing the Incomparable*

François Delaporte, *Anatomy of the Passions*

René Girard, *Mimesis and Theory: Essays on Literature and Criticism, 1959–2005*

Richard Baxstrom, *Houses in Motion: The Experience of Place and the Problem of Belief in Urban Malaysia*

Jennifer L. Culbert, *Dead Certainty: The Death Penalty and the Problem of Judgment*

Samantha Frost, *Lessons from a Materialist Thinker: Hobbesian Reflections on Ethics and Politics*

Regina Mara Schwartz, *Sacramental Poetics at the Dawn of Secularism: When God Left the World*

Gil Anidjar, *Semites: Race, Religion, Literature*

Ranjana Khanna, *Algeria Cuts: Women and Representation, 1830 to the Present*

Esther Peeren, *Intersubjectivities and Popular Culture: Bakhtin and Beyond*

Eyal Peretz, *Becoming Visionary: Brian De Palma's Cinematic Education of the Senses*

Diana Sorensen, *A Turbulent Decade Remembered: Scenes from the Latin American Sixties*

Hubert Damisch, *A Childhood Memory by Piero della Francesca*

José van Dijck, *Mediated Memories in the Digital Age*

Dana Hollander, *Exemplarity and Chosenness: Rosenzweig and Derrida on the Nation of Philosophy*

Asja Szafraniec, *Beckett, Derrida, and the Event of Literature*

Sara Guyer, *Romanticism After Auschwitz*

Alison Ross, *The Aesthetic Paths of Philosophy: Presentation in Kant, Heidegger, Lacoue-Labarthe, and Nancy*

Gerhard Richter, *Thought-Images: Frankfurt School Writers' Reflections from Damaged Life*

Bella Brodzki, *Can These Bones Live? Translation, Survival, and Cultural Memory*

Rodolphe Gasché, *The Honor of Thinking: Critique, Theory, Philosophy*

Brigitte Peucker, *The Material Image: Art and the Real in Film*

Natalie Melas, *All the Difference in the World: Postcoloniality and the Ends of Comparison*

Jonathan Culler, *The Literary in Theory*

Michael G. Levine, *The Belated Witness: Literature, Testimony, and the Question of Holocaust Survival*

Jennifer A. Jordan, *Structures of Memory: Understanding German Change in Berlin and Beyond*

Christoph Menke, *Reflections of Equality*

Marlène Zarader, *The Unthought Debt: Heidegger and the Hebraic Heritage*

Jan Assmann, *Religion and Cultural Memory: Ten Studies*

David Scott and Charles Hirschkind, *Powers of the Secular Modern: Talal Asad and His Interlocutors*

Gyanendra Pandey, *Routine Violence: Nations, Fragments, Histories*

James Siegel, *Naming the Witch*

J. M. Bernstein, *Against Voluptuous Bodies: Late Modernism and the Meaning of Painting*

Theodore W. Jennings Jr., *Reading Derrida / Thinking Paul: On Justice*

Richard Rorty and Eduardo Mendieta, *Take Care of Freedom and Truth Will Take Care of Itself: Interviews with Richard Rorty*

Jacques Derrida, *Paper Machine*

Renaud Barbaras, *Desire and Distance: Introduction to a Phenomenology of Perception*

Jill Bennett, *Empathic Vision: Affect, Trauma, and Contemporary Art*

Ban Wang, *Illuminations from the Past: Trauma, Memory, and History in Modern China*

James Phillips, *Heidegger's* Volk: *Between National Socialism and Poetry*

Frank Ankersmit, *Sublime Historical Experience*

István Rév, *Retroactive Justice: Prehistory of Post-Communism*

Paola Marrati, *Genesis and Trace: Derrida Reading Husserl and Heidegger*

Krzysztof Ziarek, *The Force of Art*

Marie-José Mondzain, *Image, Icon, Economy: The Byzantine Origins of the Contemporary Imaginary*

Cecilia Sjöholm, *The Antigone Complex: Ethics and the Invention of Feminine Desire*

Jacques Derrida and Elisabeth Roudinesco, *For What Tomorrow . . . : A Dialogue*

Elisabeth Weber, *Questioning Judaism: Interviews by Elisabeth Weber*

Jacques Derrida and Catherine Malabou, *Counterpath: Traveling with Jacques Derrida*

Martin Seel, *Aesthetics of Appearing*

Nanette Salomon, *Shifting Priorities: Gender and Genre in Seventeenth-Century Dutch Painting*

Jacob Taubes, *The Political Theology of Paul*

Jean-Luc Marion, *The Crossing of the Visible*

Eric Michaud, *The Cult of Art in Nazi Germany*

Anne Freadman, *The Machinery of Talk: Charles Peirce and the Sign Hypothesis*

Stanley Cavell, *Emerson's Transcendental Etudes*

Stuart McLean, *The Event and Its Terrors: Ireland, Famine, Modernity*

Beate Rössler, ed., *Privacies: Philosophical Evaluations*

Bernard Faure, *Double Exposure: Cutting Across Buddhist and Western Discourses*

Alessia Ricciardi, *The Ends of Mourning: Psychoanalysis, Literature, Film*

Alain Badiou, *Saint Paul: The Foundation of Universalism*

Gil Anidjar, *The Jew, the Arab: A History of the Enemy*

Jonathan Culler and Kevin Lamb, eds., *Just Being Difficult? Academic Writing in the Public Arena*

Jean-Luc Nancy, *A Finite Thinking*, edited by Simon Sparks

Theodor W. Adorno, *Can One Live after Auschwitz? A Philosophical Reader*, edited by Rolf Tiedemann

Patricia Pisters, *The Matrix of Visual Culture: Working with Deleuze in Film Theory*

Andreas Huyssen, *Present Pasts: Urban Palimpsests and the Politics of Memory*

Talal Asad, *Formations of the Secular: Christianity, Islam, Modernity*

Dorothea von Mücke, *The Rise of the Fantastic Tale*

Marc Redfield, *The Politics of Aesthetics: Nationalism, Gender, Romanticism*

Emmanuel Levinas, *On Escape*

Dan Zahavi, *Husserl's Phenomenology*

Rodolphe Gasché, *The Idea of Form: Rethinking Kant's Aesthetics*

Michael Naas, *Taking on the Tradition: Jacques Derrida and the Legacies of Deconstruction*

Herlinde Pauer-Studer, ed., *Constructions of Practical Reason: Interviews on Moral and Political Philosophy*

Jean-Luc Marion, *Being Given That: Toward a Phenomenology of Givenness*

Theodor W. Adorno and Max Horkheimer, *Dialectic of Enlightenment*

Ian Balfour, *The Rhetoric of Romantic Prophecy*

Martin Stokhof, *World and Life as One: Ethics and Ontology in Wittgenstein's Early Thought*

Gianni Vattimo, *Nietzsche: An Introduction*

Jacques Derrida, *Negotiations: Interventions and Interviews, 1971–1998*, edited by Elizabeth Rottenberg

Brett Levinson, *The Ends of Literature: The Latin American "Boom" in the Neoliberal Marketplace*

Timothy J. Reiss, *Against Autonomy: Cultural Instruments, Mutualities, and the Fictive Imagination*

Hent de Vries and Samuel Weber, eds., *Religion and Media*

Niklas Luhmann, *Theories of Distinction: Re-Describing the Descriptions of Modernity*, edited and introduced by William Rasch

Johannes Fabian, *Anthropology with an Attitude: Critical Essays*

Michel Henry, *I Am the Truth: Toward a Philosophy of Christianity*

Gil Anidjar, *"Our Place in Al-Andalus": Kabbalah, Philosophy, Literature in Arab-Jewish Letters*

Hélène Cixous and Jacques Derrida, *Veils*

F. R. Ankersmit, *Historical Representation*

F. R. Ankersmit, *Political Representation*

Elissa Marder, *Dead Time: Temporal Disorders in the Wake of Modernity (Baudelaire and Flaubert)*

Reinhart Koselleck, *The Practice of Conceptual History: Timing History, Spacing Concepts*

Niklas Luhmann, *The Reality of the Mass Media*

Hubert Damisch, *A Theory of /Cloud/: Toward a History of Painting*

Jean-Luc Nancy, *The Speculative Remark: (One of Hegel's bon mots)*

Jean-François Lyotard, *Soundproof Room: Malraux's Anti-Aesthetics*

Jan Patočka, *Plato and Europe*

Hubert Damisch, *Skyline: The Narcissistic City*

Isabel Hoving, *In Praise of New Travelers: Reading Caribbean Migrant Women Writers*

Richard Rand, ed., *Futures: Of Jacques Derrida*

William Rasch, *Niklas Luhmann's Modernity: The Paradoxes of Differentiation*

Jacques Derrida and Anne Dufourmantelle, *Of Hospitality*

Jean-François Lyotard, *The Confession of Augustine*

Kaja Silverman, *World Spectators*

Samuel Weber, *Institution and Interpretation: Expanded Edition*

Jeffrey S. Librett, *The Rhetoric of Cultural Dialogue: Jews and Germans in the Epoch of Emancipation*

Ulrich Baer, *Remnants of Song: Trauma and the Experience of Modernity in Charles Baudelaire and Paul Celan*

Samuel C. Wheeler III, *Deconstruction as Analytic Philosophy*

David S. Ferris, *Silent Urns: Romanticism, Hellenism, Modernity*

Rodolphe Gasché, *Of Minimal Things: Studies on the Notion of Relation*

Sarah Winter, *Freud and the Institution of Psychoanalytic Knowledge*

Samuel Weber, *The Legend of Freud: Expanded Edition*

Aris Fioretos, ed., *The Solid Letter: Readings of Friedrich Hölderlin*

J. Hillis Miller / Manuel Asensi, *Black Holes / J. Hillis Miller; or, Boustrophedonic Reading*

Miryam Sas, *Fault Lines: Cultural Memory and Japanese Surrealism*

Peter Schwenger, *Fantasm and Fiction: On Textual Envisioning*

Didier Maleuvre, *Museum Memories: History, Technology, Art*

Jacques Derrida, *Monolingualism of the Other; or, The Prosthesis of Origin*

Andrew Baruch Wachtel, *Making a Nation, Breaking a Nation: Literature and Cultural Politics in Yugoslavia*

Niklas Luhmann, *Love as Passion: The Codification of Intimacy*

Mieke Bal, ed., *The Practice of Cultural Analysis: Exposing Interdisciplinary Interpretation*

Jacques Derrida and Gianni Vattimo, eds., *Religion*

- So how does 1 think c̄ DuPuy... as a progressive?
  - Is 1 taking leave of the parochial (what modernity has made of relig) for the relig?

- And am 1 — in JL Nancy's sense — exiting the parochial via the deconstruction of Xianity?

- Are we generating an axial shift in our Relig Imagination (vs. our parochial sensibilities)?

Rdg List
Daniel Barber
9.1 Andijar
Bataille

Made in the USA
San Bernardino, CA
20 April 2015